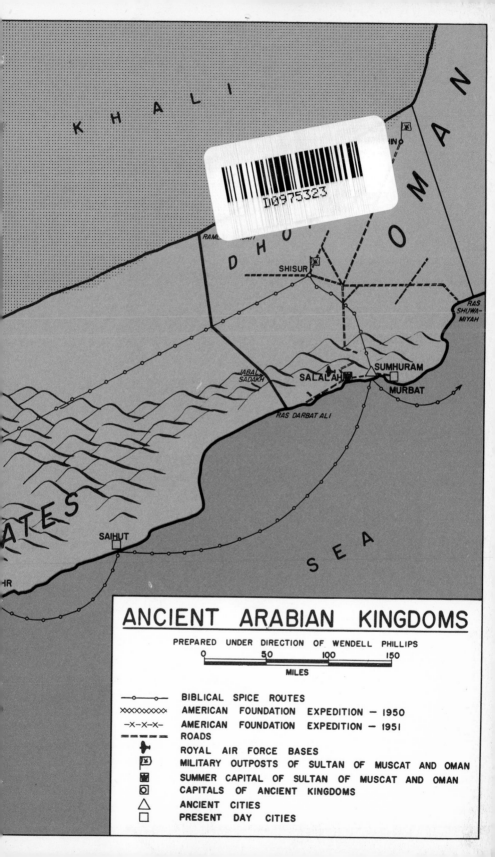

ANCIENT ARABIAN KINGDOMS

PREPARED UNDER DIRECTION OF WENDELL PHILLIPS

0   50   100   150

MILES

—o——o—	BIBLICAL SPICE ROUTES
xxxxxxxxx	AMERICAN FOUNDATION EXPEDITION — 1950
–x–x–x–	AMERICAN FOUNDATION EXPEDITION — 1951
– – – – –	ROADS
✈	ROYAL AIR FORCE BASES
⚑	MILITARY OUTPOSTS OF SULTAN OF MUSCAT AND OMAN
⊞	SUMMER CAPITAL OF SULTAN OF MUSCAT AND OMAN
◎	CAPITALS OF ANCIENT KINGDOMS
△	ANCIENT CITIES
☐	PRESENT DAY CITIES

QATABAN AND SHEBA

QATABAN
AND
SHEBA

*Exploring the Ancient Kingdoms on the
Biblical Spice Routes of Arabia*

BY WENDELL PHILLIPS

· ✳ ·

Harcourt, Brace and Company

NEW YORK

TO MY MOTHER,
WHOSE LOVE AND ENCOURAGEMENT,
LIKE HER NAME, SUNSHINE,
ARE NEVER FAILING

AUTHOR'S PREFACE

Herein lies the story of a dream, which like many dreams occasionally achieved nightmarish qualities. To some the high point of my story will lie within the Queen of Sheba's city where disaster overtook our expedition. To others the lions of Timna, the discovery of Miriam, or the Temple of Venus may take precedence over tragedy in the Kingdom of Yemen. I hope that these pages may stimulate those who, for better or worse, are born explorers, but I warn all others to whom romance, adventure, science, travel, and the lure of the unknown beckon that the fulfillment of their dreams may also bring upon them the torture of split lips, swollen tongues, frozen fingers, dysentery, fever, heartbreak, and monotony beyond compare—all major parts of the explorer's life.

Today the door stands wide open for exploration, with "Brightest Africa" presenting a field laboratory of continental proportions for scientists of the most varied specialties.

In "Happy Arabia," however, the bell has just rung and the door swings ajar, still awaiting those equipped to open it wide. For here lies one of the last of the world's relatively unknown areas. It is this land of sand and dust, Bedawi and jambiya, buried temple and mud palace, that awaits our return to bring new life and activity.

But there are great difficulties. Today portions of South Arabia are beset with political intrigues, and border disputes abound.

Whole regions are forbidden and marked insecure where blood feuds rule and the rifle is king. Throughout our four major expeditions, which are informally recorded in this book, we strove for understanding and friendship between Arabs and Americans. The Arabia of tomorrow is the heritage of the present-day Arab, and unless America and Europe contribute materially to the Arabs' well-being, our spheres of influence will wane, in accordance with the pattern set throughout this mid-twentieth century.

It is not the purpose of this account to criticize the past but to picture the present, with a prayer that the future will become as bright as Arabia was once happy. Exploitation of the late nineteenth-century variety is nearing an end throughout the present-day free world. Nothing illustrates this to a higher degree than current American enterprises throughout Arabia. These activities are built on the solid rock of co-operation and equal advantage to both major parties concerned, with the healthy existence of each partner wholly dependent on mutual satisfaction and progress. Thus ancient Arabia is entering a new and glorious era.

Few Arabs can understand charity for charity's sake alone, and fewer Europeans or Americans practice it. A unique policy of honesty with regard to the motivating stimulus for European-American intervention in Arabian affairs plus the honest admission by my Arab brothers that they in turn need us as much as we need them will go a long way toward making this land where once flourished the "Children of the Moon" a better land for all, *inshallah!*

The author wishes to make it clear that all statements and opinions expressed in this book, unless otherwise directly quoted, are his responsibility alone.

My salaams and deep appreciation to Arabia's foremost living personality and ruler—Sultan Said bin Taimur, Sultan of Muscat and Oman and Dependencies, for honoring me with the title of Mustashar.

My eternal appreciation to John Francis Neylan, the rock upon which my African expedition was built, and to Samuel F. Pryor, the Gibraltar of my Arabian expeditions.

My thanks to Secretary of Air Harold E. Talbott, to former

Under Secretary of State Walter Bedell Smith, to Senator Bourke B. Hickenlooper, and to Assistant Secretary of State Henry A. Byroade for many helpful deeds.

My thanks to the Aden government and to the Royal Air Force for co-operation and assistance.

My thanks to Dr. Robert Gordon Sproul, President of the University of California, for giving me my first opportunity at expedition leadership; to Dr. William K. Gregory, eminent paleontologist, for guiding my early footsteps along the trail of ancient man; to the late Dr. Robert Broom for crowning the African expedition with his Swartzkrans Ape Man; to Dr. Charles L. Camp for my first membership on any expedition; to James K. Moffitt, California class of '86, whose youthful enthusiasm for exploration served as a constant stimulus; to R. V. Whetsel for invaluable assistance and companionship in Dhofar; to Commander Wendell Phillips Dodge, veteran explorer and former editor of the *Explorers Journal,* for never forgetting my expeditions; to Dr. Irwin Moon and Lawrence Sherman, master movie producers, for photographic guidance; to the State Department's Richard Sanger for first suggesting the possibility of work in Beihan; to ace Middle East correspondent Wilton Wynn for paving our way into Yemen; to Louis Johnson, to Edward Eagan, to Charles Nager, to Henry Ikenberry, and to Paul Aiken, for legal advice.

So many persons have aided directly or indirectly in the preparation of this book that to mention all their names would require a separate chapter. Grateful thanks are due to members of all four expeditions for making available their invaluable field notes and to my fellow directors of the American Foundation for the Study of Man for unlimited support; to Lowell Thomas for constant stimulus, literary encouragement, and editorial guidance; to my father, Merley H. Phillips, and to Brigadier General T. A. McInerny, who never tired of urging me to write down my experiences in book form; to L. P. Kirwan, Director of the Royal Geographical Society, for co-operation with our maps; to Dr. Friso Heybroek and to Nigel St. J. Groom for specialized information and the inclusion of their maps; to Fred Bluntschli for drawing the two end-paper maps; to Jack Maigher, editor of *Chrysler Mo-*

tors Magazine, for printing our thousands of pictures; to William Terry for making each picture a work of art; to David Curtin for assistance in the selection of pictures; to Mrs. W. F. Albright, to Professor Ralph W. Chaney, to Professor A. M. Honeyman, to Professor R. A. Stirton, to Professor M. Mitwally, to Charles Inge, to Pat Kuhnel, to Hussein Adenwalla, to Keith Collins, to Ansaf Abdul Maksoud, to Joe Rychetnik, to Gus Van Beek, and to Herbert E. French for editorial suggestions; to Dr. Albert Jamme for carefully checking each page and for his translations of new Qatabanian and Sabean inscriptions; to my mother and to my sister Merilyn for carefully checking every word; to Professor Casper Kraemer for numerous worthwhile suggestions and text corrections; to Willis Kingsley Wing, my authors' representative, for his constant encouragement and advice.

My very special thanks to Professor William F. Albright, who meticulously added to and subtracted from each page, drawing freely upon his seemingly unlimited fund of knowledge, in addition to comparing Greek and Latin translations with the originals; to my lovely secretary and Arabist, Mademoiselle Eileen Salama, for the tremendous good will she created for our expeditions wherever she went, for her major role in obtaining hitherto unobtainable information first hand from leading sultans, princes, saiyids, sheikhs, and sherifs of South Arabia, and for her invaluable assistance throughout every phase of the preparation of this manuscript; and to Marshall McClintock, who helped beyond measure in the editing and reorganizing of my material, and to whom I especially owe a lasting debt of gratitude for making readable English out of what otherwise might have passed for nonliterary Qatabanian.

WENDELL PHILLIPS

FIELD STAFF

American Foundation Arabian Expeditions

I & II (BEIHAN)
III (YEMEN)
IV (DHOFAR)

WENDELL PHILLIPS	Leader I-II-III-IV
PROF. W. F. ALBRIGHT	Chief Archaeologist I-II
WILLIAM TERRY	Field Director—Director of Photography I
GLADYS TERRY	Business Manager I
EILEEN SALAMA	Arabist—Secretary II-III-IV
CHARLES MC COLLUM	Chief of Motor Transport I
	Field Director II
	Administrative Director III-IV
GEORGE FARRIER	Motor Transport Specialist I
	Administrative Assistant II-III
	Field Director IV
ROBERT CARMEAN	Motor Transport Specialist II
	Field Director III
RICHARD BUSSEY	Business Manager III-IV
DR. ALBERT JAMME	Epigrapher I-II-III-IV
PROF. ALEXANDER HONEYMAN	Archaeologist—Epigrapher I
DR. FRISO HEYBROEK	Geologist I
DR. RICHARD BOWEN	Engineer Archaeologist I
JAMES SWAUGER	Archaeologist II
DONALD DRAGOO	Archaeologist II
ELLIS BURCAW	Archaeologist II
ROBERT SHALKOP	Archaeologist II
GUS VAN BEEK	Archaeologist II
RALF ANDREWS	Archaeologist III-IV

xi

JAMES RUBRIGHT	Archaeologist III-IV
KENNETH BROWN	Assistant Archaeologist I
JOHN SIMPSON	Assistant Archaeologist II
HARRY SCARFF	Architect III-IV
DR. LOUIS KRAUSE	Physician I
DR. JAMES MC NINCH	Surgeon I
DR. VALENTIN DE MIGNARD	Surgeon II
CMDR. C. H. GILLILAND	Physician III-IV
GIRAIR PALAMOUDIAN	Surveyor—Draftsman II
OCTAVE ROMAINE	Photographer I
WALLACE WADE	Director of Photography II
CHESTER STEVENS	Photographer II
	Director of Photography III-IV

CONTENTS

✳

ILLUSTRATIONS

Contents

MAPS

QATABAN AND SHEBA

1

TURN BACKWARD, TURN BACKWARD

From the air, Arabia looks as if it had lain there, harsh and barren, from the beginning of time. This huge block of earth, wedged between the vast land masses of Asia and Africa, suggests the first groping efforts to separate the land from the sea, for it is starkly primitive, gnarled, and naked. Here is the earth's crust undressed, unornamented by lakes or forests.

Only at the outermost corners does one glimpse small patches of green, indicating that the Maker of this subcontinent realized that something more than stone and sand were needed to make the earth good for human beings. Finding that trees and even a few rivers improved the property, He made most of the other continents with those features, but left Arabia as it was, except for a few precious drops of fertility scattered sparingly among its corrugated valleys and sandy plateaus.

Despite the forbidding face of southern Arabia, it looked good to me when I made a two-week flying survey in August, 1949, for I had some idea of what lay behind the withered and emaciated mask. I saw beneath the shifting sand dunes, the parched wadis, and the tumbled rocks, a long highway stretching seven hundred miles across the broad base of the country, then turning northward and winding for more than a thousand miles to the shores of the Mediterranean and the homes of our civilization's ancestors. I looked back over my shoulder three thousand years and saw long trains of camels burdened with frankincense and myrrh and sometimes with gold, pearls, ivory, cinnamon, silks, tortoise shell, and lapis lazuli. They followed the single road because there was no other; to the north the Rub' al Khali, or Empty Quarter, offered hundreds of miles of absolute desiccation; to the south the barren plateau spread only a short distance before it plunged precipitously into the sea.

There were good reasons for the road to follow the route it did—a series of those precious drops of fertility granted so sparingly to Arabia. The camels and the traders needed water and food—commodities more valuable than gold or incense in the ancient days as now. Around these spots grew great cities exacting tribute from the caravans for permission to travel on—across sand and rubble to the next tax-levying city, with *its* water and food.

From a few ports hugging the narrow shore along the central portion of southern Arabia, trails fed into the main route. Here strange vessels with huge sails swept in on the breast of the seasonal monsoons—whose variations were an oriental secret for thousands of years—to discharge cargoes from ports to the east, from India, and from Socotra, the "Isle of the Blest," an important crossroad of sea trade between India, Africa, and Arabia even before Moses led the Israelites out of bondage. At the western corner, other harbors received goods from the nearby horn of Africa and sent them north to join the main road, which was worn deep by the flow of southern Arabia's priceless natural product—incense from the valley of the Hadhramaut and from Dhofar, the frankincense country.

Today we can scarcely appreciate the role of incense in the ancient world because, for one thing, it is difficult to imagine the odors of that world, requiring clouds of sweet-smelling smoke to cover them. Resins, gums, and spices were used in embalming, fumigation, and medicine. They were burned on funeral pyres, at weddings and other celebrations, and daily in many homes.

Religious rites, however, demanded the largest quantities of the best incense—frank (or real) incense. Frankincense was sacred, and the country from which it came, in southern Arabia, was a sacred land, supplying the ancient world with its most holy and precious product. In the twelfth century B.C. Rameses III of Egypt had a special building for storing incense for the worship of Amon. The temple in Jerusalem contained a holy chamber for keeping incense under guard. In Persia, Darius received from the Arabs a yearly tribute of a thousand talents, or more than thirty tons, of frankincense. In Babylon, the altar of the god Bel was enveloped in the pleasant vapors of nearly sixty thousand pounds of frankincense each year. Hindus and Buddhists, Greeks and Romans—the gods of all demanded the hardened oozings of a certain kind of tree that grew mainly in one small area of southern Arabia and across the gulf in Africa.

For a thousand years, and perhaps much longer, southern Arabia prospered beyond belief, winning its classical name of Arabia Felix (Happy Arabia), which has seemed such a bitterly ironic description to all who have looked in recent centuries at this sterile and withered land supporting a handful of people with grudging stinginess.

The profits of trade were added to the profits of incense production, for southern Arabia was the great carrier of goods, the middleman between East and West. During the centuries when the Indian Ocean was a bustling center of maritime commerce—before the Mediterranean became the world's busiest shipping lane—the Arabs held a virtual monopoly of traffic between two civilizations that never came in direct contact with each other. Ships from India and Ceylon might stop at Arab ports on the Arabian Sea or barter in Arab-controlled regions of East Africa, where it curved in neighborly proximity to the Arab homeland. But they could never pass beyond that narrow strait between the two, which we now call Bab al Mandeb, the entrance to the Red Sea. On the other hand, the ships of Egypt and other countries to the north could sail the Red Sea at will, but were generally kept from going beyond Bab al Mandeb into the Indian Ocean. The middleman's position could be maintained only by keeping producers and consumers apart.

So a great many of the Orient's luxuries were added to the loads of frankincense on the camel caravans from southern Arabia, and the long highway to the markets of the Western world be-

came an even more coveted possession. People fought for control
of the road as bitterly as they battled for the incense country itself. From the second millennium before Christ to early in the
Christian era there was a succession of kingdoms that rose and
fell, amalgamated, conquered, and submitted. Saba, Ma'in, Qataban, Hadhramaut, Himyar—strange and unfamiliar names to most
of us, as are the names of the rich and thriving cities that were
their capitals, Marib, Qarnaw, Timna, Shabwa, Zafar. We know
something about Saba, of course, in its other spelling—Sheba—
whose queen, according to the Bible, visited King Solomon and
brought many wonderful gifts, including frankincense. The Old
Testament gives us a few other glimpses of southern Arabia, so
brief as to tantalize rather than inform, and serving only to confirm the existence in ancient times of wealthy, warring nations in
a region that has for almost twenty centuries been a stagnant back-
wash of the main stream of history.

Facts get buried deep in twenty centuries, but a few clues survived the neglect and erosion of time. Many of them, it is true,
are contained in legends and folk tales which are dubious combi-
nations of fact and fancy. But even poetry may contain historical
truth, as Schliemann found when he located and unearthed ancient Troy on evidence in Homer. More reliable are the statements about southern Arabia in Herodotus, Pliny, Strabo, Era-
tosthenes, and other classical writers, even though they are sketchy
and based on hearsay. *The Periplus of the Erythrean Sea,* a fac-
tual account of a Greek sea captain in the first century A.D., is
dependable as to the coast but tells little about the interior.

These clues to a fabulous past were too few to attract many explorers or scientists to brave the sandy wastes and feuding tribes
whose only point of agreement was their hostility to foreigners,
above all Westerners and Christians. But in the past century a
few courageous men and women have penetrated the region and
have described the ruins of the great dam at Marib, one of the
wonders of the ancient world, the remains of a temple here and
there. These, and a few hundred inscriptions, proved that the old
tales and vague reports were based on fact.

Knowing all this, I could scarcely believe that the hundreds of miles of barren wastes I viewed from my plane had once supported wealthy cities and a profitable world trade. Every grain of sand seemed to say, "No, not here!" It was hard to believe that a land which had been almost useless for two thousand years could have been important and valuable at any time.

What had ended southern Arabia's long period of greatness? There were many factors, of course, including the decreasing use of incense as Christianity replaced the pagan religions. But if there is one primary factor, it was probably a Greek sailor named Hippalus, who in the first century B.C. discovered that in the Indian Ocean the monsoon winds blow east toward India in the summer and west toward Africa in the winter. Soon Roman ships were bypassing southern Arabia, carrying goods from East to West largely by water at far less cost than overland by camel through the tax-levying cities.

Southern Arabia has been bypassed ever since, as the center of civilization moved ever further away to the west and north. The great movements of history surged back and forth on the other side of the Empty Quarter, as empires rose and fell without causing a ripple in the isolated pool of South Arabia's history, a pool that grew smaller and smaller until it dried up like the parched wadis that crisscross the country. Time fell asleep here, and the husks of ancient civilizations were buried in deep sand, preserved like flowers between the leaves of a book. The land looked forbidding, but it was rich with the spoils of time, and I wanted to unearth some of those riches, digging down through sand and centuries to a glorious past.

2

SEARCH FOR A SITE

The R.A.F. plane from Aden made a bumpy landing on the little landing strip in the Wadi Beihan, and I tried to make my stomach settle down comfortably in its accustomed place. In a flight around the world I had not yet felt uneasy until this brief jaunt to inspect the sand-covered ruins of the ancient South Arabian capital of Timna. Now I pulled myself together for the warm greeting of Sherif Saleh bin Naser, as picturesque and dignified an Arab as I could have wished to see.

The Sherif had two beasts of burden to offer for the seven-mile ride to our destination—a camel and a small horse. The camel was a vicious-looking beast, and as I approached him I heard Gargantuan subterranean noises rumbling from his mid-section. I turned to Charles Inge, Director of Antiquities for Britain's Crown Colony of Aden, who had accompanied me, and asked if he would like to ride the camel. He obligingly agreed, and enjoyed a pleasant ride. I chose the horse, which was equipped with a saddle that seemed upholstered with rocks and stirrups so short that my knees almost banged my chin as we bounced along over the broad, dry watercourse between barren cliffs.

Under the circumstances, I could not arouse much interest as we approached the huge mound of earth and sand known as Hajar Kohlan. This ruin of a once-great city was about half a mile long and a thousand feet wide, covering close to sixty acres. This was what I had come to see, but I centered my attention on the nearby mud palace, which comforted and cooled me the moment we stepped inside. We were greeted by its owner, Sherif Awad, brother of the actual ruler of Beihan. He was a rather fierce-looking, handsome man who could easily have enacted the role of the brave but villainous sheikh in a Hollywood movie. Awad was a romantic figure, a wanderer who liked to hunt and fight. He called himself "King of the Empty Quarter," the vast stretch of desert to the north where almost no one lived and few ventured.

Sherif Awad entertained us with a lunch served in typical Bedouin style. After we had seated ourselves on the floor, a large bowl was brought in, escorted by a swarm of flies. I peered inside and saw that it was filled with a strange mixture that looked something like mush, arranged like a huge doughnut, whose hole was filled with a yellow liquid. As I looked, hands stretched from all sides, each one scooping up a fistful of the mushlike substance, then dipping it into the yellow liquid. From here the hand traveled to the mouth, followed by a few of the flies that detached themselves from the main cloud over the bowl.

I have eaten many strange foods served in many styles, but it was with difficulty that honor and diplomacy forced me to take a few bites. The next course revived my spirits somewhat, for it was a bucket of broth that proved to be quite savory. I felt that the next installment, a serving of mutton, might bring me back to normal, but this particular mutton was served in a fashion I had never encountered before, with the internal organs of the sheep spread out before me like a fan. I did my best, but my best was not very good. When Charles Inge told Sherif Awad in his fluent Arabic that I was an American, my host nodded understandingly, as if that explained everything.

In the afternoon I inspected the mound of Hajar Kohlan containing the ruins of Timna, once capital of the Kingdom of Qataban, which Charles Inge had recommended as the most promising archaeological site in all southern Arabia, with the exception of the Queen of Sheba's ancient capital, Marib, and the ruins of Sirwah located in forbidden Yemen. Convinced that Timna offered great possibilities, I discussed with Sherif Awad such questions as the availability of native workers, the rental of his mud palace for an expedition, and other matters. By the time I returned to Aden that evening, I felt sure that Beihan could reveal significant discoveries about the people of South Arabia in the pre-Christian era—their life and loves, their religion, language, customs, government, business, and their relations with the rest of the ancient world.

But I did not yet want to rule out other possible sites, so I decided to continue my tour of inspection. Meanwhile I had a talk with the acting governor of Aden—the governor himself was away—Mr. A. R. Thomas. This gentleman was most co-operative, assuring me that an expedition would be welcomed in the Aden Protectorates—the long stretch of land along the southern coast of the Arabian Peninsula in which most of the tribes have made treaties with the British.

But he ruled out one site that had been on my list of prospects. This was Shabwa, ancient capital of the Hadhramaut, which was not only claimed sporadically by the neighboring independent kingdom of Yemen but was occupied by Arabs who apparently wanted nothing to do with Britain, Yemen, or any other outside power. As the authorities put it, security was very bad in and around Shabwa.

Why was I so determined to dig somewhere in South Arabia? For one thing, it was almost virgin territory. It had beckoned scholars and scientists for generations, but sand, drought, and native bullets had kept most of them away. The archaeological prizes lie primarily in regions left rather blank by map makers, with firm international boundary lines turning into vague dots and question marks. This means that the intruder is likely to be shot at by two or three claimants. In the past two decades, however, British treaties of friendship had ended numerous old feuds, although many regions were still labeled "Security Bad." Some travelers had made their way inland, and the first real excavation had been carried out in the Hadhramaut, where Gertrude Caton Thompson unearthed a moon temple at Hureidha, dating back to the fifth to third centuries B.C. I decided that a full-scale expedition might at last enter South Arabia with reasonable safety.

My attention first turned to South Arabia during a twenty-six-month African expedition which I led under the auspices of the University of California. In the course of the expedition, more than fifty scholars, scientists, and technicians, utilizing twenty-five trucks, an airplane, and a motorboat, had covered the entire continent, working on research problems in tropical medicine, paleontology, geology, anthropology, archaeology, and other fields.

Many things conspired to bring South Arabia into my mind during the African expedition. East Africa, for instance, has many close ties to Arabia, and Somaliland was one of the ancient sources of incense, some of which was shipped to Arabian ports and thence up the incense route to the Mediterranean world. The islands and towns of Africa's east coast contain many Hadhramis from the Wadi Hadhramaut. The Sultan of Zanzibar, with whom I had a pleasant lunch, was a cousin of the Sultan of Muscat and Oman, in southeastern Arabia. Finally, at one stage of the African trip I met and talked with the Right Honorable Sultan Sir Mohammed Shah, better known to the world as the Aga Khan.

This fabulously rich gentleman had established a camp in the Serengetti Plains, heart of the finest big-game country of Tanganyika, consisting of a 4,500-yard airstrip for his safari's two planes, twelve elaborate tents with private baths, electric lights, hot and cold running water, plus sixty native servants, five gunbearers, twenty personal servants, four cooks, and five of Nairobi's best white hunters. After inspecting this equipment for a little hunting trip, I was no longer worried by criticisms which had been voiced occasionally as to the unwieldy size of my own expeditions.

As a former president of the League of Nations Assembly, the Aga Khan was interested in the international character of my expedition, with scientists of many nationalities and faiths working together as a team. He heartily endorsed a project that had been formulating itself in my mind—an expedition to microfilm the thousands of priceless documents in the Monastery of St. Catherine at the foot of Mount Sinai. Most important, perhaps, he suggested

South Arabia as one of the most essential remaining areas for archaeological work.

Not long before, I had met the acting foreign minister of Saudi Arabia, who had apparently looked favorably on my casual suggestion of a future expedition into his country. Thus events, people, and the lure of the unknown led me to South Arabia—in my mind. The problem was to get there with a well-staffed and equipped expedition that could accomplish something worthwhile.

Such an expedition, as well as the microfilming project in Sinai, required an organization of scope and substance. After careful planning and much help, I established the American Foundation for the Study of Man, with Professor William F. Albright, Ph.D., Litt.D., D.H.L., Th.D., D.H.C., LL.D., the world's leading Biblical archaeologist and chairman of the Oriental Seminary at Johns Hopkins University, as first vice-president.* This organization, formed specifically to conduct world-wide research on the origins, development, and history of man from the earliest times to the present, won the support of many men of vision and influence, as evidenced by our Board of Directors—Fleet Admiral Chester W. Nimitz (1949-52), Samuel F. Pryor, Lowell Thomas, Brigadier General T. A. McInerny, Walter E. Ditmars, S. Bayard Colgate, James K. Moffitt, and Charles Nager.

So far, so good. But where in South Arabia would our first expedition excavate? The region was so rich and at the same time untouched that many possibilities tempted us. Professor Albright and I were in touch with H. St. John B. Philby, the foremost living explorer of Arabia, who wanted us to start our program in the Nejran area of Saudi Arabia, home of the ancient kingdom of Ma'in. This prospect was soon crossed off our list, however, by a confusing combination of politics, international business interests, and a competing project of another institution, which never materialized.

One amusing note relieved this disappointment. Somehow, the Saudi ambassador in Washington became suspicious that the ulte-

---

* Professor Albright is the author of over eight hundred books and articles on the Bible and the Middle East.

rior motive of our expedition was to promote Zionism in Saudi Arabia. This is an example of the kind of nonscientific problem the leader of a scientific expedition encounters. He must also expect to be accused of spying, planning naval bases, inciting revolution, stealing gold, and searching for uranium.

We crossed a second name from our South Arabian list almost as quickly as that of Ma'in. This was Marib, capital of ancient Shebaland and definitely the most tempting and promising of all archaeological sites, but it lay in the forbidden kingdom of Yemen.

I decided to have a look at three possible sites that remained, so I flew around the world on Pan American Airways, with stop offs in Istanbul, Cairo, and Alexandria to make final arrangements for the Sinai expedition, which by this time had won the support of the Library of Congress. In Cairo I had lunch with St. John Philby, who, despite the Saudi Arabian difficulties, encouraged me and agreed that I should consider the Wadi Beihan, site of the capital of the old Qatabanian kingdom.

I chartered an Arab Airways *Rapide,* an old canvas-covered plane with Peter Colvin of Cairo Shell at the controls, and flew to Luxor, Port Sudan, Kamaran Island in the Red Sea, and landed at Aden, Britain's Middle Eastern Gibraltar. This noisy and busy semimodern city probably has an ancient history, but most of its clues to antiquity have been obliterated. There I met Charles Inge and had my talk with the acting governor. Looking askance at my *Rapide,* he put at my disposal an R.A.F. plane to fly me into the Wadi Beihan for my first visit to the mound that covered ancient Timna. I was grateful, for my mind kept recalling that morning in 1947 when my paleontologists had noticed a strange reflection glistening in the Egyptian desert. Upon investigation a plane was found, all of whose passengers and crew were in a mummified state, their safety belts still fastened, with the pilot's log portraying the terrible isolation of the desert, for its final entry was dated 1943.

By the time I left Aden everything looked favorable for Beihan as an excavation site, but there were still some problems to be answered. The only way to reach Beihan at that time by land was long and roundabout, over a few hundred miles of road—or so it

was called—from the seaport of Mukalla northward into the Wadi
Hadhramaut and then westward, largely over plains and desert
with no road at all. Despite the fact that much of this region was
unmapped, investigation convinced me that properly equipped
trucks and some experienced desert drivers could get through all
right.

That was not the problem so much as were the governmental
authorities in Mukalla. Although this city was the chief port of
the Eastern Aden Protectorate, under British influence, it was the
seat of a nominally independent government controlling the
town itself and much of the country in the Wadi Hadhramaut
through which we would pass. This Qu'aiti government—so named
from the family that established and enlarged it—was at least independent enough to maintain its own customs and collect duties.
The Sultan of Mukalla might feel that he should collect duties
on the trucks and equipment I moved through his country—a pen-
alty that might stop the expedition before it started unless I could
get our materials through as scientific equipment of a totally non-
commercial nature.

So I flew from Aden to Mukalla, where the British advisers were
most helpful and took up the matter of customs with the Qu'aiti
officials. I learned, to my dismay, that since £54,000 were to be
spent during the next year on improvement of 800 miles of road,
and our expedition would traverse 240 miles of road, the Qu'aiti
government thought we should pay a duty of £16,200, about $45,-
000.

It was several minutes before I could recover the power of
speech, perhaps a fortunate thing, for otherwise I might have
blurted out that I did not want to buy 240 miles of road for my
personal possession. I just pointed out that this amount of money
might finance entirely a fair-sized expedition and would certainly
prevent my considering Beihan as a possible site.

Finally it was suggested, in the best of spirits, that if I could
donate a steam-roller or similar piece of equipment to the road-
building program, the expedition might enter the country duty
free. While this was no small problem, I thought it might be handled, and thanked the officials for their generosity.

I flew back to the United States and spent three months getting together the expedition's staff, enough funds to keep us going, and such items as trucks, cameras, food, refrigerators, electric power plants, gasoline, oil, typewriters, recording machines, guns, radios, medicines, and other essentials, plus transportation to Arabia—but no steam-roller. I found American business and industry willing to contribute their products not only from a philanthropic desire to aid the expedition but also to test materials and machines under new and grueling conditions. Money was harder to raise, except for the Sinai expedition, which appealed to financial contributors because of its Biblical connections and the obvious importance of microfilming more than two million early manuscript pages.

3

THE ESSENCE OF MUKALLA

The thousand-ton SS *Velho* steamed out of Aden with most of the staff and some of the equipment—including about two bushels of hard money—of the First Arabian Expedition of the new American Foundation for the Study of Man. Two men had preceded us to supervise the landing of the bulk of equipment at Mukalla and to establish a base, explore part of our overland route, and lay down gasoline dumps along the way. They were Kenneth Brown, an old high-school friend engaged primarily as assistant archaeologist, and young George Farrier, motor transport specialist and general pinch hitter.

In addition to our regular staff, we had with us Charles Inge, who planned on spending a few weeks with us in Beihan, and Jama Ishmail, hired in Aden as the expedition's head Somali, in charge of household management and servants plus other duties which later included saving the lives of all of us. Over six feet tall, quiet and smiling, Jama was a man of substance and experience, having been with Hugh Scott on his naturalist's expedition into Yemen. Jama spoke not only his native Somali, Hindustani, and English, but also Arabic in numerous dialects—a skill certain to prove of help despite our possession of one of the greatest linguists in the world, Professor Albright with his twenty-five languages.

The governor of Aden had insisted on sending along with us fifteen Bedouin government guards under the command of the indomitable Captain Mubarak Abdallah, respected and feared throughout the Aden Protectorates. His fame rested in part upon a dramatic tale of numerous killings to save "face" according to tribal law. I heard the story in several versions and always dismissed his alleged murder of his entire family as a gross exaggeration. The truth about the killings, in Arabia always elusive, favors the following: Mubarak once sent a guest to a wedding at his uncle's encampment. The guest was murdered. Mubarak thereupon purchased a new rifle and a quantity of ammunition, and within a year had avenged his guest and cleansed his blackened honor by eliminating the three men responsible, though they were his kin. Captain Mubarak instilled in me immediate confidence, which was heightened later when I witnessed his excellent marksmanship.

While I appreciated the governor's concern about our security on the journey to Beihan, I had been dismayed at my first talk with him. Sir Reginald Champion informed me, with the pleasantest of smiles, that if he had been present during my survey trip he would not have agreed to let the expedition into the Protectorates—there were just too many political and security problems involved. "However," Sir Reginald had continued, "since you and your party have now arrived I wish to welcome you and will do all I can to make your stay as enjoyable and successful as possible."

Thirty-six hours after leaving Aden we saw Mukalla, a white city crowded onto a narrow shelf between the blue harbor and tall red-brown cliffs. From about two-thirds of a mile away, where we cast anchor, it was lovely. Its whitewashed buildings, of four or five stories, accented by the taller minarets of thirteen mosques, seem to rise up out of the water. Blue decorations on the houses pick up the color of the sea, and four tiny white forts atop the cliffs complete the pictorial composition. On closer inspection, the white houses turn gray and look cramped and dingy, the water becomes dirty, and all remembrance of beauty is obscured by clouds of flies and the all-pervasive smell of fish—dead, drying fish.

At first we were too busy to pay much attention to either beauty or ugliness. Out from a cluster of dhows on the water of the harbor darted a small canoe containing George Farrier, scarcely recognizable because of an impressive beard which he had no doubt grown to make him look a little older than his nineteen years. He came aboard, and was soon followed by our second advance man, Kenny Brown.

There had apparently been some minor difficulties in connection with the landing, as I learned when George Farrier took me to one side.

"For heaven's sake, don't try to bring in anything that gurgles, not even a bottle of hair tonic," he whispered. "We've been accused of rumrunning!"

"Of what?" I shouted.

George gently broke the news that the hawk eye of a minor Qu'aiti official had noticed three cases of Log Cabin Syrup and, never having heard of this essential American commodity, immediately accused the expedition of attempting to smuggle whisky into their "bone-dry" state. In a desperate effort to demonstrate the truth, George had opened a container and accidentally poured warm syrup over the uniform of the senior customs official, who immediately became the prime attraction for every fly in the neighborhood.

I was trying to check over in my mind what gurgling items we might have on the *Velho* when the loading of the dhows began, a precarious business requiring the prayers and crossed fingers of the entire staff. A dhow is really an overgrown rowboat with a twenty-five-foot mast and two banks of oars, intended in Mukalla primarily to convey grain. Our electric power plant and refrigerator were not so easy to handle, although the major problems were two Dodge Power Wagons weighing 5,600 pounds each. Kenny Brown's assurances that eleven similar trucks had gone safely ashore this way did not make me feel any better when I saw one right front wheel suspended over the edge of the boat a few inches above the water.

Unloading was even more difficult, however, as Bill Terry, our field director, saw while he was taking movies of the job. Bill had come from Sinai, along with his wife, Gladys, to help get the Arabian expedition started. Through the viewer of his Ciné Special he saw the rear end of a truck suddenly appear where the front end should have been, as native workmen tried to haul it from the dhow to the embankment. The heaving and hauling of many

Expertly trained Arab government guards loaned to the expedition for its first overland journey to Beihan, on which the convoy passed through areas of doubtful security around disputed Shabwa

Captain (Rais) Mubarak Abdullah, master rifleman, who once liquidated a considerable portion of his family for a breach of Arab etiquette

Arab dhow transporting loaded expedition Power Wagon from ship to shore at Mukalla

First half of the expedition's convoy of Dodge Power Wagons climbing the steep Ma'adi Pass en route to Hadhramaut from Mukalla

sweating Arabs saved the precious Power Wagon from a watery grave.

Among the unusual items unloaded were two gunny sacks weighing more than 150 pounds and containing two thousand large silver coins stamped with the shining countenance of the Empress Maria Theresa and the date 1780, although they had obviously been minted recently. We had to carry them because in the interior of South Arabia the Maria Theresa dollar, or riyal, was the only sizable coin accepted, despite the fact that Indian rupees and annas were legal in Aden and official in the Qu'aiti and Kathiri states. The natives, except for those in the cities, still preferred the big and impressive M.T. dollar, and did not really feel that they were getting money unless they saw the picture of the great empress of a nation of which they had never heard.

The coin probably became current in Arabia by filtering down through Turkey long ago. Its value fluctuates with the value of silver, and was worth about fifty cents American when we were there, but the Bedouins of Hadhramaut and Beihan knew nothing of exchange rates. They knew only that they wanted Maria Theresa, although for small change they accepted almost any small coins—local buqshas or money from India or the East Indies.

When everything was safely ashore from the *Velho,* we headed for our base and got a closer look at Mukalla on the way. It is a city of almost no vertical depth, somewhat resembling Alexandria in the way it is spread thinly along the sea front, but having a strong flavor of Zanzibar. It is not a truly ancient city, since it was not in existence during the first century A.D. when the author of the *Periplus* made his voyage along the coast. At that time Cana, probably some distance to the west, was the principal port by which men and goods reached the Hadhramaut and the old incense route. Since its founding in the Middle Ages, however, Mukalla has been a busy place with the usual cosmopolitan population of seaports. Indian influence is evident everywhere, among the high officials, in the dress of the ruling family, and in some of the architecture, notably the Sultan's new palace on the western outskirts of the town. Near the palace is the fine residential section, called Bara as Sida. The old palace, now a government office building, is in the old city, along with most businesses, the prison, and some

Somali slums. The worst slum quarter is at the eastern end of town, under the cliffs, through which we passed on the way to our base.

Here the cliffs come very close to the water. Only at the western end is Mukalla open to attack, where in the old days they built the only fortified wall required for protection of the city. We slipped between cliff and sea, heading east on our way to a summer palace generously loaned us by His Highness Sir Salih bin Ghalib al Qu'aiti, K.C.M.G., Sultan of Shihr and Mukalla. Before reaching it, we passed through a new suburb called Khalf, created not long ago as a center for the fish-drying industry. Here, spread out over rocks and beach, lay millions of fish, drying in the sun. The smell that rose from them must have reached as high as the unused forts on the cliffs above. The odor penetrates clothes, hair, and lungs so that you carry the essence of Mukalla with you for some time after leaving it.

Our palace sat in a beautiful spot on the edge of the sea, but it had almost no windows and few modern conveniences. While we tried to make ourselves comfortable Charlie McCollum, our chief of motor transport, checked over trucks and equipment. Dr. James R. McNinch, Jr., the expedition's physician, and Octave Romaine, our photographer, fitted Lyman telescopic sights to our rifles and sighted them in. And I prepared myself for a meeting with the finance secretary of the Mukalla government—to discuss steam-rollers.

Charles Inge had warned me that the government really expected the steam-roller, or a duty of 15 per cent on the value of everything I brought in. Since this would have bankrupted us at once, I had to find a way out. Fortunately, the finance secretary listened understandingly as I explained that in three months for the organization of two expeditions I had been unable to obtain a steam-roller. But since we planned on spending at least two seasons working in Beihan, I would surely get one, or something as valuable for the road-building program, before we had completed our work. He was obviously disappointed, but decided that nothing could be accomplished by holding the entire expedition in Mukalla until I found a steam-roller.

4

THROUGH THE HADHRAMAUT

It was two o'clock in the afternoon on Monday, February 20, 1950, before we had packed all equipment and supplies into our thirteen specially built Dodge Power Wagons and started for the interior, with our Explorers' Club flag No. 143 pointing the way from the nose of the lead vehicle. Our convoy picked its way slowly down the long street of Mukalla that runs parallel with the water front and finally rolled through the city's one gate, in its western wall. As we passed the big camel park, a crowd of Bedouin camel men gathered to stare at us with expressions far from friendly.

We had been warned that the owners of camels resented motor vehicles as threats to their trade and livelihood. Farther north, in Saudi Arabia, the discovery of oil had so quickened the tempo of westernization that many roads were built and trucks imported. Since camel owners had no capital to invest in trucks, they went out of business or subsisted on leftover crumbs of trade. News of this development had traveled the Bedouin grapevine—a mysteriously efficient and rapid means of communication. One of the chief obstacles to the laborious building of a road from Mukalla to the Hadhramaut had been the fierce antagonism of the camel men, who sometimes displayed their annoyance with bullets. Even at the time of our first trip, a few years after completion of the road, Bedouins sometimes took potshots at passing or stalled trucks. A massed convoy like ours, however, was not likely to be attacked in the daytime.

Turning inland from the park, we started climbing a rather steep grade to a limestone plateau, where the road turned eastward and led us down several natural terraces and through small wadis that were surprisingly green. The clouds of locusts we saw would not leave them green for very long.

We spent the first night near a small airfield maintained by the R.A.F. at Riyan, then drove on the next morning to the spot where the road joined that from the port of Shihr. Heading north again, we passed the Sultan's tobacco gardens near Gheil ba Wazir and began to climb the steep Ma'adi Pass. By noon we were 4,000 to 5,000 feet above sea level, and stopped for lunch and a brief rest. Although we were not near anything that looked like a settlement, a small band of boys appeared from nowhere selling coconuts.

In the afternoon we labored up ridges and through precipitous gorges, past the village of Ma'adi, and up a long series of breathtaking hairpin turns that lifted us onto the enormous tableland called the Djol, over which we would travel until we neared the Wadi Hadhramaut.

The Djol is cut by many deep valleys, and the geological formations are marvelously exposed. There is no vegetation to hide the rocks and except on the wadi bottoms no deposits to obscure the visible history of the earth's crust. During our brief stops, I often explored a bit with Dr. Friso Heybroek, of The Hague, the expedition's geologist and chief map maker. My early training as a paleontologist had not been entirely obliterated by the work and worries of organizing and leading expeditions, so I was excited when Friso and I found a few fossil Foraminifera—tiny shells of prehistoric ocean-dwelling protozoa—some pecten clams, echinoid spines, and corals from the Eocene epoch some fifty-odd million years ago, when portions of Arabia lay under the sea.

We suffered our second night on the Djol, seventy-six miles from Riyan. At an elevation of about 3,000 feet, the afternoon was cool, but as soon as the sun sank we found ourselves shivering in a temperature close to freezing. Feeling like pioneers on the old Santa Fe trail, we arranged our trucks in a protective hollow square, inside of which we prepared meals, ate, and slept.

Captain Mubarak regularly rode beside Gladys Terry, who took

The expedition bedded down inside a protective hollow square formed by the Power Wagons, while outside the pick of Aden's Arab government guards stood watch to prevent any possible surprise attack

Gladys Terry, expedition business manager, sitting on the bumper of her Power Wagon. During the following week she became the first American woman explorer to reach Hadhramaut and Beihan.

over the second position as convoy pace-setter. Although she occasionally got out of sight around a turn or over a hill, I was never worried about her. I knew she was safe as long as Mubarak drew breath, for he was a tremendous admirer of her driving. To an Arab, anyone who can drive or fly is a superior person, and Gladys is superb at either the wheel of a truck or the controls of a plane.

She had handled the field accounts of three major expeditions, totaling about eighty-three scientists, scholars, and technicians, and approximately three hundred native assistants, operating in more than two dozen countries. She had driven a two-and-a-half-ton truck with trailer from Cairo to Capetown, and set an all-time record for the Middle East by making six trips in ten days from Cairo to Mount Sinai in the driver's seat of a Power Wagon. In the words of Jefferson Caffery, the American ambassador to Egypt and her passenger on two of these journeys, "she is indeed an unforgettable young woman." To top it all, Gladys is a beautiful blonde. On the trip to the Hadhramaut, Gladys's pace-setting was so expert that not a truck blew a tire or broke a spring on that rocky road, a feat I would have thought impossible.

The success of any expedition often depends more on the strength and skill of its nonscientific staff than on its scholars. This is certainly true when the expedition operates in an area like South Arabia, of difficult accessibility and doubtful security. The men who save the day then are the logistics experts, the motor transport specialists, and the medical men. If they falter, the whole expedition falters, and the scholars cannot do their work. These considerations had made me pick several young men for my staff, despite the head shaking of some who insisted that experience was essential. Perhaps I leaned toward young people because I was not yet thirty myself.

After dinner one evening we heard soft music from the campfire of the government guards. The song or chant was strange to our ears, as the music of totally different cultures usually is, but it grew in meaning and beauty as we listened. The guards sang together as if they were a trained choir, and many of us walked nearer to listen. Soon we were sitting around the fire with them, and when they asked us for a song, we complied with some hesitation. They answered with another Arabian piece, and we sang again. I felt rather ashamed to realize that our best was far below the musical standard of their worst, but it was a thoroughly enjoyable evening.

Professor Albright became ill, but since we were only sixty miles from the sizable city of Seiyun, where there would be good accommodations, we drove on. We encountered thick accumulations of silt framed on either side by impressive scarps. Irrigated fields of barley, interspersed with date gardens, showed green against the arid landscape. Between the villages of Nuwedre and Skedan we were amazed to see the rarest of sights in South Arabia—a beautiful flowing stream of crystal-clear water, filled with fish.

Village followed village with greater frequency as we neared the Wadi Hadhramaut near the center of its most fertile area, which extends for about sixty miles out of its total length of close to 360 miles. A wadi is not really a valley but rather a dried-up watercourse. Many wadis are not dry all the time, but become raging torrents after heavy rains, when water pours down the cliffs and over the rocks unchecked by vegetation.

For eleven months of the year, or often for several years on end, not a drop of water may be seen in many wadis, but subsurface water may remain that can be reached by wells. There are many wells in the sixty-mile stretch of the Wadi Hadhramaut, near its source, accounting for the cluster of towns and villages in this area. At some points here the wadi is close to forty miles wide, but it narrows down to four or five miles beyond Tarim, the easternmost of the cities in this fertile stretch. Here it changes its name to the Wadi Maseila, although it remains geographically the same wadi all the way to its outlet near the sea close to Saihut. In a presumed pluvial period, twenty to twenty-five thousand years ago, the Wadi Hadhramaut was a great river flowing eastward, fed by countless tributaries that are now the smaller wadis leading into the Hadhramaut.

Hadhramaut itself is referred to in Genesis under the Hebrew name "Hazarmaveth," which is supposed to mean "Enclosure of Death." Genesis also refers to the sons of Joktan, and today one finds tribesmen of the Hadhramaut proudly stating that they are the descendants of Joktan, supposed by them to be Qahtan, great-great-great-grandson of Shem, son of Noah, and the legendary ancestor of all South Arabians.

Turning left as we entered the Wadi Hadhramaut, we drove a few miles to the beautiful city of Seiyun, capital of the Kathiri state. It is more spacious than most South Arabian cities, less packed and cramped, with many open spaces lined with graceful date palms. Arrangements had been made for us to stay at the rather bizarre but sumptuous palace of Saiyid Abu Bakr, of the powerful and wealthy Al Kaf family, financial rulers of Kathiri and builders of the road from Mukalla and Shihr into the Hadhramaut. The Saiyid was away in Singapore, where the Al Kaf family has many relatives and extensive business interests, but we were welcomed by another prominent member of the family, Saiyid Jemalalleil of Tarim, who also invited the entire party to lunch at his palace the following day.

The Arabs of the Hadhramaut fared well in the great days of the incense trade, but when the rich kingdoms fell after transfer of the traffic to the sea, the wadi could not support its population. Hadhramis began to seek their livelihoods in other lands, where they became tradesmen, real-estate owners, moneylenders, and brokers in such distant places as Kenya, Tanganyika, Zanzibar, Sudan, Egypt, Saudi Arabia, Abyssinia, Singapore, Penang, and the former Netherlands East Indies, where the largest Hadhrami colony flourishes, numbering today about seventy thousand. Wherever they went, however, they kept a deep love of their homeland. They all wanted to return home some day loaded with wealth gained abroad. Despite the Hadhramaut's isolation, there has always been a good deal of movement of people and money and goods between it and Hadhrami colonies in other lands, producing in the midst of desert land a region of sky-scraper cities, roads, sumptuous palaces with many modern conveniences, jewels, imported foods, and a college-educated upper class. As a result of the admixture of blood between Hadhrami Arabs and, in particular, the East Indians, Hadhramaut has been called the "Land of the Javanese Princesses."

The Sultan's home in Seiyun was seven stories high, although built principally of mud, and whitewashed to a gleaming beauty. In Tarim, a city of aristocrats and fine homes, we found Saiyid Jemalalleil's mansion with electric lights, running water, Western-style furniture, baths, toilets, and telephones. This city is the religious heart of the Hadhramaut, with a reputed 365 mosques, one for each day of the year. We climbed the spiral staircase in a minaret 175 feet high and enjoyed a wonderful view of the spacious city, surrounded by a wall with five gates and more than twenty forts.

Tarim's religious importance comes from the fact that it is a city of saiyids, and saiyids rule the Kathiri state. The term "saiyid," in South Arabia like that of sherif, is a hereditary title somewhat equivalent to that of lord, with deep religious significance because it is borne by those who claim descent from the Prophet Mohammed through his daughter Fatima. Saiyids are spiritual leaders rather than political or military chiefs, but some have gained great power through force of personality or wealth. Even the poorest of the saiyids, however, is regarded with respect and even reverence.

Saiyid Jemalalleil spread before us the most elaborate of the banquets we had enjoyed. We took our places in a great hall, whitewashed and decorated with brilliant colors, sitting cross-legged on the floor. Down the middle stretched a beautiful rug, on which lay lovely dishes filled with strange food.

I turned to George Farrier. "Look, George," I said. "Some of this food may not appear too appetizing to you, but don't let American prestige down. Dig in and make out that you're enjoying it, will you?"

George nodded, but at that moment a plate was set before him. "Eyeballs!" he gulped. "Eyeballs and—"

"Yes," I replied, smiling, "as honored guests we get the best."

Later I turned from a conversation with the Saiyid to see George obviously obeying orders—and with gusto. His big right hand emerged from a bowl of rice, then plunged into a bowl of honey. He managed to get the dripping food into his mouth with astonishingly few grimaces and with evident satisfaction. George was not attacked by flies because of the waving palm leaves in the

The enchanting Hadhramaut residence of Saiyid Abu Bakr of the powerful and wealthy Al Kaf family in the city of Seiyun, which served as temporary expedition headquarters

Shibam—South Arabia's most spectacular skyscraper city—whose many-storied buildings constructed mainly of mud were built over the centuries for defense against attack by surrounding Bedu tribes

hands of several small boys who stood behind us throughout the meal.

Dessert consisted of a thick paste made from year-old dates, with unleavened bread soaked in black honey. But then we were led into the next room where we found cake and tea. While doing our best with this last course, we saw the enactment of a traditional custom of the Kathiri state. The doors of the banquet hall were thrown open to the *meskeen* who had gathered. These are the poor, maimed, blind, and other unfortunates, about two dozen of whom were immediately at the food with noisy appreciation.

After this excellent feast, we did not have much appetite for the afternoon tea at the magnificent home of Saiyid Omar bin Sheikh Al Kaf. His palace was fascinating, however, above all the huge inlaid bathtub which was surrounded by colorful murals of young women in various degrees of undress and interesting positions.

About twenty miles west of Seiyun we came to Shibam, the most spectacular skyscraper city of Arabia. Tall mud buildings cluster so close together that they seem to be one structure, of almost uniform height—except for the Sultan's brown-and-white striped palace, which dominates the town. With their plastered tops gleaming white in the morning sun, the gray buildings looked more imposing than they really are, for their massive walls, sloping back slightly from their foundations, rise abruptly from an elevation above the flat wadi bed. Actually, most of them are only six or seven stories high, although they appear to be twice that because each floor has a double row of windows, one above the other.

Inside the city, one sees why the buildings appear to be built on top of each other. They almost are, for no real streets separate them, only alleys in which three people might find it difficult to walk abreast. Narrowness is not the only obstacle to a stroll down these alleys, for they are generally dark, damp, full of people, and their gutters—running down the center—are used for the disposal of garbage and sewage. Long chutes project out and down from upper floors of the buildings for carrying waste matter, which bounces off a kind of buttress at street level in the general direction of the gutter. One must step lively at any sound from above. When the gutters are not completely clogged, they carry sewage to a main cesspool, principal feature of the one open square of the city.

Despite its abominable sanitation and overpowering odor, Shibam is the most important commercial town of the Hadhramaut. For centuries it has been the chief market for all surrounding tribes, and in recent decades has profited as the inland capital of the Sultan of Shihr and Mukalla.

Our convoy pushed on for Gouda, through a wadi that grew ever wider, although it was still bounded on either side by towering cliffs. A bad stretch of deep sand slowed us down, but we reached the settlement in time to load the precious gasoline deposited there by our advance staff, and to put more mileage behind us before stopping for the night.

At Gouda we saw the arrival of a long train of several hundred camels, which came to be watered and taxed. Each petty Arab state levies taxes on camels and their cargoes which travel over tribal boundaries, and Gouda's lone well was sure to attract all caravans moving in that region. Thus we witnessed, on a very small scale, the process by which several kingdoms had grown rich in the days of the incense trade.

While the gasoline was being loaded, Dr. McNinch treated a severe local case of gonorrhea with sulfadiazine and dispensed handfuls of aspirin, for most of the population of Gouda suddenly developed headaches upon learning that a doctor was available. When Charlie McCollum signaled that the convoy was ready to move, Bill Terry took movies of our departure for Bir Asakir, where we hoped to spend the night. Two Bedu guides accompanied us for the ostensible purpose of keeping us on the correct route. No member of the expedition had traveled beyond Gouda, and there was little that could be called a road at all. The Wadi Hadhramaut grew so broad that it scarcely resembled a wadi any more, and we entered upon the eastern edge of the Ramlet Sabatein, a vast sandy plain extending from near Marib in Yemen on the west almost two hundred miles into the opening of the Wadi Hadhramaut on the east, and from Timna in Beihan northward to some vague point at which it merged almost imperceptibly into the huge desert, Rub' al Khali. Ramlet Sabatein, incidentally, means "Plain of the Two Sabas," and suggests an ancient time when the kingdom of Saba (Sheba) may have conquered Qataban and perhaps much territory to the north and east.

From here on Bill Terry and I, old hands at running truck convoys, had the thrill of our expedition lives, for it was now possible to travel thirty-five to forty miles an hour over the hard-packed sand and gravel of the Ramlet Sabatein. It was an unforgettable sight to see our convoy spread out in echelon, traveling at this undreamed-of desert speed, with Bill clinging to the top of the photo van desperately trying to shoot movies in all directions.

Making such good speed, we covered three times as many miles on this day's drive as on any other, and arrived at Bir Asakir long before dark. I was glad, because the gleaming white fort there makes a romantic picture, looking like something out of the Hollywood version of *Beau Geste*. There is nothing else at this ill-chosen spot except a well—*bir* means "well" in Arabic—so we started to unpack our cooking and sleeping equipment and make camp outside the walls of the fort.

The firing of shots in the distance interrupted us, and some looked uneasily for their guns. But we were just being introduced to the customary desert greeting of southern Arabia. About ten men of the Al Amr section of the Bal Ubeid tribe approached us shooting into the air, and we returned their salute with volleys from shotguns, carbines, and revolvers, then shook hands all around. The Arab of the desert, who lives by his rifle and might soon die without it, uses it also for his warmest welcomes. If he likes you he will probably shoot at you, and the nearer the miss the greater his show of affection. A few weeks later I was deeply affected by the display of brotherly feeling on the part of a sheikh in Beihan, who, while clasping my hand with his right, simultaneously fired with his left, the rifle bullet passing some inches in front of my nose.

Later that evening the rest of the Al Amr group came along, and Charles Inge and I were invited to join them around their campfire. There, over cups of strongly minted coffee, we were told that their tribe had twenty-six members, and twenty-four murders to its credit. I looked wonderingly around the campfire trying to spot the two who had not been holding up their share of the tribal honor.

We left Bir Asakir very early the next morning because we wanted to make this last and most difficult leg of our journey to Beihan in one day. On the first portion, we had to drive across the plain north of forbidden Shabwa, then cut down southwest when we calculated that we had bypassed the ancient town sufficiently. But no one knew how far away we should keep. The Karab tribe, some sections of which control most of Shabwa, consists of nomads who wander over an area of several hundred square miles. They had been known to attack trespassers, far from the town itself. Part of Shabwa was owned by the Bureiki, a clan of holy sheikhs who had served for countless generations as keepers of sacred places. The tombs of two of their patron saints were at Shabwa, which remained the Hidden City for centuries and even today has been visited by only a handful of Westerners.

Our expedition's size and armament, with its fifteen government guards under Captain Mubarak, were good insurance against attack. I am sure that we could have driven directly into the town and looked at everything we wanted to see, provided we stuck together. But there might have been an exchange of shots—an "incident"—and that is what we wanted to avoid. So we drove over the plain three or four miles to the north of the old capital of the Hadhramaut, accompanied by two sheikhs of the tribes living at Shabwa, who had been obtained by Charles Inge to serve both as guides and hostages—a common practice in South Arabian travel.

There has been some confusion between the words "Shabwa" and "Sheba." In antiquity, Shabwa was probably the least important and the youngest of the capitals of the four great South Arabian kingdoms, and had absolutely nothing to do with the Queen of Sheba. It was located in an arid country incapable of supporting a large population, which is not the case with Timna or Marib. Its possession of salt mines and above all its key position

Revolver practice was temporarily interrupted when this pretty Arab girl appropriated the expedition's tin can target.

The expedition obtained fresh water from the deep well at Bir Asakir, last western outpost in Hadhramaut, manned by the British-trained Hadhrami Bedouin Legion.

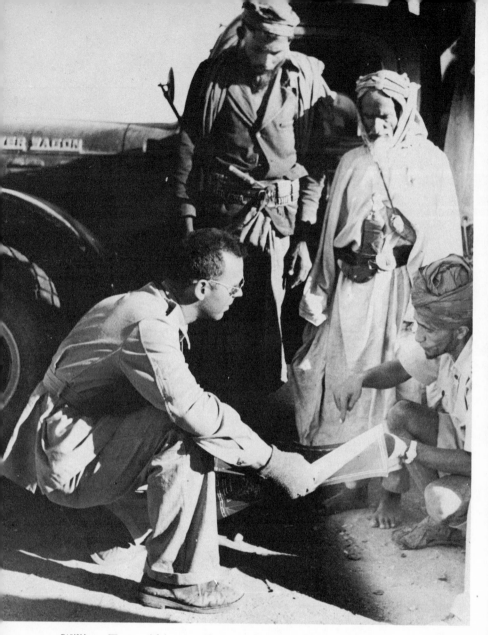

William Terry, African explorer and photographer, checks the route around disputed Shabwa with two local tribal sheikhs serving as combination guides and hostages.

on the old incense road made it important. That position also explains why the capital of the Hadhramaut lay so far west of the main wadi. It could catch all the trade coming north from the ancient seaport of Cana as well as that coming along the valley.

By the time we pulled into the Beihan village of Aseilan, the ceremonial rifle greeting, which sounded like the landing of the Marines at Tarawa, was incapable of arousing very much emotion in us. We were just too tired and too relieved at being a mere two miles from "home."

A large part of the population of the Wadi Beihan was on hand to look not so much at us as at our Power Wagons and to beg rides for the remainder of our journey to Hajar Kohlan. They climbed on running boards, fenders, hoods, and grinned happily as our trucks moved over the sand.

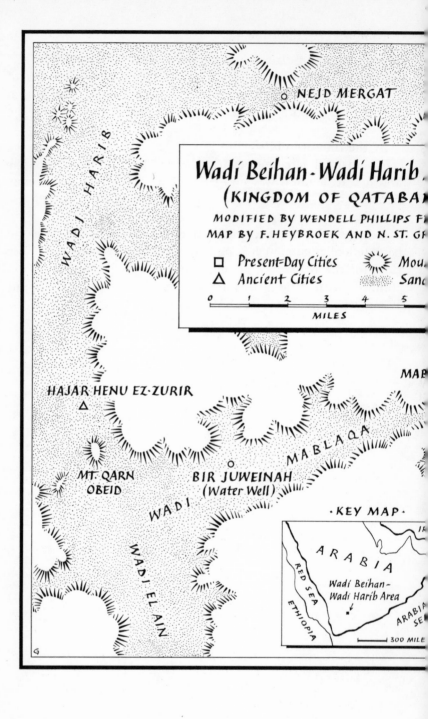

NEJD MERGAT

WADI HARIB

Wadi Beihan - Wadi Harib
(KINGDOM OF QATABA
MODIFIED BY WENDELL PHILLIPS F
MAP BY F. HEYBROEK AND N. ST. GR

☐ Present-Day Cities   ☼ Mou.
△ Ancient Cities   ░ Sand

0   1   2   3   4   5
MILES

HAJAR HENU EZ-ZURIR
△

MABLAQA

MAP

MT. QARN
OBEID

BIR JUWEINAH
(Water Well)

WADI

WADI-EL-AIN

·KEY MAP·

ARABIA

RED SEA

ETHIOPIA

Wadi Beihan-
Wadi Harib Area

ARABIA
SE

300 MILE

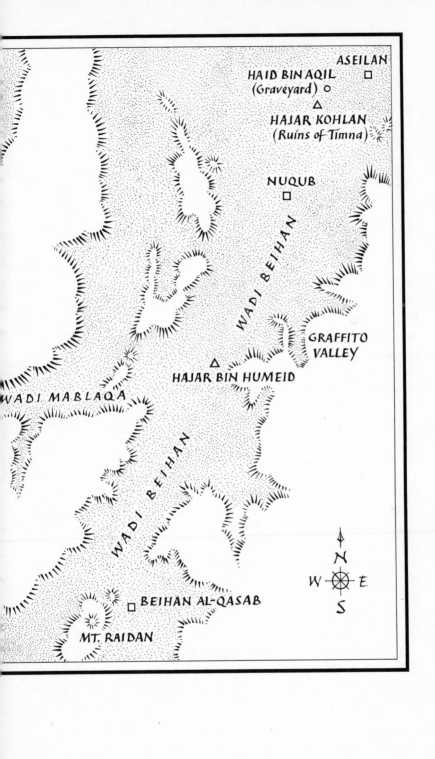

ASEILAN □

HAID BIN AQIL
(Graveyard) ○

△

HAJAR KOHLAN
(Ruins of Timna)

NUQUB
□

WADI BEIHAN

GRAFFITO
VALLEY

△
HAJAR BIN HUMEID

WADI MABLAQA

WADI BEIHAN

N
W ✶ E
S

□ BEIHAN AL-QASAB

MT. RAIDAN

5

THE DIG

Our host and landlord in Beihan, Sherif Awad, called on us
the next morning to take us on a tour of our new home and
headquarters. He was quite proud of the many changes he had
made since my survey trip the year before. The whitewashing of
the upper part of the house pleased us, but we were particularly
impressed by the murals in a large reception banquet room on
the ground floor. The friendly and understanding purpose of these
pictures touched us, for they evidenced his sympathy with both
Great Britain and the United States while displaying his knowledge of world events far beyond the Wadi Beihan. One of them,
for example, portrayed—graphically if not artistically—President
Truman and King George dropping atom bombs on Marshal
Stalin.

Sherif Awad served tea to his tenants, with the assistance of
extremely polite local residents of importance. I relaxed comfortably on the carpeted floor and welcomed the cup of tea brought
me by a smiling Beihani. But as my hand reached out for the
cup, he snatched it back with mumbled apologies, scowling at
the struggling green fly on the surface of my beverage. His smile
returned as he cleverly rescued it with only one grimy finger and
triumphantly handed the cup to me.

Although the main archaeological program had to wait for the
arrival of Professor Albright, who had stayed in Seiyun until he
recovered from his illness, the rest of us inspected the area and

made preliminary plans. We wanted to select projects that might
bring significant results in the six weeks before the heat became
too intense. Here was a city covering more than sixty acres and
itself covered by thousands of tons of sand. Unearthing the entire city was a project of a decade or more, and one that we had
never contemplated. We had to choose two or three small areas
that would disclose the greatest amount of information about the
Timna of antiquity.

One spot had really been agreed upon already, the South Gate,
where Charles Inge and Kenny Brown set to work at once. This
southern edge of the mound had always revealed a tempting portion of its structure above the sands. Here in 1936 Stewart Pe-
rowne, then political officer for the Beihan, had found an inscription starting, "I, the King of Qataban, in my city of Kohlan . . ."
and giving the names of regions he claimed as part of his domain.*

The Qatabanian inscriptions are written in a language which
differs slightly from that of the inscriptions from other parts of
South Arabia. The royal names and the earliest inscriptions indicate a mixture of the dialects of Saba (Sheba) and Qataban.
These facts suggest a period when Qataban was ruled by the Sabeans. The native Qatabanian language was closely related to that
of Ma'in to the north, and to the language of Hadhramaut, dif-
fering slightly from that of Saba. It is likely, therefore, that the
people who spoke the language of Ma'in, Qataban, and Hadhramaut had lived in this region before the Sabeans and that the
latter then conquered the area and strongly influenced its language and personal names.

The alphabet of ancient Himyar and earlier Arabian kingdoms
is consonantal, and as a rule no vowels are expressed. It is actually quite easy to read—far easier than Arabic. Southern Arabic
preserves the most consonants and the most archaic sounds of all
the alphabets derived from Canaanite. For example, the Hebrew
alphabet has twenty-two letters, the Greek twenty-four, with six

---

* In 1924 an Austrian scholar of Greek extraction, N. Rhodokanakis, assembled all the known Qatabanian inscriptions and proved that the mound
called Hajar Kohlan, in Beihan, was actually the site of ancient Timna,
when it was a powerful city on the incense road to the Mediterranean.

Chart of South Arabian Letters

	1	2		1	2
ʾ			m		
b			n		
g			s		
d			ʿ		
ḏ			ġ		
h			f		
w			ṣ		
z			ḍ		
ḥ			q		
ḫ			r		
ṭ			š		
ẓ			ś		
y			t		
k			ṯ		
l					

Chart of South Arabian Letters Prepared by Dr. Albert Jamme, W.F.

There were twenty-nine letters in this alphabet, which was originally borrowed from the Canaanite-Phoenician-Hebrew alphabet of Syria-Palestine in the fourteenth or thirteenth century B.C. Like it, the South Arabian letters represented only consonants. The order of the South Arabian alphabet was different from that of the northern script and resembled that of the derived Ethiopic (Abyssinian) alphabet closely, as we know from parts of alphabets found on pavements of the temple at Timna, dating from about the third century B.C. The chart includes: (1) formal lettering on stone and metal; (2) scratched or cursive lettering from graffiti on rock scarps, etc. The direction of letters in inscriptions was generally either left to right (chiefly before the seventh century B.C.), right to left (nearly always after the fifth century B.C.), or alternately right to left and left to right (boustrophedon style, dominant in the eighth to fifth centuries B.C.).

vowels, the English twenty-six, with five vowels, the Arabic twenty-eight, whereas the ancient Himyaritic alphabet had twenty-nine letters without vowels.*

Nearly fifty years ago the great Egyptologist, Sir Flinders Petrie, discovered a previously unknown alphabetic script at Serabit el-Khadem in the Sinai Peninsula. These now famous Proto-Sinaitic inscriptions have illustrated in various ways the close relationship between the South Arabian dialects of our early inscriptions and the Canaanite dialects of the north. For example, the Serabit el-Khadem letter B looks almost the same as those in early inscriptions from southern Arabia. The significance of this fact was pointed out by our own Professor Albright, who, a few years before, on our African expedition, had climbed the steep cliffs at Serabit el-Khadem to visit the ancient Egyptian turquoise mines, on whose walls he could study the controversial Proto-Sinaitic inscriptions. He showed that this language represented a Canaanite dialect of about 1500 B.C., which was like parent Hebrew and was probably the language spoken by the Hebrews in the land of Goshen in the Nile delta before the Exodus.

Professor Albright reached Timna sooner than we had expected, and we were all delighted to see him strong and healthy, so eager for immediate work that he was somewhat disappointed to learn that we had not already taken care of all diplomatic formalities. Nevertheless, he enjoyed as much as the rest of us the visit we paid to Sherif Hussein, *de facto* ruler of Beihan, in the town of Beihan al-Qasab, about seventeen miles south of Timna.

The dominant personality of the Wadi Beihan, and perhaps for an area extending a good deal beyond it, is Sherif Hussein bin Ahmed, a tall and handsome man who loves shooting, good food, his wives, and bright colors in his clothing. A leader of great charm and tact, with intelligence and forthrightness, he has

---

* The alphabet of the ancient peoples of South Arabia was first worked out independently more than a hundred years ago by two German scholars, Erwin Roediger and Wilhelm Gesenius. It was Gesenius who also completed the deciphering of Phoenician (closely related to ancient Arabic) and who first put our knowledge of Biblical Hebrew on a sound scientific basis. The first complete collection of proper names in southern Arabia was published in 1934 by Professor G. Ryckmans of Louvain, and the first real grammar in 1943 by Dr. Maria Höfner of Tübingen.

reached his position as virtual ruler of twenty to twenty-five thousand people by the force of his personality and the wisdom of his father, Ahmed bin Muhsin. Sherif Ahmed had gained stature through his position as mediator in the disputes of the Bal Harith tribe, of northern Beihan, and the Musabein, of the south. It was he who brought them together sufficiently to negotiate one of the earliest treaties between Arab groups and the British at Aden. The Bal Harith and Musabein, each with dissident groups, had been a difficult crowd for Sherif Ahmed to hold together, but in the main peace had been kept in the Wadi Beihan, despite its proximity to the contending kingdom of Yemen, and most of the people liked the idea of peace instead of killing—as ordinary people usually do everywhere.

Sherif Ahmed's biggest problem, as he grew old, was the succession to his power. He had three sons, but the most commanding and able of these was the youngest, Sherif Hussein. Old Sherif Ahmed decreed, shortly before his death in 1934, that his successor should be his grandson, Saleh bin Hussein, who would be brought up as ruler from the time of his boyhood. Saleh bin Hussein—"bin" means "the son of"—was the son of the strongest and brightest of the old Sherif's children, who naturally became regent upon the old man's death. In this way Sherif Ahmed saw to it that Hussein ruled Beihan, without inviting bloody feuds carried out by the older brothers. Sherif Hussein had ruled well, apparently, for under him Beihan enjoyed greater peace and stability than ever before. His son, called by the title of emir, was now in his early twenties, but seemed content to leave state affairs in his father's hands.

When we arrived at the Sherif's ample home, we were ushered into a brightly lit room whose floor was completely covered with beautiful Arab rugs, with dozens of assorted pillows strewn around the outer edges. After tea, the party paraded into a nearby room in which dinner was served. My skepticism about southern Arabian meals vanished with the serving of a banquet of such excellence and variety that any person could have found good food to his taste—with lamb, chicken, rice, hard-boiled eggs, bread, honey, sliced pineapple, and different kinds of hot sauces.

Professor W. F. Albright, chief archaeologist of the expedition, measuring a
broken Qatabanian water jar

Sherif Hussein bin Ahmed, ruler of Beihan

After dinner we moved to a third large room, where Sherif Hussein made a somewhat lengthy speech, which was translated on the spot by Professor Albright. The main points were that he was extremely happy that we had come to his part of the world, that we were to consider his home our home, and that his one desire was to make our stay a happy one. As his later actions proved, he meant every word of it. I replied with as many nice things as I could think of on the spur of the moment, choice literature which the Professor may have made nicer in the translating but which certainly turned out shorter.

At the end of the speechmaking, Sherif Hussein presented to Bill Terry and me two magnificently carved jambiyas, or Arab daggers. The Sherif apparently sensed that although the Professor was the most important personage of the expedition, he was not the type of man to want or require a jambiya. Curved knives of the type Sherif Hussein gave us are now almost impossible to obtain, since they used to be made by the Yemen Jews, who have left their homeland of many centuries to settle in Israel.

Finally, in a large open courtyard, two dancing girls from Yemen entertained us. Their swaying bodies, a full moon, several small twinkling lanterns, a reed flute and two tom-toms, carried us back to the days of Scheherazade and the Arabian Nights' Entertainment. The girls wore long, vividly colored skirts and blouses, and carried on their necks, ankles, and wrists a heavy collection of silver jewelry that tinkled and clanked as they moved. In the background stood several hundred of Sherif Hussein's bodyguard, tall and fierce-looking men with jambiyas stuck in their full cartridge belts and rifles in their hands. It was an exotic atmosphere, until the dancing girls swooped close to my nose and I smelled the camel urine with which they set the curls in their hair. Anyway, the dancing became monotonous after ten minutes. After two hours, all one could admire was the girls' endurance.

Our first experience with gypsy dancing girls had occurred two years before, at the Abu Zeneima rest house in Sinai, when we gave a party to celebrate our discovery of the approximate location of Moses' crossing of the so-called Red Sea. No such celebra-

tion was complete without gypsies, who consisted in this instance
of two male musicians and three women dancers. The girls were
quite remarkable, for each one possessed complete muscular control of the four major sections of her stomach. They would lift
their stomachs to the upper right, shift over to the upper left,
then drop to the lower left quarter, and so round in a circle. If
favorably inclined, they could also rotate in reverse. As Professor
Albright was obviously the most elderly man present and the girls
had been told by fun-loving Henry Field that he was loaded with
piasters, the dancers directed most of their activities in his direction. It was quite a picture, with our Professor sitting there,
Gladys perched on the arm of his chair, and the gypsies dancing as
close as possible to him. The Professor's face became redder and
redder, and his one comment on the performance was "My, what
marvelous control!"

Sherif Hussein's gypsies apparently had no such remarkable
talents. While they were dancing, Gladys Terry paid a visit to the
Sherif's harem, under the guidance of the twenty-year-old Emir,
who spoke some English. We eagerly awaited her return to hear
about the prize beauties of Beihan—for the Sherif had his choice
from all the valley.

"There were twelve women in the room I visited," Gladys reported, "but it was hard to tell whether some of them were wives
or children."

Beihani girls marry as young as twelve years of age, and while
we were in Beihan, Sherif Hussein was presented with a fourteen-
year-old girl as a birthday gift. He promptly took her as his wife
—his twentieth marriage!

"What did the women look like?" I asked Gladys.

"Like Theda Bara—olive-skinned, bangs, wide mascaraed eyes;
and shy and pretty."

Emir Saleh, Gladys went on, had introduced her to the oldest
of the wives, his own forty-year-old mother, and then, while the
others stared, established her on a high pile of cushions in one
corner of the room. One by one the women arose from their own
cushions and gathered around her. They were not dressed in the
common black or indigo muslin of most Beihani women, but in

Typical Beihani family entertaining visiting gypsy girl seated in the center of the tent

George Farrier recording songs and music of a mixed group of roving South Arabian gypsies visiting Beihan

Dancing girls visiting Beihan from Yemen. Each strand of their long black hair was carefully dipped in camel urine which not only set the curls but also made their hair glisten.

silk jersey, dresses of beautiful colors. On their hips they wore elaborate belts.

After a long silence one of the wives took off her heavy belt of solid silver and handed it to Gladys. Arabs give only when they have accepted you as a social equal, and when they do, they expect gifts in return. With a smile, Gladys took off her beloved turquoise bracelet and handed it to the girl who had given her the belt.

We spent the night at Sherif Hussein's house, and most of us left for Timna early the next morning. Bill and Gladys Terry, with a few of the others, stayed a while to take motion pictures of the dancing girls in the daylight.

On the way back to our headquarters, Charles Inge pointed out a mound about nine miles south of Timna, where he hoped the Professor would dig. We stopped for a look at this oval-shaped elevation about seventy feet high, with a few patches of hairy grass on its round sandy bank and some gnarled trees at its base. Charles told us that Hajar bin Humeid, as the mound was called, must have been an important town in antiquity, although not as large as Timna, to which it was subject. It stood at a fork of the incense road, one branch of which had led off toward the Hadhramaut and Dhofar, the other to ports near the present city of Aden.

Human beings have a strange habit of sticking to the same spot when they build a city. Even if a settlement is completely devastated, it must have valuable assets for the few survivors—wells or foundations or building materials—because the new city is usually built on top of the old one rather than started from scratch a mile or two away. Thus city is superimposed on city until in the end the final city has a good view from the top of a hill made of its predecessors. This habit makes it convenient for archaeologists, who can dig down through one ancient mound and study the remains of civilization after civilization.

One side of Hajar bin Humeid had been carried away by erosion, exposing about fifty feet of the layer cake of antiquity. The strata that signified perhaps a dozen different cities, their remains preserved in sand, invited the Professor to investigate.

"Looking at it is like pressing your nose against the window of history, isn't it?" I said. "But it will take a lot of sorting before we can read the full story."

The Professor just nodded, but I saw a light in his eye.

"How far back do you suppose these strata go?" I asked.

"Certainly back to Sheba's time, in the tenth century B.C.," he replied, "and perhaps to Abraham. Maybe even further."

Hajar bin Humeid became the second spot chosen for excavation—a special cross-section dig with the primary purpose of establishing a time sequence of ancient Qatabanian civilization. The first was at Timna's South Gate, and the third was established the next day, at a small but rather high mound near the northern city wall. At this spot an Arab had claimed to find, two years before, a small bronze plaque depicting a camel and containing an inscription. The text was dedicated to the Sabean god, Dhu-Samawi, and its script indicated that the plaque had been made some time about the first century B.C.

We now knew where to dig. The next step was to find men for the digging.

6

MOUNTAINS AND CLOUDS
OF SAND

It takes a great many men to dig up and carry away the accumulated sands of two or three thousand years, but Sherif Awad had assured us that there would be a plentiful labor supply in the Wadi Beihan. When we sent out a call for workers, more than a hundred appeared the first day, but apparently someone had decided that working for the Americans would require neither brains nor brawn. We were confronted with an astounding assortment of cripples, mental deficients, and very young boys. If Beihan had possessed hospitals, we might have thought they had been emptied at our call for workers.

Possibly the able-bodied men of the population sent out first the unemployable dependents of their families, for when we rejected a majority of the first applicants and asked for more volunteers, we found some likely prospects. The typical Arab of the desert and the wadis is a tough and intelligent human being, sometimes scrawny by our standards but wiry and strong, alert and quick. Within a short while we had a working force that varied between two hundred and fifty and three hundred men and older boys who not only worked hard but took a real interest in all that was going on. Many of them felt personal pride in work well done or in accomplishing more than the next fellow. Several times we actually had to stop a man from carrying a stone too heavy for him and let others help. The work was not easy, but hot, dirty, heavy, tiresome, and repetitious.

The biggest job, of course, was carrying sand. At first our workers followed the approved Aden method of sand hauling, with
two men at each end of a loaded gunny sack stretched out length-
wise. Loading was tedious, half the sackful spilled, and not much
could be carried per trip. We decided that wicker baskets would
do the job far better, and although we had none, this was one item
we could procure locally. We placed a rush order for a large quantity in the neighboring village of Aseilan. When the baskets began
to arrive, work went faster and more smoothly until a disagree-
ment developed about the best way for the men to carry their
loads. Professor Albright, out of the wealth of his experience, insisted that baskets should be carried on the hips. Charles Inge and
I thought baskets belonged on the head. The Professor said our
method would lead to much spilling of sand not only on the
ground but on the heads in question, while I retorted that hip
carrying would lead to curvature of the spine, or at least cramped
muscles.

The workers themselves agreed with Professor Albright, as they
had always carried loaded baskets on their hips. Once, however,
when the Professor was away, I persuaded a few of the men to try
carrying the baskets on their heads. They liked it, so the rest of
them followed suit. When the Professor returned, he must have
been amazed to see lines of workers marching from the dig to the
dump with baskets balanced on their heads. But he said not one
word, and I didn't quite dare ask what he thought about it.

Digging and dumping present problems just as great as carrying
sand. When searching for archaeological treasures, you cannot tell
an ignorant worker just to dig here, and let it go at that. All shovel
work must be under the supervision of a man who knows where
to dig, how deep, what to look for, and above all, when to stop.
We had hoped to have a crew of Guftis, Egyptians from the town
of Guft, trained in archaeological work for generations, since Sir
Flinders Petrie first went to that country. They make ideal foremen on a dig, but we didn't have time to arrange for hiring and
transporting them. That meant staff members had to supervise,
but some of the more intelligent Beihanis caught on very quickly
and moved up to positions as straw bosses. Their most important

task was to see that shoveling stopped when signs indicated the approach to something worthwhile. The signs might be only broken pieces of pottery that most Arabs would not look at twice. Professor Albright, however, might learn approximate dates from them.

Dumping would at first glance appear to offer no difficulties. Finding the right place to put sand in a desert should not be puzzling, but actually the location of dumps is one of the worst archaeological headaches. Nine times out of ten the place where one decides to dump sand and debris is exactly that spot at which one wishes to excavate later, as a result of clues gained at the first excavation. Carrying the sand beyond the reach of archaeological potentiality takes too much time, although we did use trucks, loaded with wicker baskets, to get much of the sand some distance away.

A special dumping problem confronted us at Hajar bin Humeid, the mound south of Timna with the eroded cross section. The obvious solution was to throw the sand and debris down the face of the cliff, but at the bottom of this cliff there was an irrigation ditch. It was bone dry at the time and looked useless, but our workers explained that it would be filled with beautiful nourishing water when the rains came, and they expected heavy rains soon. They objected to the idea of our filling the ditch with tons of sand and rock.

But when you stand on top of a small mound, where else can you dump anything but down the side? There was, of course, the other side, but that meant carrying sand up and over the hill. The lower we went in our work, the more the men would have to climb up to reach the top from which they could throw debris to the other side—an obviously inefficient operation. We finally decided on a method that sounds silly but actually was the most practical. We dumped everything down the cliff and then at the end of the day put a small crew to work to clear out the irrigation ditch. It all seemed useless as weeks went by without a drop of rain, but when the water finally came we felt justified and the local population was happy.

By the time our first pay day came around, we were not in full operation, by any means, but we were digging, hauling, and dumping sand at three locations. The workmen lined up Thursday night —Friday is the day of rest in the Moslem world—to get paid. Professor Alexander M. Honeyman, Oriental scholar from St. Andrews University in Scotland, who had the thankless and complicated task of keeping our employee accounts straight, started handing out money. Wages were two-thirds of a Maria Theresa dollar per day for the men and half an M.T. dollar for the boys —hardly exorbitant by C.I.O. standards but excellent pay for South Arabia. In addition, we paid small amounts as baksheesh, or rewards for the finding of valuable objects such as inscriptions, pieces of pottery or metal, and anything of possible archaeological value, the size of the baksheesh depending upon the worth of the discovery. It was a matter of prestige as well as finance to win baksheesh and this incentive made the workmen eagle-eyed and careful. It added enormously to Sandy Honeyman's bookkeeping, however, for small change was a never-ending nuisance. We used Arabian buqshas in seven different coin sizes—half buqshas, buqshas, two buqshas, two and a half buqshas, four buqshas, five buqshas, and ten buqshas. Forty buqshas equaled one Maria Theresa dollar, which was worth half an American dollar.

It grew dark as the men were being paid on our first Thursday. Some of the staff were helping Honeyman, and I stood by to see that everything went smoothly. The line gradually grew shorter, and the men with money in their hands wandered away to the right, where I saw them gathered in small clusters. From the ejaculations and growing hubbub, I judged that something was not as it should be. I sauntered a bit closer and saw that many of the boys and even some of the men had extremely unhappy expressions on their faces and were muttering darkly to themselves. One of my spies—there is never a shortage of good spies in Arabia—informed me that a pious and dignified old gentleman with a white beard had organized a little racket by which he managed to extort one buqsha from each boy and from some of the younger men as soon as they were paid. My limited knowledge of Arabic did not

One of our best Beihani diggers, looking like an Old Testament patriarch

Above, Beihani basket boys lined up outside excavations, and, *right,* Beihani workers dumping sand at the South Gate of Timna

enable me to understand the basis of his extortion demands, but I was more concerned with stopping it than understanding it.

Disguising myself slightly by removing my shirt and jingling a few buqshas in my hand, I walked toward the old fakir, who was completely surrounded by other young workmen. When I was close enough for him to hear the pleasant sound of buqshas, his arm instinctively darted out and his hand grabbed mine. My tightened fist resisted his efforts to snatch one buqsha, so he looked up at me, somewhat annoyed. The other workers had already recognized me and stepped back, so the old man and I faced each other in the middle of an ever-widening circle. His expression of annoyance and greed changed instantly to one of horror. He snatched his hand away from mine as if it burned, then turned and fled— moving rather briskly for such an old gentleman. I did not say a word. He never appeared again, to the gratification of the boys, who looked at me with greater respect for my quick disposal of a menace that was too much for them to handle. I never did find out why they thought they had to give him money.

Another old man was a different sort altogether. He had worked three days on Professor Albright's dig at Hajar bin Humeid before I noticed that he was totally blind. He was so industrious and careful an excavator that we wanted to keep him, but his blindness was certain to make him cause trouble with the shovel in time. The Professor finally put him to work with a stick cleaning around the stone blocks of new walls as they were uncovered, where care had to be exercised to prevent damage to ancient materials. This was an excellent idea, but one day he industriously cleaned all the supporting sand from the base of a sagging stone wall, nearly bringing the whole structure down on top of us.

Hajar bin Humeid was full of surprises for Professor Albright and Dr. Albert Jamme, our Belgian epigrapher from Louvain, who expected to find quantities of broken pottery but instead encountered at the outset extensive stone walls of houses and a possible temple. While this was an interesting development, it threatened to slow down the work so that the desired cross section of the mound could not be completed the first season. The top layer uncovered turned out to be of the medieval Arab period, between about A.D. 1000 and 1400, rather than Himyaritic, as expected. The Himyarites flourished in South Arabia during the first centuries of the Christian era, as successors of the ancient kingdoms of Qataban, Sheba, and Ma'in, which are correctly designated as pre-Himyaritic. A huge broken vase of typically Arab design, along with many other items uncovered in the top layers of the mound, provided much enlightening information about the Middle Ages in this region, but the existence of Arab levels put our goal that much deeper.

The chief purpose of Professor Albright's work at Hajar bin Humeid was to establish a sound scientific chronology for Qatabanian and related Arabian civilizations. Any houses, temples, inscriptions, implements, and art objects found would be welcomed eagerly, of course, but there was no effort here, as at Timna, to lay bare a city or even a portion of it. Excavation of a scarp section is a sampling procedure. A rectangular cut about sixty feet square was made from the top downward, like drilling a well and bringing up samples at different levels. In this case, cutting the section was simplified by the previous erosion, which had washed away one face of the mound.

Professor Albright and his crew would completely clear one occupation level of the mound within their sixty-square-foot cut. Pieces of pottery and other objects of interest would be gathered and taken to headquarters. Then Dr. Richard Bowen, engineer-archaeologist from Rhode Island, would map the uncovered level carefully and Ocky Romaine would photograph it from all angles. Next, the Professor would be removed from the area, forcibly if necessary—for his safety and a much needed rest. Although he invariably protested at going back to headquarters, he knew it was best for him to be out of the way when the demolition squad went to work. Otherwise he would have tried to be right in the middle of things, plunging in eagerly to get a glimpse of something in the next level before the wreckers had finished their work.

Doing archaeological work alongside Professor Albright is no mean task, for he is always up and cheerful at five in the morning. Within a few minutes, in his eagerness to get everything assembled for the day's work, our Professor manages without fail to rouse the entire expedition into an unwelcome state of wakefulness. On top of this, being a charter member of the old school, he believes that anything beyond the barest necessities is a sign of inherent weakness.

Under the direction of Charlie McCollum and George Farrier, the strongest workers removed the heavy blocks from the stone walls that had been exposed and examined, rolling them over the slope to disappear in a cloud of dust below. When everything had been cleared down to the designated level, the demolition team departed, the Professor returned, and archaeology as such took over again at Hajar bin Humeid.

A paleontologist goes through much the same process in his study of fossils in rocks, and he obtains essentially the same thing— an accurate chronology for a particular area together with a correlation of that area with others far removed. He may uncover, for example, a little four-toed horse, Eohippus, from the Eocene in North America. If he finds a similar four-toed Eohippus in another part of North America—or anywhere else—he concludes that the rocks are of the same relative age in both areas. He knows this because other studies have shown him that four-toed horses lived during only one epoch of the earth's geologic history, that three-toed and one-toed horses lived at later epochs, all over the world, and that a four-toed horse is never found associated with three- or one-toed horses. Mr. Paleontologist finds, as he works up to the present from sixty to forty to ten million years ago that horses progressively lose their toes, lengthen their legs and teeth, becoming more and more like the race horses at Epsom Downs. After that, fossil horses—or fossils of almost any kind—enable him to date the region in which he finds them. He has a fossil index.*

Archaeologists search for a pottery index. They use many other methods, also, for establishing accurate dates, including inscrip-

---

* The paleontological evidence before us today clearly demonstrates ordered progressive change with the successive development of new faunal and floral assemblages through the changing epochs of our earth's history. There should be no real conflict between science, which is the search for the truth, and Christ's teachings, which I hold to be truth itself. It is only when scientists remove God from creation that the Christian is faced with an irreconcilable situation.

tions, alphabets, materials, the way stones are cut and used, and now the radiocarbon examination of charred wood or ashes. A pottery index, nevertheless, is almost an essential to proper fixing of chronology. One of Professor Albright's major archaeological achievements was his establishment of the first correlation of pottery of different periods and areas throughout the history of Palestine. He now hoped to establish a similar pottery sequence for South Arabia, which would form the frame of reference for all future archaeological investigations, our own and others.

The method of learning dates from bits of pottery, sometimes with a high degree of accuracy, is a scientific procedure requiring knowledge in many fields, great skill, and wide experience, but an example can be given to show how it is done. We know that the burnishing of pottery by the wheel rather than by hand developed in Palestine and Syria in the ninth century B.C. and lasted to the early sixth century. Southern Arabia had close relations with Palestine during that period, but it would take some years for new techniques to travel that distance. Therefore, when pottery fragments of the wheel-burnished type with similar shapes of vessels are found in ancient ruins of South Arabia, a date contemporary or a little later can be placed on the level in which they are found, providing other evidence substantiates this finding.

After the first levels at Hajar bin Humeid had been disposed of, Professor Albright began to encounter much more pottery, greatly to his satisfaction. He also uncovered an obviously pre-Arab Himyaritic wall, the finest we had seen to date. Since it was at one side of the section, this wall might be excavated without having to be demolished along with the rest of its occupation level, so I decided to tackle this job. The Professor believed that this might turn out to be a temple, as the revealed wall was already nine feet high on one side, more than the average house. Hopefully, I set to work.

That's how I happened to be near the top of Hajar bin Humeid when one of the worst sandstorms I've ever encountered struck—and I have sat through some bad stone blizzards in various parts of the world. It came up rather suddenly. Only a few minutes after the wind freshened into a stiff breeze, we felt the first stinging assaults of sand pellets on our hands and faces. Then the sky grew dark and the sun went into partial eclipse as a thick cloud enveloped us, a cloud that seemed made of very solid stuff traveling at jet-plane speed.

There is only one thing you can do in a sandstorm—find the most sheltered spot and close every possible aperture in your body. You still have to breathe, so something must be left open, and that is where the sand goes. I was grateful for the back apron of my turban, which I wrapped around my face like a veil. We all sat against the wall of our dig, and I watched sand blow in around the walls we had been excavating. It was easy to see how a great city could disappear in a short time in the desert, for the sand reached into every crack and crevice and tried to fill up depressions as if it were a liquid.

Four hours seem like twenty-four when you are sitting out a sandstorm, and that is how long our blow on Hajar bin Humeid lasted. When it ended I was amazed to find that it was not even quitting time, so we set to work again. Just before five o'clock the reward for our will power and fortitude appeared when one of the Arabs excitedly uncovered a beautiful alabaster table of offerings, decorated along one side with a row of carved ibex heads. The ibex was an animal of special veneration among the ancient peoples of Arabia, and frequently adorned sacrificial tables of offerings to the gods, such as the one we found. The same workman also found, beside the table, a heavy copper bracelet.

By the end of a week we completely cleared the inside of our supposed temple and found it to be partitioned into small rooms. Inside the entrance-way, an orange-colored plaster floor was uncovered, extending for several feet and looking very much like a Y.M.C.A. foot pool. Had we found a bathhouse, then? We could not decide, but our last and best find at this spot suggested that even if the building was not a temple, it may have had some connection with religious affairs. It was late Saturday afternoon when one of my best Arab excavators excitedly cried, "Baksheesh! Baksheesh!" From the debris I saw one corner of a smooth stone with inscriptions on it. We removed the surrounding sand and rock carefully and brought forth a truly beautiful dedication stone inscribed to the moon god.

The moon was the chief deity of all the early South Arabian kingdoms—particularly fitting in that region where the soft light of the moon brought the rest and cool winds of night as a relief from the blinding sun and scorching heat of day. In contrast to most of the old religions with which we are familiar, the moon god is male, while the sun god is his consort, a female. The third god of importance is their child, the male morning star, which we know as the planet Venus.

There were innumerable minor gods, and in addition there were private or family gods whose worship was carried on in the home rather than in temples. Beyond these few facts, we knew little of the religious ideas, ceremonies, and rites of Qataban and other southern Arabian kingdoms. One of the chief purposes of the expedition was to learn more, because the religion of a people is a revealing clue to its character. The table of offerings and dedication stone told us very little that we did not already know, but they raised hopes that we were on the right trail and that somewhere during the course of our work we might enter an actual temple of the ancient Qatabanians and re-create the rituals expressing their beliefs, their ideals, and their spiritual yearnings.

7

"WEAKNESS OF THE BONES"

All is not archaeology on an archaeological expedition. One of our problems was getting some of the appurtenances of modern civilization into the medieval world in which we were working. Gasoline is essential to a motorized expedition, and there are no filling stations in the land of the horse and camel. At first, Aden Airways found that it could not fit gasoline drums into its Dakotas, so the fuel was carried in the planes' tanks. The same planes also regularly delivered—and carried away—mail and people.

A few weeks after starting work I received an unexpected letter in Arabic, mailed from Egypt:

> After compliments, I am a British subject. I beg to inform your good self that I am in possession of books written in the Arabic language about antiquity places in Aden. I am ready to supply you with these books as a guide provided you pay me $50,000 as insurance before supplying the books in question. If the books mislead you and your endeavors are frustrated, you have the right to obtain a refund of the money from me. On the other hand, if your research is successful, it then becomes my money and you have no right to claim it. I must also be informed by wire what sort of antiquities you have and whether all went well or not. If you are agreeable, please let us complete our agreement through the British Consulate at Port Said. Please accept my profound respect.

I had to admire the high goal this confidence man set for himself. He was not interested in small change, and he thought no

American would be interested, either. Regretfully, I was unable to take advantage of this golden opportunity.

Captain Mubarak and our fifteen government guards returned to Aden on the first Dakota to visit us, having seen us safely into the hands of the sherifs of Beihan without firing a shot except in greeting. Bill and Gladys Terry also took off; they were long overdue at the Mount Sinai expedition, which was their special charge.

Byron Wardle of the American consulate, who had kindly consented to handle our mail and shipments from Aden, flew up to visit us. When he heard that many of the equipment items we ordered had never arrived, he turned around without leaving the airfield and flew back to Aden to look after the expedition's needs. The State Department can indeed be proud to have had a representative such as this, whose every action and thought was directed toward creating and maintaining American good will abroad.

One plane brought to us Dr. Louis Krause, of the University of Maryland, who came to spend three weeks as a member of the expedition. His arrival was greeted with special warmth by Dr. McNinch, who was having more than his hands full looking after the health of the expedition members as well as countless ailments, real and imaginary, of the local population. Dr. Krause joined his young colleague in the gloomy old storeroom on the ground floor of our house, which Dr. McNinch had converted into a field hospital and over the door of which hung a sign, UNIVERSITY OF MARYLAND HOSPITAL—ARABIAN DIVISION.

With two doctors now available, sickness seemed to increase among the Beihani. Two hundred patients a week came through the doors of the hospital with a multiplicity of diseases that would have taxed a big clinic. Despite the fact that many came out of curiosity and others to be fashionably ill, our doctors estimated that fully 70 per cent of their patients had genuine ailments. Certainly they saved several lives, eased much pain, and preserved sight and limbs for those who might have lost them. In addition to the great and measurable good they did, the good will gained for our expedition and for America was incalculable. The news of our doctors and their hospital spread for many miles over southern Arabia.

The Arab women were somewhat suspicious and would not speak out readily, but Drs. Krause and McNinch understood their shyness and knew that probably not one of them had seen anyone but an Arab before, and many had seen no male but immediate members of the family. Our doctors were patient until the shyness was overcome, and then they were subjected to a deluge of talk, as if dams had been broken. Some women went on endlessly about innumerable ailments and troubles until the doctors could not figure out just what complaint had brought them to the hospital at this particular moment. Finally, if the women received what they considered an insufficient amount of medicine or too brief a treatment, they complained bitterly and at great length.

The minor complaints of the local population seemed to run in cycles. At the outset there were hundreds of headaches, for which the hospital handed out aspirin tablets. Then someone had what he called "weakness of the bones," a vague disorder which Dr. McNinch thought might mean a vitamin deficiency. So he gave the patient some beautiful red vitamin capsules. Immediately an epidemic of "weakness of the bones" broke out in the Wadi Beihan, and there was a run on the red capsules lasting for several weeks. After Dr. Mac had treated two or three women for syphilis by injections, several others came in proudly demanding injections for syphilis, obviously without having any idea of what was implied. The injections hurt slightly and this pain made the treatment popular. Like most patients the world over they thought that if it hurt it must be effective.

Strangely, many of the tribesmen actually believed they had syphilis, although our doctors observed only two or three genuine cases during the first season. One young swain insisted that he must have syphilis, because, as he declared loudly and with appropriate gestures, he had enjoyed all the women of his village and all the women had enjoyed him.

Among serious complaints, eye and skin diseases led all others. The eye troubles ranged from very mild virus types of conjunctivitis to trachoma and a surprising number of cataracts. Five or six new cases of cataracts turned up almost every day during our

stay in Beihan. Most of the skin diseases were minor, although
we did encounter one Beihani tribesman suffering from leprosy.
Dr. Krause, an authority on the history of medicine and well
versed on medical references in the Bible, pointed out that the
leprosy found in the world today is probably not the leprosy of
ancient times, at least as it is described in the Bible. A common
Biblical phrase is "a leper white as snow," but no modern form
of leprosy fits this description. In all probability, the Biblical
term, "leprosy," covered various skin ailments such as psoriasis,
a disease in which the lesions become covered with white scales.

The infant mortality rate is a little more than one-third, which
is surprisingly good for such a region. During our African expedition in the Sudan, we had found an infant mortality rate of
around 50 per cent, and among the Congo Pygmies of the Ituri
Forest, four out of five babies die during their first year.

A week after we arrived a fifteen-year-old camel boy, Abdullah
bin Hussein, came to the hospital. He shyly stretched out his
right arm, which was swollen up and badly infected with gan-
grene. Most startling, the hand was missing. Young Abdullah explained that one of his camels had bitten him eight weeks before and that his hand had hung by its tendons for about ten
days before it dropped off. The only treatment Abdullah had
given the arm was soaking the stump in camel urine. Dr. Mac
immediately cut off the two protruding bones, cleaned up the infection, and prepared Abdullah for further amputation. The lad
wound up with no arm, but also with no excruciating pain. And
he seemed to understand that unless the doctor had acted dras-
tically, he soon would have had no life.

One Sunday morning a runner arrived at Timna with an urgent plea for our doctor to visit a small village seven miles south
of Beihan al-Qasab near the Yemen border. After a two-hour
drive through deep wadis and between sand dunes, Dr. McNinch
found an Arab who had recently been wounded in a frontier
tribal battle. The bullet had gone in the left groin and emerged
from the man's right buttock. The hardy individual had staggered to his feet and walked four miles down the mountain to

his village, where he received first-aid treatment of camel urine as a disinfectant and sand as a controller of hemorrhage.

When Dr. McNinch arrived, he could accomplish little because the man was too shy to let the doctor examine the wound, which was certainly in an embarrassing spot. All Dr. Mac could do was to give the man aureomycin to stop the infection and an analgesic to relieve the pain. Encouraged by the good results, the man eventually overcame his shyness and submitted to full treatment, followed by complete recovery.

A Bedouin girl came to the hospital one day asking for some medicine for her mother, who could not straighten out her fingers. Dr. McNinch examined the old lady and found what he suspected—arthritis, which is as common in the Wadi Beihan as it was in the days when Jesus was preaching in the synagogue on the Sabbath and "behold there was a woman who had a spirit of infirmity for eighteen years and she had been bowed together and could no wise lift herself up," a classic description of arthritis. An interesting fact about this disease is that it is as common here in dry, dry Beihan as in parts of the world with damp climates—in contradiction to many theories about it.

Some of the local treatments and cures were interesting to our doctors, who admitted that camel urine was a fair disinfectant even though they did not recommend its use. Many Arabs apply antimony to their eyelids, explaining that it not only prevents eye disease but adds to beauty. This practice has continued for at least a thousand years and probably longer. For almost any pain that lasts some time, the sufferer is branded with a red-hot iron. Dr. Krause encountered a heart case in which the hot iron had been placed over the apex of the heart, exact location of the trouble. It marked the spot, but did not improve the heart condition.

The chief complaint of the Arabs was exemplified by a man close to eighty who urgently asked Dr. McNinch for some medicine that would correct his condition. He did not, he said, enjoy his wives as much as he once did. In spite of the inability of our doctors to cure this particular ailment, there was a steady pilgrimage toward our headquarters on foot and camel throughout the season.

One day Kenny Brown was driving from Hajar bin Humeid to Timna when he saw a young Arab girl of ten or eleven by the side of the road waving frantically at him. He stopped the truck and she limped forward to climb in. He learned then that she was on her way to visit the *hakim,* Dr. McNinch. Kenny's Arabic was becoming quite fluent, so he was delighted with this opportunity to carry on a conversation with someone new.

The girl would say nothing in answer to his questions, however. She just shook her head and looked fixedly at the road ahead. Kenny was beginning to have doubts about his Arabic when he saw the girl put her head in her hands and realized that she was carsick. The obvious became evident even before Kenny could slam on the brakes, and when the truck stopped the girl threw herself on the sand and wept bitterly. When Kenny helped her back into the truck and they drove off again, she simply could not understand why he was not angry with her. For the remaining two miles she prayed fervently for Allah to bless him, his wives, his children, and entire tribe. At Timna she stepped down, kissed his hand, and scuttled, still praying aloud, to the door marked "Hospital" in both Arabic and English.

Another visitor to our hospital will never be forgotten by any of us who saw him. He was an Arab boy with no face—or at least with nothing that could be called a face. There were jaws and some teeth, two holes where a nose had once been, and a mass of diseased flesh. Only the two big eyes remained, and the forehead above them. The eyes now stared fixedly at Dr. McNinch, who explained to me that the boy's face had been eaten away by yaws.

As Dr. Mac began the urgent treatment required to try to save the boy's life, I saw a shadow move in one corner of the room. I recognized there a tall Arab who had for some time been one of our worst troublemakers at the South Gate. Mac pointed out that he had been showing up at the hospital almost every day for the past month with a vast assortment of ailments, some real and some imaginary, but not serious. Now it turned out that all this time he had allowed his pitiful young brother to remain at home without receiving the medical care he so desperately needed.

Dr. McNinch told me that he held out little hope for the boy's life. "When you come back next year, I probably won't be along," he said. "Try to find out about the boy, if you can, and let me know. I've never seen anything like this and I want to know the outcome."

Among the many problems that were neither archaeological nor medical with which we had to cope the most distracting was the invasion of the spiders. A new word should be invented for these creatures in Beihan, for the word "spiders" calls to mind something from a quarter of an inch to two inches, at most, in diameter. Our spiders were not of this puny race. Several of them were measured by accurate instruments proving them to be more than seven and a half inches across. The biggest of all could not be measured, for he was a squashed mass by the time a ruler arrived, but I would swear he was close to nine inches. Their bodies were round, fat, and hairy. Their legs were the size of matchsticks—the big kind. And there were scores of them.

I remember the time I was sitting at my desk discussing the day's work with Charles Inge. Suddenly a huge shadow crossed the wall on our left, and I looked up to see a monstrous spider passing within a few inches of Charles's head. I yelled and came up with my Colt Peacemaker, while poor Charles dived for the other side of the room, undoubtedly more afraid of the six-shooter than of the spider. I was so fascinated to see the speed with which Charles moved that the spider got away.

We were assured by the local Beihanis that the spiders were not poisonous, but most of us felt that a spider that big had no need of poison. Kenny Brown saw one bite the middle right out of a giant locust that was trying to escape. The ordinary swatting device is useless against such giants. I had the feeling that the spider would snatch the swatter away and strike back. Guns were effective, and shooting a moving spider was good target practice. However, the best and safest spider killer was the foot of a small Arab boy named Naser, whom Kenny Brown had more or less adopted, and who had immediately been renamed

Nausea by Dick Bowen. Nausea was a prize, always willing to undertake any job, no matter how unpleasant, and he delighted in killing spiders.

One evening several of us were talking in one of the large rooms of our palace, while Professor Albright was working at a desk nearby. Someone suddenly saw one of the huge spiders on the wall and let out the yell that usually came with such a sight. From the shadows Nausea appeared, made a running leap through the air, and with his bare left foot smashed the spider against the wall. The rest of us felt somewhat shattered by the experience, but the Professor was so absorbed in his work that he did not even look up.

Professor Albright was singularly unconcerned about the spiders, especially when he had removed his glasses. At such a time, he is quite nearsighted and spiders disappear from view, which was perhaps the most effective way of handling the whole situation. But it was hard on the rest of us. One evening I passed the Professor's room as he was about to retire. He was sitting on the edge of his bunk, and his glasses had been laid aside. To my horror, I saw a huge Beihani spider leisurely walking across the Professor's pajama leg, unknown to him.

Instinctively I reached for my Colt, but since shooting off the Professor's leg just to get a spider was out of the question, I held my fire and concluded that unless the spider actually picked up the Professor and carried him away the chances were that neither would do the other any harm. This was indeed true, for the spider continued on his way unhindered—probably to my room—and the Professor lay down and fell asleep to dream of inscribed potsherds.

Even in South Arabia we had landlord trouble. Financial negotiations are endless and must conform to a kind of elaborate ceremony in this part of the world, so I had never settled with Sherif Awad the amount of rent the expedition should pay for his mud palace. Finally, not long before the end of the first season, he came to see me with a "Where, oh where is my rent?" expression on his face. This time we managed to come to an agreement. George Farrier hauled into my room several bags of Maria

Theresa dollars and dumped a sizable quantity on the floor. With great ceremony, we paid Sherif Awad three hundred M.T. dollars as rent for the season. The Sherif solemnly gave thanks for the money and then as an afterthought reminded me of something I had never realized in the first place. It seems that we owed him for nineteen baskets for which he had acted as broker, plus rent for the use of four cows which had been employed to haul away loose sand at the South Gate. Thus another thirty-seven M.T. dollars changed hands and everyone was happy except our accountant, George Farrier.

George should not have been surprised at this transaction for he had become quite accustomed to the Beihani way of doing business, having served as the expedition's chief commissary officer for some time. With the help of our head Somali, Jama, George did the shopping once a week in Aseilan or Beihan al-Qasab, the chief city, pleasant and green. Once Kenny Brown went along when they were going to buy a goat, and found himself fascinated by the procedure.

After finding a fat goat to their liking, they began to bargain with the animal's owner who, knowing they were Americans, set his price absurdly high—at fifteen M.T. dollars. George and Kenny came back with an absurdly low offer of five M.T. dollars, which sent the goat salesman into a story, with words and gestures, about how desperately poor he was and how his wives and children were starving. George and Kenny raised the offer to seven dollars, whereupon the goat owner threw up his hands and shouted in a loud voice—there was a good-sized audience at this entire transaction—that George and Kenny were trying to starve his family and ruin his business.

At this point George and Kenny turned as if to move on, but the agile Arab grabbed their arms and said in the most mellifluous of voices, "Oh, Americans, you have won the goat! It is yours for thirteen dollars."

Astounded that this magnificent offer did not produce the desired effect, the Beihani threw in his final ace in typical Arab strategy. Leading the goat by its mane, he presented it to George, saying in a ringing voice heard by everyone around, "This admirable goat, the finest of my herd, is yours for nothing, my gift to the Americans."

The boys were now the owners of a goat, as Arab etiquette made refusal impossible. This same etiquette also required that a gift of equal value be presented to the former goat owner. My two clever bargainers, who had been beautifully outmaneuvered but not cheated, presented the grinning Arab with ten dollars, amid the cheers of half a hundred onlooking townsmen.

Finally, there was the theft of the two Colt revolvers. I kept them wrapped in their original boxes in the bottom of my suitcase, and one morning, I discovered that they were missing. When I reported the theft to Jama he was heartbroken because he felt fully responsible for allowing a thief in our midst, even though he had no idea who it could be. Day after day went by without a clue to the Colts, so I finally reported the matter to our landlord, Sherif Awad, who was properly concerned and reported the theft to his brother, Sherif Hussein, who nodded and said he would look into the matter. Now in Beihan when Sheriff Hussein says he will look into a matter, that matter is taken care of.

Several days passed, however, before Jama came to my room and told me that Sherif Hussein was downstairs having tea and would be pleased to have me join him. When I exchanged amenities and sat down, Sherif Hussein dramatically put in the center of the table a heavy bundle wrapped in a huge handkerchief. Opening it, I found the two revolvers covered with sand but none the worse for wear, along with twelve boxes of Winchester .38 Special cartridges. This was a special surprise, since I had not realized that ammunition was stolen, too.

When I asked the identity of the thief, Sherif Hussein shook his head sadly but bravely and pointed to himself. He had taken them, he said, but later repented of his criminal action and had to return them. I accepted his story as graciously as I could, but I had little doubt about the true identity of the culprit who was for some reason being protected by the Sherif. Our pock-marked Beihani houseboy had disappeared the day before the Sherif's visit, and he never returned to collect his salary.

Some of our staff were disappointed at this anticlimax, for

Sherif Awad had proposed bringing a holy man from Yemen who would perform an elaborate ceremony to determine the thief. The chief feature was to be the heating of an iron to white heat. The suspects would line up, stick out their tongues, which would then be touched by the white-hot iron. The one who cried out was obviously guilty.

Sherif Awad had an explanation of all this that was more than mere hocus-pocus, but I would not like to put it to the test. The guilty man obviously knew he was guilty. He would therefore be frightened and his saliva would cease to flow, leaving his mouth dry. His tongue, not being moist, would be burned by the white-hot iron. The others, being unafraid and wet-tongued, would not be burned. It was all so simple, said Sherif Awad.

8

BAL HARITH TRIBESMEN

*

Every few days we saw a long caravan of camels ambling down the flat wadi bed from the north, carrying loads of rock salt. After stopping for water they went on their way south, toward Yemen, where the salt was sold. The salt came from mines near the mouth of the Wadi Beihan, in the territory of the Bal Harith tribe. For hundreds of years these mines had been an important factor in the economy of Beihan, and we knew that they would be interesting geologically. We wanted to visit them, but hesitated because they were so inaccessible that even Sherif Hussein had never been there. He encouraged us to make the trip, however, because he wanted to come along.

Finally eight of us decided to go, along with Sherif Hussein, Sherif Saleh bin Naser, and Captain Alan Denny, the officer in charge of government guards in the Beihan area. One Monday morning we set out with four trucks, heading north. Our first stop was in the village of Aseilan, where Sherif Awad joined us after making sure that his five personal bodyguards and one goat were loaded into the truck following his. With a smile, he explained that the five guards were for our protection, as life was not always secure among Allah's children. The goat would serve as the main course for dinner that night.

The first thirty miles of our journey made us feel that the difficulty of reaching the salt mines had been exaggerated, for we followed the road down the wadi by which we had arrived. The last seven miles, however, made up for everything, for we drove across vast expanses of rolling sand dunes. There was a trail to follow—the trail made by the camel caravans from the salt mines. But we soon decided that camels were the vehicles intended by nature for such terrain, in spite of the fact that our four-wheel drive Power Wagons and our Goodyear sand tires carried us ahead very nicely. Almost too nicely, in fact, for we went at a speed which turned the parallel ridges of the sand dunes into waves remarkably like those on the ocean. I was just about to become seasick, which I rarely do even on the sea, when we entered rather abruptly onto a flat plain which sloped gradually upward to a low ridge of mountains. We churned up the slope and dropped over the ridge into a saucer-like basin. Here were the salt mines of Aiyadin.

There were five visible cracks in the saucer, wide cracks that meant salt mines. Only two of them, however, looked new, and in these men were working, working in the same way they must have worked for a century or more. Their digging made aesthetic patterns in the walls of salt, but was very inefficient by our standards. We saw lines of men swinging long tools as they faced a wall of salt. The tools were pointed metal sledges fitted over slender three-foot handles, which they swung with such precision that they could hit a spot one inch below the previous blow each time. These vertical slashes of the sledge cut beautiful grooves in the wall of salt and piled the chipped salt up at their feet, to be carted away in bags as it accumulated. With the tools they had, they did beautiful work, but one month's work with modern machinery and dynamite would have taken care of all the sweating and straining of thousands of Bal Harith miners for the past two hundred years.

According to our geologist, Friso Heybroek, these mines were cut into a dome of pure Jurassic salt, impregnated with oil shale, which rose in a gentle arc from deep in the earth until it almost broke the surface of the ground in several places. We all noticed the strong bituminous smell from the oil in the salt. One of the workmen told us that during the summer months the oil actually leaks out of the salt. The natives soak it up in rags and use it for cooking.

There is no regular working force. Members of the Bal Harith tribe leave their homes on occasion for a shift at working the mines—for periods of one to three months. Sometimes there are as many as forty men on the job, although there were just twelve when we were there. While on the job, each man receives about a quarter of an M.T. dollar for every camel load of salt—between three and four hundred pounds. With an average of five hundred camels a month leaving the Aiyadin mines for Beihan and Yemen, that means a great deal of salt but not much money for a lot of hot, hard work on the part of the tribesmen. Still, the total income in a year's time is considerable for an isolated tribe like the Bal Harith. The best guess at yearly production is 2,400,000 pounds of salt, which brings about one M.T. dollar per hundred pounds, or a total of 24,000 M.T. dollars, equivalent to about $12,000 American at the time we were there.

Not all of the salt goes for dollars, however. Since there is no water near the mines, some of the returning camels must bring back that essential liquid for the workers. Two hundred pounds of salt may be exchanged for eight goatskins of water, with each worker needing a goatskin every two days. Some loss is suffered from hijackers, too, for the long strings of salt-laden camels winding their way slowly across sand dunes on thirty miles of open desert make an attractive prize for raiders from neighboring tribes in Aulaqi, Yemen, and the Hadhramaut. News that a raiding party has set out often travels faster than the raiders, and then the Bal Harith tribesmen grab their rifles, leap on their camels and set out to protect their salt. A force of five hundred Bal Harith warriors is something most tribes will not trifle with.

The Bal Harith are camel raisers, owning large herds that bring in some income when they are rented for the carrying trade between Yemen and Hadhramaut. They are great travelers, like most desert Bedu, and claim to have emigrated from the northern deserts of Nejran centuries ago. This sounds reasonable, as their fine stature and excellent physique are those of northern desert tribes. A good deal of their traveling is done in search of fodder for their

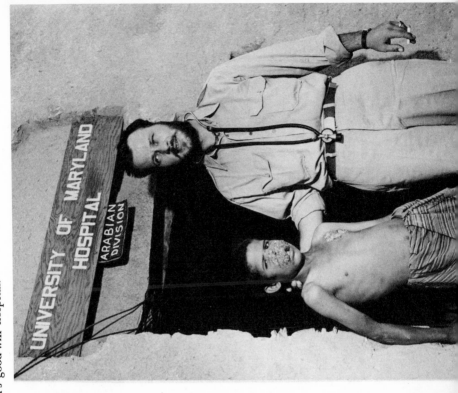

Left, little Beihani girl displaying the latest in South Arabian hair styles. *Right*, Dr. James M. McNinch, Jr., boy whose face has been eaten away by yaws. Through the miracle of penicillin Dr. McNinch cured this dread disease, leaving another living testimony of the expedition's good-will hospital.

Left, the matchless beauty of the sand dunes of Arabia. *Right*, Bal Harith tribesmen mining salt at Aiyadin. Lines of workers swing long pointed sledges with perfect precision forming beautiful parallel grooves in the wall of salt.

camel herds. The rich loam of the wide "delta" area of the Wadi Beihan, where it extends into the Ramlet Sabatein, is luxuriantly fertile when there is enough water, but that is rare indeed. Only the largest *seil,* or flood, will reach as far as the delta area of the Bal Harith, but when that miracle occurs, the water is diverted by irrigation canals into the fields, which become green with miles of ripening wheat.

Light floods are spent long before they reach Bal Harith country, and during some bad years no water may reach it at all. The camel herdsman always keeps his eye out for a distant cloud that may spill its water miles away. When he hears that the desert has "drunk" in some particular area, he looses the hobbles on his camels and drives them quickly to the favored spot, hoping to reach it before the sun withers the plants that have sprouted after the rain. Most of the time his camels live off the *rak* bushes that thrive in the desert—an adequate but not a choice food, for it sours the milk of the camels and gives them diarrhea. The herdsman himself uses the *rak* berries as a purge.

The harshness of the country in which he lives, the vast tracts of waterless desert, the sand that burns his feet, the dust storms of the *simoon,* and the merciless day-long glare have toughened the fiber of the Bal Harith, as of all desert tribes. They have made him hard, self-reliant, and fiercely independent. The constant struggle for survival against drought and disease, the threat of raids and the ever-present menace of intertribal feuds have built into his character stubbornness, bravery, cruelty, and sometimes treachery.

The demands of the desert have forced these sand dwellers to develop among themselves a code of honor and chivalry, but the desert law that regulates their behavior and enables them to survive should never be interpreted according to our own standards. It is severe, practical, not always moral as we see morality, and it is often broken in the flame of anger, the heat of battle, or the fire of greed. There is romance aplenty among these desert Bedu, but it is romance that is not always pretty, a colorful picture within a framework of savagery.

The paramount sheikh of this Bal Harith tribe is sixty-year-old

Sheikh Ali bin Munassar al Harithi. Sheikh Ali once explained to me that there are today some four to five thousand Bal Harith in Beihan and that they have lived there for eleven generations. After a little coaxing Sheikh Ali repeated from memory, while counting on his fingers, the names of his ancestors—bin Munassar, bin Ali, bin Ahmed, bin Husseyan, bin Mohammed, bin Zaeyal, bin Badr, bin Ghassar, bin Mohammed, bin Huthair, bin al Harithi.

The other main tribal group of the Wadi Beihan are the Musabein, who live in the south, chiefly at the head of the wadi. Where the Bal Harith are desert Bedu, the Musabein are a hill tribe and largely settled. The Bal Harith, although divided into eleven separate sections of different size and power, are closely knit in a political sense; the Musabein, on the other hand, are scattered through mountains, plateaus, and fertile wadis and are not so homogeneous or united. The Bal Harith live for the most part in black goat's-hair tents, the Musabein in stone forts. The Bal Harith are tall, black-bearded, and deep-throated, wearing long, wide, desert robes and possessing the eager jauntiness that comes of the desert. The Musabein clothe themselves in colored turbans and futas from Aden, or smear their half-naked bodies with indigo dye; they are smaller and in some there is a mixture of Negro slave blood.

While the Musabein are a larger tribe than the Bal Harith, they are more sharply subdivided and subject to feuds. Despite the maintenance of peace for the past eight or nine years, much of the bitter antagonism of different sections remains, for the feuds are as old as time. There is one small section, for example, that consists of only six male survivors, yet it is still nominally feuding with thirteen different groups of neighbors. In the Wadi Ain, a tribe exists of which there now remains but one small boy, a sheikh over no one but himself. The fact that the Musabein are more or less settled farmers and shepherds makes their feuding no less bloody than that of the wild Bal Harith. But they are not as open about their grievances, so they appear less passionate and fiery. Their battles and intrigues are carried on with less dash and fewer scruples. They repress public exhibition of their hostile feelings and rely more on cunning and treachery.

Aside from the two main tribes in Beihan, there are some thousand slaves in the region who have refused to accept their freedom, preferring to raise families and livestock while remaining in their masters' service. Because the slave traffic has been virtually wiped out in the Red Sea area, their numbers are steadily decreasing. Those who are no longer slaves are given places to pitch their tents on their former owners' lands, where they plant and harvest crops, sharing the proceeds. The free man, if he is skilled, may also set up shop as a rugmaker, silversmith, or dyemaster, thereby becoming a member of the restricted middle class. Of the two Jews remaining in Beihan when we arrived, the old man died and his young son was adopted by Sherif Hussein and became a Moslem.

This is the assortment of human beings to whom the Sherif of Beihan and his very capable family had brought peace and order. Eight years ago it was unsafe, in much of the Wadi Beihan, to leave one's house by daylight. Rival factions crouched in their small forts and fired at each other spasmodically, or went on raids to plunder, kill, and destroy. By night, people emerged to plow their fields or burn down the palm trees of their neighbors, creeping along the bottoms of narrow irrigation ditches to get away safely. Some of the forts possessed underground tunnels to their wells, so that water could be drawn at all times without danger.

Within five years all this was changed. The big factional feuds stopped and the bitter enmities between groups tempered to a friendly aloofness. There were occasional shootings, of course, but as isolated incidents or the results of raids from tribes outside Beihan. The change came with only a small force of fifty government guards, a radio operator, and a political officer, Peter Davey. The guards had no fighting to do, but served as a token of the power of the Sherif of Beihan. There was no pitched battle, no open clash, no sudden submission on the part of hostile groups. The war was a cold one, a long series of political maneuvers against cunning and intrigue. Shots were sometimes fired, but mainly from a distance, serving as warnings or demonstrations rather than intents to kill. The Sherif wanted above all to avoid bloodshed, since one more dead man might mean the start of a new feud. Slowly, group by group and section by section, the people were won over.

To almost the whole population, it marked the inauguration of a new era, for most of the people, who had never tasted peace before, found it good.

Peter Davey, incidentally, had been transferred to the territory of Dhala a few years later, 1947, where he found his task much more difficult than in Beihan. The ruler of Dhala was of a different cut from the Sherif of Beihan, holding his position through oppression and brutality, which brought constant civil war. After ejecting this Emir Haidera, Davey began to get somewhere in bringing order out of chaos, but many tribal leaders fought every step he took. One of the worst offenders was Sheikh Mohammed Awas of the Ahmedi tribe. Davey finally decided to make an example of him, and gathered a handful of tribal and government guards to arrest him. The party set out by night and marched hard, hoping to take the Sheikh by surprise.

Mohammed Awas and several followers were in one of his fields, but stepped into a nearby wadi bed when they saw the approaching party. Davey stopped and stated simply, "I have come to arrest you." There was no parley. The Sheikh suddenly raised his rifle, fired, and Peter Davey fell mortally wounded, while a slave of the Sheikh fired again. A government guard immediately shot Mohammed Awas and his brother on the spot. During the sharp battle that followed, Davey's body was rescued before the government forces withdrew.

Dhala is the source of most of the qat used in the Western Aden Protectorate. This is a narcotic introduced into South Arabia from Abyssinia many centuries ago, and has proved one of the scourges of that region. Its production has been forbidden in Audhali, Yafa, and Fadhili, as well as Beihan, but its use is not illegal, unfortunately.

Qat is a narcotic stimulant found in young leaves of the evergreen shrub *Catha edulis*. When the leaves are chewed, the user feels alert, confident, and is quite garrulous. There is no hang-

over, as such, but the aftereffects are drastic, in that they produce
a mind scarcely capable of working at all. In time, the user suf-
fers from sleeplessness, loss of appetite, and extreme constipation,
and addicts are easily recognized by a wan discoloration and tight-
ening of the skin. Many of the shootings that still occur in the
Wadi Beihan come when qat addicts become too cocky and decide they can lick not only their enemies but the world.

A few killings are straight business—murder for a price—for this
profession exists in southern Arabia as in more civilized parts of
the world. In South Arabia, an assassin's fee may range from a
few to many thousand Maria Theresa dollars, and there are often
complications in payment because there are two types. The *diya*
or blood money fee remains constant at 707 dollars, but most self-
respecting assassins consider it a loss of face to accept the blood
money right away after doing their work. They will accept, however, the *lo'am* or *hashem,* which might be translated as the honor
or respect payment. When a sultan or ruling sherif is killed, this
may go as high as 20,000 M.T. dollars, for an important sheikh
3,000 dollars, for an *aqil* or sectional leader 100 to 1,000 dollars,
and for a *qabili* or tribesman from 50 to 500 dollars.

The price varies according to the personality and power of the
victim, his standing, and the circumstances of the murder.

Just which type of shooting Alan Denny was preparing for as
we camped near the salt mines of Aiyadin I do not know, but I
was happy to see him check his machine gun and set it in a favorable position despite the well-known peace of Beihan. The
camp was a pleasant one, being high on the side of a mountain,
far from the camel ticks that swarmed near the mines where the
camel trains were loaded. We pitched our tents, lighted our fires,
and had tea while the goat was being expertly skinned and prepared for dinner.

It was getting dark, but that did not prevent us from having
our usual evening shooting match. I knew that Sherif Hussein
and Sherif Awad were happy indeed, for they had just drunk tea
and now prepared to shoot, the two favorite occupations of the
Bedouin. Most of us shared their love of good marksmanship and
weapons. Our new arms and seemingly unlimited supplies of am-

munition created a sensation wherever we went. The best good-
will gifts brought by the expedition into Beihan were its rifles,
carbines, and revolvers.

In Beihan, good marksmanship is not only a method of obtaining personal satisfaction or food, but at a moment's notice it may
mean the difference between life and death. This was the case, at
least, until recent years, and the men of Beihan have become so
used to that situation that they still would not dream of being
without rifles. When Sherif Awad, for instance, visits our headquarters he first leans his rifle against a wall and then sits down
nearby. If he should go into the next room for even three minutes, he would not think of moving without first picking up his
rifle.

As it was growing dark, Sherif Hussein introduced us to a new
kind of target shooting. After setting up glowing embers in the
sand ninety yards away, we lined up to see who could shoot them
out. Sherif Saleh bin Naser then performed one of his circus
tricks. This dignified old gentleman held his rifle upside down,
with the stock resting on top of his head, and hit his target.

Dinner was ready, and we ate around the campfires, under a
sky bright with stars and a new moon. Just as we were leaning
back comfortably, the Bal Harith tribesmen from the mine came
to serenade us. Holding hands in a long line about a hundred
yards away from us, they began to chant, and as they sang moved
forward, then back again. Their chants are strange, repetitious,
and possess an eerie quality that soon seems thoroughly suitable
to the desert night.

When they departed, we told a few stories before turning in.
From Sherif Hussein, with explanations by Alan Denny, I heard
a tale about a Beihani customs post which the Sherif had built
to collect taxes on salt going into Yemen and on Yemeni products coming back into Beihan. The Yemeni authorities, in the
person of Ashami, Governor of Beidha, said this was an aggressive act. John Allen, Deputy British Agent at the time, replied
that it was not aggressive but was on the contrary perfectly normal and legal, solely a matter of internal administration of Beihan.

The Yemenis replied to this by allegedly building a fort for the seemingly sole purpose of preventing the Sherif's customs post from functioning. Worst of all, according to the British view, the fort was on Beihan territory, although Yemen has never really recognized the existence of a boundary line at that point. After a great deal of talk and many exchanges that got nowhere, the R.A.F. rocketed the Yemeni fort from the air, since its strategic location made land assault difficult. The fort was destroyed with no casualties except one man who was scratched on the cheek by a stone splinter.

The ground campaign was interesting because it involved over two hundred men who were engaged in battle for three weeks with no fatalities on either side. This remarkable result is attributed to the long range at which they were firing and does not reflect on their marksmanship or on their earnest desire to drill holes in one another.

Before the actual rocketing, there was a solemn exchange of messages between Mr. Allen and Ashami, which illustrated some of the unique features of politics and war in this part of the world. In an effort to settle the differences, Mr. Allen, his wife, and a political officer traveled to Beidha in Yemen and spent the night there. At the conclusion of a long discussion, Ashami told Mr. Allen that he thought the British were entirely wrong on every point, but would he kindly send from Aden a doctor to see his sick baby.

Back in Aden, Mr. Allen dispatched a doctor at once, with a letter to Ashami saying it was a shame that they had been unable to come to some agreement, but he hoped the baby would be all right. The doctor returned with a letter from Ashami saying he thought Mr. Allen a dictator and warmonger, with a postscript thanking him very much for sending the doctor, who had helped the baby a great deal.

Later Mr. Allen sent a telegram to Ashami saying that he would unhappily be required to take air action if Ashami would not withdraw the fort, with a postscript saying that he was glad to hear the baby was better. Then Mr. Allen dispatched a plane to drop leaflets over the fort, warning the people to clear out before rocketing started. Attached to one of the leaflets was a small parcel containing sweets and toys for Ashami's baby. Shortly afterward a reply was received from Ashami by road, thanking Mr. Allen very much for the sweets and inviting him to come and visit Beidha again, bringing his wife and children; there was a postscript to the effect that the coming air action was completely inexcusable and illegal.

9

THE LIONS OF TIMNA

The ancient graveyard of Timna was located on the slope of Haid bin Aqil about a mile and a half from the main city mound. Although cemeteries are often rewarding sites for archaeological excavation, we had not started here before because of the number of other promising spots and also because this particular burial place had been plundered and robbed extensively both in antiquity and in more recent times. Charlie McCollum and I investigated it, however, set to work at a likely looking spot, aided by Abu Bakr, our antiquities guard, who was also a Yafai tribesman and expert at digging graves. As might have been expected, we found our grave had been thoroughly rifled centuries before, but it contained thirteen new inscriptions.

When further work on Professor Honeyman's hoped-for temple on the north side of Timna proved it to be only a cluster of houses, we decided that more rewarding finds might be made in the cemetery, plundered or not, so he set to work vigorously at Haid bin Aqil.

The day Sandy Honeyman began working at the graveyard, I received word that the chief of our tribal guards, who had been looking after our security, had been called away unexpectedly by Sherif Hussein for duty elsewhere. The next afternoon I received from him the following letter written in Arabic:

Dear Sir:

I beg to inform you, O Friend, that I have reached Beihan al-Qasab at 10:30 hours this morning on transfer. I thank you very much for your kind treatment, for which tablets of gratitude will be engraved in my heart forever.

Abdrubbuh Ali

Excavation at the South Gate was from the beginning the most exciting and rewarding work. At the outset the area in front of the gate itself was covered with sand and debris to a depth of about fifteen feet, with only the tops of the gate towers visible above the surface. Charles Inge and Kenny Brown set to work there, limiting themselves to an area forty feet wide and a hundred feet long at the gate itself and adjacent walls.

After removing several feet of sand in front of the gate, with only a few ancient objects turning up, they reached a stratum of heavy burning which contained many artifacts such as potsherds, beads, bits of inscribed stone, and pieces of bronze and iron. We saw streaks of ashes with layers of clean earth and sand in between, then another layer of ashes with more bits of stone inscriptions, pieces of alabaster with rows of beautifully carved ibex heads, and other objects. It was evident almost from the start that the city of Timna had suffered a catastrophic destruction, in which fire played a major part.

As the wall and gate towers were revealed, several monumental inscriptions were discovered, one of which caused a momentary flurry of excitement because it contained the word WBLQS. If supplied with the correct vowels, this might read Bilqis, the traditional name of the Queen of Sheba. On the face of it, this was a reasonable assumption, since we were in the neighborhood of the glamorous queen. But our hopes, combined with the universal allure of this fabulous visitor to Solomon, ran away with us and carried us several centuries farther back than our excavations had actually taken us. Professor Albright, called to examine the inscription, studied it briefly and announced that the name Bilqis made no sense in association with the rest of it. Further study might reveal the meaning of WBLQS but we definitely had not discovered a reference to the Queen of Sheba.

Feeling a little let down, we all went back to work. Actually, the inscriptions found at the South Gate were of first importance, even if they did not make sensational headlines. Most of them were public decrees mentioning the names of various kings of Qataban, among whom was featured one Shahr Yagil Yuhargib, who ruled Qataban when it was at the height of its power about 75 B.C.

As more and more of the South Gate was revealed, Dick Bowen, our engineer, pointed out that we would soon have to apply some type of protective shoring to keep it from collapsing on us. I was astounded to see how the great granite blocks had decayed and how they began to crumble as soon as they were cleared of sand and exposed to the atmosphere after so many centuries. In a particularly bad state of preservation were two large columns of inscription of about twenty-five lines each. The reddish granite of these stones was extremely friable, a condition which had been made worse by the burning of the city at the time of its destruction. Sandy Honeyman spent three days under the burning sun making an accurate hand copy of the inscriptions. Then photographs were taken and, after allowing the wind three days to remove loose particles, a latex squeeze was taken.

After the weak points were shored up, digging continued. At the twelve-foot level, the façade of the gate had been completely cleared except for its foundation, and the wall for a length of seventy-five feet was exposed to view. This was badly destroyed, but there was a well-preserved revetment sloping outward beneath it, which must have been strikingly beautiful in the great days of Timna, for there was evidence that it had originally been covered by gleaming white clay or plaster.

By the end of the first three weeks of excavation, the area in front of the South Gate and its adjoining wall had been entirely cleared. The gateway itself was flanked by two massive towers constructed of rough blocks, some as large as eight by two feet. The masonry work was good but not smoothly finished, indicating that the gate was built before the flowering of Qatabanian civilization, when more polished work was done. Certainly it was made not later than the fifth century B.C. Many inscriptions were found on the big blocks of the towers, and there was also evidence of two vertical grooves for gateposts and another for a heavy cross-beam. Charred wood still remained in parts of these grooves.

Now we had our first glimpse, infinitesimal but still a glimpse, of ancient Timna. It was not too difficult to approach the massive South Gate and imagine ourselves part of a camel caravan loaded with frankincense, on our way from the lands of the East to the Mediterranean. We were more eager than ever to enter the city, but at this point Charles Inge, who had supervised work at the South Gate, had to return to his desk in Aden. Kenny Brown took over for him, under the direction of Professor Albright, and with his troop of Arab irregulars began the invasion of Timna itself. Carefully they cleared away small mountains of sand, layers of ashes, huge blackened building stones, broken pottery, and charred timbers of great size. At a depth of ten feet, just inside the gateway, they reached a pavement of smooth flagstones, still intact and in good condition.

The excavators followed the pavement northward into the town, carefully leaving a strip of debris on the right side of their clearing so that a complete stratified record for later study might be preserved. They widened the path until they realized that they were in a paved courtyard just inside the city gates. On either side they unearthed built-in stone benches. Here, no doubt, was a fine outdoor meeting place for the elders of the town, or a favored spot for conducting business. Here, perhaps, the most notable warriors of Qataban gathered to tell each other tales of the mighty battles between Qataban and the neighboring kingdoms of Saba, Ma'in, and Hadhramaut.

Turning left shortly after entering the gateway, Kenny Brown and his crew cleared a path until they came to the well-preserved wall of a building, designated Building A, but soon named House Yafaam as a result of two inscriptions giving the name of the building and that of the king for whom it was built.

A wide trench was now excavated northward along this wall until another building was reached, Building B, whose inscriptions gave it the name House Yafash. This structure's wall was partially cleared in a trench that followed it eastward until it ended and turned abruptly north. Here the men came to the corner of the second building facing on the square or courtyard, and Professor Albright made one of his frequent visits of inspection to decide just what digging should be done next. At this interesting point, Kenny Brown came down with a fever and was confined to bed by Dr. McNinch, much against his will. I took over immediate direction of the South Gate work until he should be able to get on his feet again.

We had now dug around three sides of a courtyard, but not to the pavement in every place, by any means. And the center was still filled with debris. This first excavation had been in the nature of an exploratory operation, to find dimensions, structures, contours, on which we could base subsequent digging. In our trenches next to the walls, we had dug down only about four feet in most places. Professor Albright decided it was time to clear most of the court area and go deeper. This operation required the greatest care, not only because we were excavating through a stratum of heavy burned debris and might with one careless stroke smash a fine vase or statue, but there was also danger of digging right through the original ground level inadvertently.

By this time, however, many of our workers were well trained, eager to cart away as much debris as possible but more determined not to miss or ruin one archaeological treasure. Salim, our native truck driver hired in Mukalla, had recently been promoted by Professor Albright to straw boss over a group of diggers in the South Gate area, and proved himself more capable every day.

At this point a series of illnesses hit the expedition staff. Kenny Brown was followed to the infirmary and bed by Dick Bowen, Professor Albright, and then Dr. Jamme, who spent twelve hours a day in the boiling sun studying inscriptions and wound up with the fever one would expect after such an experience. I thought that our mud palace looked more like a front-line receiving station than an archaeological headquarters, but work had to continue, even if at a somewhat slackened pace. The rest of us just doubled up, but as usual in such circumstances, extra complications arose beyond the expected.

One day, I wearily went up to my room, where I had hoped to do some essential writing before going back to work at the South

Gate. But our head Somali, Jama Ishmail, rushed by me shouting something important and exciting in a mixture of Arabic, Somali, and English. I jumped up and out the door, almost killing myself in the process, for Beihani doorways are made either for midgets or people crawling on their hands and knees.

Holding my aching head, I staggered out on the landing and there found Salim, half standing, half sitting, and apparently about to drop from exhaustion. But I could scarcely see Salim because of something he held in his arms, something that looked like a green lion with a creature riding on its back. Ascribing this sight to the crack on my head, I shook it and looked again. Salim began to slump toward the floor, saying, "Sahib, Sahib Phillips," followed by something completely unintelligible in Arabic.

The green lion and rider were still in Salim's arms, and I knew that a great find had been made.

"Where did you get it?" I gasped in Arabic.

"By House Yafash, Sahib," said Salim.

I helped Salim set the green figure on a nearby army cot. Then I ran to get Professor Albright out of bed, Dr. Jamme out of bed, Kenny Brown out of bed, and Dick Bowen out of bed.

We all stood and stared at the figure that lay before us. Then Professor Albright threw a bit of cold water on my excitement by asking how the lion happened to be lying on a cot in my room. When I told him that Salim had carried it to me, he shook his head in disapproval.

"Very bad archaeological practice," he muttered.

He was right, of course. All our workers had been told over and over again to leave any find intact without touching it and to call a member of the staff immediately. Many objects broke even with the most careful handling by experts, and we never wanted a workman or even a straw boss like Salim to handle a find without careful supervision. Salim generally obeyed orders, but he knew that in the green lion he had found something so important that his one thought was to get it to me in a hurry. Luckily, it was cast in such heavy metal that even rough handling did not damage it.

After getting the matter of bad archaeological practice out of the way, we could all look at the statue with more appreciative eyes. It was a bronze lion, and on its back sat a fat cupid holding in one hand a dart and in the other a broken chain leading to a collar fastened around the lion's neck. At the base of the statue there was a complete inscription in ancient Qatabanian characters. As we were looking at the inscription, Sandy Honeyman, who had just arrived from the graveyard, joined our party and gasped audibly at the sight before him. Then the heads of Professor Albright, Dr. Jamme, and Professor Honeyman were bent low over the figure, while the rest of us waited.

I heard brief mutterings exchanged between the three, and then Professor Albright slowly straightened up with words that I shall never forget.

"Wendell, we've got it. By Heaven, we've got it!"

Drs. Jamme and Honeyman nodded in agreement, smiling. I had never seen Professor Albright so excited.

"Got what, Professor?" I asked.

"A date. Look!"

He leaned over and pointed to the inscription on the base of the figure. Slowly he read it aloud.

"*Thuwaybum wa 'Aqrabum dhuway Muhasni'im shayyamu Yafash.*"

"That means," he continued, "that Thuwaybum and 'Aqrabum, members of the family Muhasni'im, who decorated the House Yafash, also made these lions, or had them made."

"So?"

"So this discovery is unique in the annals of South Arabian archaeology, and will straighten out our chronology, help fix the dates of the kings of Qataban, and enable us to date our masonry with reference to the development of civilization in South Arabia."

I took a deep breath and hesitantly inquired, "How?"

"This lion is a copy of a Hellenistic original and couldn't have been copied much before 150 B.C. because the Greeks were not making them long before that. If King Shahr Yagil Yuhargib had the House Yafash redecorated, as we believe we have learned, he also had this lion installed, because the same two craftsmen did both jobs. So Yuhargib lived in the second or first century before

Christ, and not the fifth, sixth, seventh or even eighth, as has been thought. This clears up our main lines of history in South Arabia."

Now this was quite a statement even for our Professor and was enough to send us all to the South Gate at top speed to see where the lion had been found. Salim pointed out the exact place near the wall of the House Yafash where the lion had been buried in ashes and charred wood. When Timna was destroyed, the lion must have been immediately covered over by ashes, falling stones, and burning beams so that it was not seen by the invaders in the excitement of finding other loot. Otherwise, it certainly would have been carried off and melted down for bronze.

No one felt like going back to bed after this discovery, but Dr. McNinch insisted that Professor Albright and Dr. Jamme return to their rooms. He allowed Kenny to be up and about for a few hours, so we worked together at the South Gate excavation for a while. About three-thirty I sent him back to his room.

Half an hour later, Abdullah, one of our best workmen, cried, "Baksheesh, baksheesh, ya sahib!" I walked slowly over to him, sure that nothing else of importance would be found on such a day of days and expecting the usual small inscription or corroded bracelet. Abdullah was pointing to a bit of green metal which appeared through the burned layer a few feet from the spot at which the bronze lion had been discovered.

The moment I took over the task of exposing this buried object all our workmen gathered round to watch the fun, which so enraged foreman Salim that we almost had bloodshed on the spot. Carefully I brushed away some ashes from the top and saw another ridge of green metal. I brushed more, and for a time this served only to add to my confusion, for what I uncovered were many narrow ridges of green metal leading off in all directions.

Charlie McCollum came up at this stage, having just finished greasing several Power Wagons. Together we continued the cautious uncovering of the object before us. Ashes, sand, bits of rock were brushed away, and finally a piece of charred beam four inches thick. Then I sent Salim for Kenny Brown, who had missed the first big find because of his illness. If this turned out to be impor-

Left, totally blind old sheikh, once one of Beihan's chief assassins. If someone wanted a person eliminated, and the price was right, this gentleman would take care of the business immediately—until trachoma destroyed his eyesight. *Below*, the bronze lions of Timna (approximate date 75-50 B.C.) excavated outside House Yafash at the city's South Gate lowered existing Qatabanian chronology by several centuries and contributed materially to placing the ancient history of South Arabia on firm ground for the first time.

Professor A. M. Honeyman holding the beautifully formed head of a young woman carved in translucent alabaster, dating from approximately the first century B.C. It was named "Miriam" by the Arab workmen who dug it out of the Timna cemetery, and is the finest female head known from South Arabia.

tant, I wanted Kenny to be on hand. And I asked him to bring along Ocky Romaine and his Speed Graphic so that he could take pictures of the object as we revealed it. Meanwhile Charlie carefully measured the exact position of the piece in relation to the wall of the House Yafash. When Kenny and Ocky arrived we completed the unveiling operation, more cautiously than ever as we saw that the object was broken.

We all began to suspect what we had found before any of us dared speak it. The size and shape seemed about right for another lion, but it looked nothing like the lion we had found. The reason, of course, was that it was buried face down and all we saw were the ridges of bronze on the back of the statue, where it was affixed to the wall originally. Finally, to our amazement and joy, we lifted it carefully from its centuries-old bed, and saw that it was truly another lion and cupid, identical with the first except that it faced in the opposite direction. The cupid had broken from his place, and there was other damage, but it was all there, complete and beautiful. This was indeed the expedition's day of triumph.

Back at headquarters, Professor Albright pointed out that the original objects from which these lions and cupids were copied by Qatabanian craftsmen probably came from Egypt, where they were made in the Hellenistic period. Many details of technique and artistry told Professor Albright the period of original creation accurately. The subject itself was popular in Pompeii and elsewhere during the Hellenistic period—sexual love in the form of a little Cupid, taming a ferocious lion and then riding, leading, or holding it by a chain.

This suggested the idea that the House Yafash might have been an establishment for the conduct of sacred prostitution. Pagan priestesses practiced sacred prostitution in many parts of the ancient world. Was it practiced in Qataban? Was the House Yafash its temple? We hoped to learn the answers to these and many more questions as our work progressed.

The workmanship in the two statues was excellent. They were cast by a process the French call *cire perdue*. This method was known to the ancients and then lost for many centuries, and is

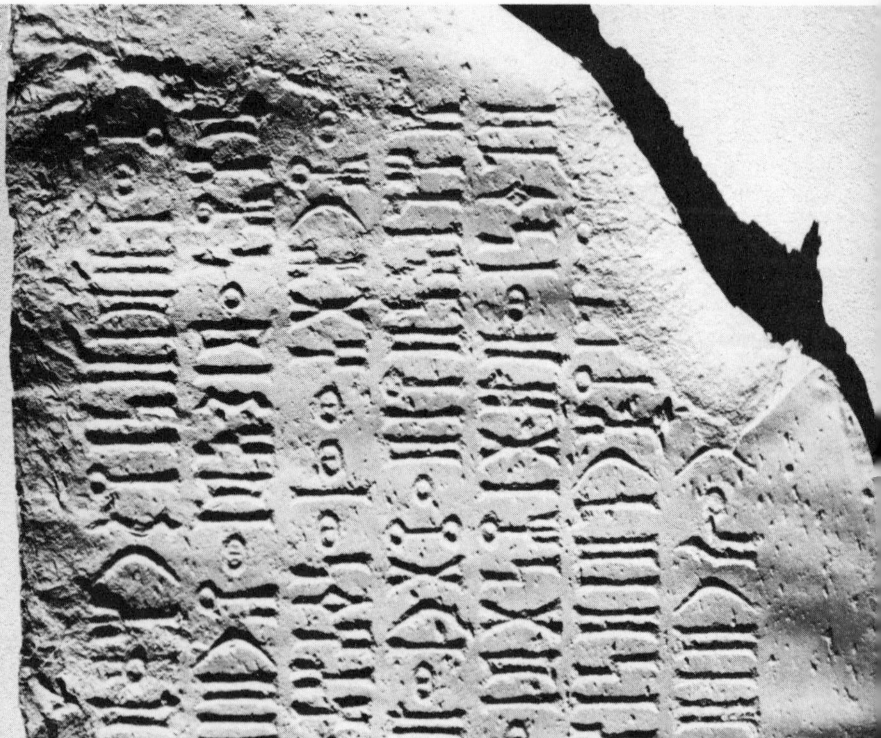

Qatabanian Inscription from House Yafash

Translation by Dr. Albert Jamme, W.F.

Each line of the inscription reads from right to left: *

1. Thuwaybum, son of Yashrih'amm, and Sabhum and Hawfi'amm, these

2. of (the family of) Muhasni'um, bought and consecrated his house Yafash and all its workrooms

3. and its superstructures and its roof-terrace and its veranda, all together,

4. according to the rules of Anbay. By Athtar and by Amm and by Anbay and by Warafu,

5. He of Lafan, and by Dhat-Santum and by Dhat-Zahran, and by his lord Sha-

6. hr Yagil Yuhargib, son of Hawfi'amm Yuhan'im, king of Qa-

7. taban, and by Fari'karib, he of (the clan of) Dharhan, paternal uncle and regent of Shahr

* This latex squeeze shows the lower right corner of the inscription missing. Subsequently the pieces completing the text were discovered by the author in the debris below the wall.

This latex squeeze was made from an unpublished Qatabanian inscription engraved on a stone in the south wall of the House Yafash in Timna (Wadi Beihan) and mentions the purchase and dedication of this house, different parts of which are listed in the text. The final invocation includes the names of the following divinities: the star god Athtar, the moon and chief god of Qataban under the two appellations of Amm and Anbay, the god of landmarks Warafu, and finally the sun goddess variously called Dhat-Santum, "she who fixes" and Dhat-Zahran, "she who appears in her splendor"; this invocation ends with valuable historical information attested in South Arabian epigraphy for the first time: Fari'karib, founder of a new dynasty, was almost probably a usurper, since his name is not followed by his father's name, but by the name of the clan to which he belonged; he was also the paternal uncle and regent of Shahr Yagil Yuhargib, son of Hawfi'amm Yuhan'im, who was thus brother of Fari'karib. This inscription also provides conclusive proof that the two bronze lions with riders were cast in the reign of King Shahr Yagil Yuhargib, since several of the same persons belonging to the same family are mentioned in the inscriptions on the lions. Since the bronze lions are late Hellenistic in date, this fact proves that the reign in question cannot be earlier than the first century B.C.

said to have been rediscovered by the great Italian sculptor of the
sixteenth century, Benvenuto Cellini. The craftsmanship of the
lions of Timna confirmed better than anything previously known
the statements of the Greek geographer, Strabo, in the last century
B.C., regarding the high metallurgical skill of the South Arabians
of his time.

That evening Professor Albright repeated for the other members of our staff the significance of the lions. Along with other
finds, they proved that the king under whom they were constructed
could not have lived before about 150 B.C., although he had previously been dated by scholars as early as 700 B.C. It was inconceivable that Hellenistic lions could possibly have been imitated
from Alexandrian originals in South Arabia centuries before there
was any such Alexandrian art to copy.

The reason for the Professor's confidence about the precision
of the date was first and foremost that the bases of the two statues
bore identical inscriptions which could be read throughout. They
named the two craftsmen who had decorated the House Yafash,
built in the reign of King Shahr Yagil Yuhargib, who could be
fixed in a dynasty which included several important kings, some
three of whom struck gold coins also in imitation of Hellenistic
models. Thuwaybum, the principal craftsman named on the lions,
is also named in the inscription on the wall of the House Yafash
describing its reconstruction under King Shahr Yagil Yuhargib.

Across the courtyard from House Yafash was the house called
Yafaam, which contained masonry and inscriptions later in date
than those of Yafash. The total of these day-to-day discoveries,
combined with the information the lions of Timna gave us, supplied a relative chronology both for script and masonry between
the fourth century B.C. and the destruction of Timna about the
time of Christ or a little earlier.

Ancient Happy Arabia was slowly showing itself through the
sands of time and neglect. Our knowledge of the history of the
civilization of early South Arabia was on firm ground for the first
time.

10

THE QUEEN OF SHEBA

One morning Dr. Bowen was investigating some interesting small mounds north of Hajar bin Humeid when a Beihani clothed in rags and a sharp curved jambiya approached him. Between uncertain Arabic and sign language, Dick gathered that the Arab wanted to show him something of great importance. Dick was far from excited, since he rightly doubted the Arab's judgment as to objects of archaeological significance, but he also knew better than to dismiss any clue without investigation.

He climbed in his Power Wagon, motioned the Arab up beside him, and set off, following the Arab's directions. Three miles north up the wadi they swung east into a rocky gorge, which narrowed until the truck had to be left behind. Going forward on foot, the Arab led Dick Bowen through a narrow canyon mouth bounded by hard metamorphic rocks. Here Dick was startled to find something far more rare than archaeological ruins in South Arabia—several deep pools of water. The hard rocks and the narrow gorge sheltered from much of the sun combined to make this little valley, known as Wadi al-Fara, the only place to hold surface water in the whole Beihan area and one of the few such spots in all southwest Arabia.

The Arab led Dick up a steep slope, where he proudly pointed out an ancient Qatabanian inscription cut in the face of a rock. Dick knew that the inscription might be interesting, but he was far more excited about other things he saw on the walls of the canyon—great numbers of graffiti, or shallow carvings in the rock surface. These graffiti contained short inscriptions with personal names—the equivalent of our "Kilroy was here" scrawls on walls or carvings on trees. This is the plain, simple stuff of which real archaeological treasure often consists.

Dick Bowen hurried back to headquarters to locate Dr. Jamme, our epigrapher, and that afternoon they both went back to the Wadi al-Fara. Jamme was as excited about the discovery as Dick had thought he would be, and spent the afternoon studying all the graffiti he could locate. His excitement was still high that evening when he announced that in Graffito Valley he had discovered a hitherto unknown and very ancient type of inscription on the rocks. This was a graffito in three lines written from left to right instead of the usual boustrophedon or ox-turn style. In boustrophedon writing, the first line reads from right to left, the next line from left to right, and so on—and this was the method of writing or inscribing that was universal in ancient South Arabia. As Professor Albright pointed out, Jamme's inscription took us back to the earliest phase of Arabian inscription in which the writing ran from left to right just as in Greek, Latin, or modern European languages.

Dr. Jamme's graffito was the earliest thing so far known from the ancient Qatabanian kingdom, dating back probably to the ninth or tenth century B.C. It contained three names that were also found in the Bible. "Nabat" is the Hebrew name of the father of Jeroboam, first king of Israel. "Ali" is the same name as Eli, the high priest mentioned in the first chapter of First Samuel. "Yagur" was the name of a place in Judah. The connections between South Arabia and the Biblical lands seemed closer than ever before, as we heard these names.

Early the next day several of us visited the Wadi al-Fara to see this remarkable graffito for ourselves. On our arrival, Dr. Jamme sat down with his back against a huge boulder and proceeded to study the opposite walls of the canyon through a pair of binoculars. Graffiti are not deeply etched into the rock and are hard to locate. While Dr. Jamme looked for his prize, the rest of us decided to go further up the valley searching for tombs or other signs of ancient ruins. When we returned about two hours later we were astounded to see Jamme seated in precisely the same position, binoculars still in hand, staring intently and somewhat angrily at the opposite wall of the canyon.

When Dick asked what had happened, Dr. Jamme rather curtly replied that he had lost his precious graffito. We all stood around dumbfounded, wondering how such an epic discovery could be so easily mislaid, especially when it was securely fastened to the side of a huge cliff. Then a remarkable thing happened. As Dr. Jamme stood on the rocky side of the canyon pointing vaguely and exclaiming in Belgian English, "It should be right there!" the marvelous graffito suddenly appeared, just where he said it should be. It was not a miracle, but rather a trick of the light against the rock. Just as Jamme spoke, a nearby Arab shifted his position so that his shadow was cast on the rock toward which Jamme was pointing. In partial shadow the scratching on the rock showed up clearly. In direct light it was really invisible from where we stood. When Dick Bowen and Jamme had found it the afternoon before, the sun had been sinking and the rock was in shadow, making the graffito easy to see.

With a joyous and booming *"Voilà!"* Jamme hailed the rediscovery of his prize and then, perhaps for the first time in nearly three thousand years, the walls of the Wadi al-Fara echoed with the ancient Qatabanian lines as he slowly spoke the words of the inscription.

Dr. Jamme continued his work in the valley, studying about a hundred and fifty more graffiti on its rock walls. Many were very old and many were enlightening, but none had the antiquity of his first great find. Several, however, were so old as to show a new form of Aleph, the first letter of the Semitic alphabet and the source of our English letter A. This letter and several others showed strong resemblance to the ancestral Canaanite alphabet, from which Phoenician-Hebrew and South Arabian descended. Professor Albright has long been convinced that the South Arabian script split off from the Canaanite in the north somewhere around the thirteenth century B.C., and these ancient graffiti with their Canaanite-like letters brought us much closer to the time when the two scripts diverged.

While our excavation work had slowly carried us backward in time—to the destruction of Timna, and on to the first, second, third, and even fourth centuries B.C., Graffito Valley whirled us past five or six more centuries and brought us close to the ancient days of the Bible, close to the time of the Queen of Sheba, who had lived in Marib, just forty miles away. Nothing in that part of the world had previously gone back to her time, which was probably around 950 B.C. Now, after looking at the rock scratchings of a man who might well have been alive when she was, we could not help thinking and talking about her.

Many legends have grown up around the Queen of Sheba, who was first mentioned in the tenth chapter of I Kings, which told of her famous visit to King Solomon in Jerusalem. At this time Solomon, whom Professor Albright dates from 961 to 922 B.C., had extensive shipping operations on the Red Sea and the Indian Ocean. As narrated in Kings, the Queen of Sheba came north by camel caravan. Her visit was undoubtedly of great commercial importance, for she "gave the King a hundred and twenty talents of gold, and of spices a very. great store, and precious stones; there came no more such abundance of spices as these which the Queen of Sheba gave to King Solomon."

It was no accident that this journey occurred not long after the domestication of the camel and the greatest expansion of trade through camel caravans in ancient history. As Isaiah puts it, "The multitude of camels shall cover thee, the dromedaries of Midian and Ephah; all they from the Sheba shall come; they shall bring gold and incense and they shall show forth the praises of the Lord." To date there is no direct evidence of the existence of camel caravans much before the eleventh century B.C. The first actual representation of a man riding a camel dates from the tenth century B.C.

Some scholars have held that the Queen of Sheba was really a northern queen reigning over a nomadic tribe in northern Arabia rather than the ruler of the nation whose capital was Marib. Although there are more Arab queens than kings mentioned in the Assyrian cuneiform inscriptions from 800 to 600 B.C., this does not prove that queens were to be found only in North Arabia. It proves only that in those days the Arabs apparently preferred queens to kings. Motherhood was easy to establish, whereas fatherhood was open to question; or, as the Latin proverb puts it, *Mater certa pater incertus.*

The Queen of Sheba may have been the ruler of the Sabeans while they were still a nomadic tribe and before they settled down, but there is no reason to place her in the north rather than the south. The first chapter of Job refers to the Sabeans as a raiding tribe. "And the Sabeans fell upon them, and took them away; yea, they have slain the servants with the edge of the sword; and I only am escaped alone to tell thee."

Actually, all we really know about the Queen of Sheba is found in the Bible. No inscription has been found in South Arabia, even at Marib, which refers to any Sabean ruler earlier than about 800 B.C., a good century and a half after the famous Queen's time. The earliest rulers of which we have knowledge were mukarribs,* priestly rulers, such as were found in most South Arabian kingdoms in their early days. They preceded the kings of Saba during at least three centuries. Thus the Queen would represent an entirely different type of ruler, but not a type unknown in ancient days. Arab legends identify the Queen of Sheba with the name of Bilqis, but there is not the slightest evidence for any of the fabulous tales that have grown up about her. They indicate, however, the great allure of this Queen for all people.

One story tells how, a few days after the Queen's arrival at the court of Solomon, that great King was shocked to hear the rumor that she possessed feet like a goat. Rather than embarrass the lady by asking her to lift her skirts and show him, Solomon conceived a clever plan. His architects built a great crystal floor looking exactly like water. The day came when Solomon, standing on the opposite side of the crystal floor, invited the Queen of Sheba to join him. Believing that she had to cross water, our Queen lifted her robes in ladylike fashion and stepped forth. Solomon saw, to his immense relief, that she possessed quite normal feet.

An Ethiopic legend is that the Queen, being a very virtuous woman, continually resisted the amorous advances of the King.

---

* Mukarrib (MKRB) is a title of which the meaning is still uncertain—it may also be translated as "uniter."

Solomon in desperation fed her some highly seasoned food one night, and then placed a jug of cool water by his bed and an empty jug by hers. After she had retired, the spices did their work and heightened her thirst. Finally the Queen tiptoed into the King's room to borrow some of his water, thus innocently placing herself within reach of His Majesty, who was eagerly awaiting her.

The legends may be fabricated, but there is no reason to doubt that the Queen was real. Some day archaeological research will confirm her existence and tell us more about her, just as it has in recent years confirmed numerous other Biblical stories of this same general period—for example, Solomon's chariot city uncovered during the excavations at Megiddo, his copper refineries recently revealed at Tel el-Kheleifeh, and the demonstrated expansion of the tenth-century (B.C.) Phoenicians in the Mediterranean Sea.

Archaeology has also furnished details illustrating Solomon's voyages to Ophir. The Bible describes Ophir as the land of gold, and says that ships sailing from Palestine took three years (one year and parts of two others, according to Hebrew usage) to make the round trip. In 1948, the ancient site of Tell Qasileh near Tel-Aviv yielded a large potsherd with an inscription dating from the eighth century B.C. It mentions thirty shekels of gold from Ophir—the first reference to Ophir and its gold found outside the Bible.

There has been much confusion between the words "Ophir" and "Punt," both of which have been applied to South Arabia. Actually, Ophir is the Hebrew name for Somaliland and neighboring areas, while Punt was the Egyptian name for the same region. There is no reason to believe that either name ever covered a geographical area extending into South Arabia.

Thirty years ago, our Professor Albright pointed out for the first time that the words for "apes and peacocks" (I Kings 10:22) brought from Ophir are the same Egyptian words as the names of two different kinds of monkey brought from Punt by the Egyptians. The rendering "peacock" comes from an old guess which connected Ophir erroneously with India.

11

MIRIAM AND THE GOLD NECKLACE

The graveyard of Timna, at Haid bin Aqil, has been a good source of income to some Arabs for a long time. Even though no serious excavations in South Arabia had been undertaken before Gertrude Caton Thompson's work at Hureidha and our own at Timna, antiquities had been reaching a ready market for many years—the finds of Bedouin treasure hunters who poked around in the sand at likely spots and came up with some remarkably fine pieces.

In Aden there is an excellent collection owned by the wealthy Indian merchant, Mr. Kaiky Muncherjee, who once offered it to an American museum for $100,000. Our suspicion that a majority of the antiquities in collectors' hands had come from Timna was partially confirmed by my recognizing two fragments belonging to the monumental inscription at the right side of the South Gate. Even more pieces have come from the graveyard at Haid bin Aqil.

I was once the house guest of one of Timna's most successful grave robbers, who presented me with a few of his best pieces as we parted. Their scientific value was greatly increased when he pointed out to me the exact spots at which they had been found— the graveyard of Timna.

Most of the Arabs of Beihan have little conception of the age of the antiquities around them. One primary reason for this is that these things belong to the Days of Ignorance, before Mohammed, and in the eyes of the old-fashioned Moslem are unworthy of attention. Even the great Arab scholars of the Middle Ages did little significant work on the inscriptions left by their ancestors.

Once, at the Timna cemetery, Professor Honeyman reproved a workman for undermining a skull rather than clearing the debris from the top of it. The Arab replied that by this method he might not have found the skull so soon. Honeyman replied that since it had already lain there for two thousand years, it could have survived another half hour. The Arab's only comment was, "Wallah, was it two thousand years?"

In spite of the extensive looting of the graveyard over the years, Honeyman's work there progressed beautifully, with more good finds than might have been expected. He began his investigations of certain selected tombs, some high on the hillside and others lower down, determined to explore each one thoroughly rather than do a more cursory job on the whole cemetery.

Late one afternoon, when the sun was beginning to beat less fiercely on the sandy slopes and the workmen were singing to encourage one another for the last hour's effort, one of them broke off to call loudly, "Ya Sahib!" Honeyman extricated himself from a nearby tomb and walked over to see a small white ring showing through the surface. It looked for all the world like a waxen human ear.

Honeyman took over the digging immediately but did not work on the dirt and sand around the ear. Instead he began removing the debris from the slope above so that there would be no rockslide as he unearthed his ear and whatever might be attached to it. Finally he and Abu Bakr took their knives and scraped away sand and earth in a wide area around the waxen ear, filling basket after basket which were passed up to an Arab worker on the next level above for disposal. It was well after the closing hour of five when Abu Bakr handed to Professor Honeyman a heavy shapeless lump of soil and stone.

Bit by bit the earth was cleaned away until there was revealed to Honeyman's eyes a beautifully formed and well-preserved head of a young woman, carved in translucent alabaster. He beamed with joy, but his pleasure was nothing compared to that of the

Unique gold necklace discovered near "Miriam" in the cemetery of Timna (Haid bin Aqil). The upturned crescent moon represents the moon god of Qataban.

The tombs of Timna after excavation. These tiered chambers were probably not places for actual burial of bodies but served as ossuaries where bones of the dead were heaped.

Arab workmen. They were happy not only for the baksheesh due them but for the beauty of the thing they had found. Never in their lives had they seen a statue as fine as this, and the loveliness of this girl stirred them. On the spot they decided that she was Professor Honeyman's daughter, and without consulting anyone else they christened her Miriam. Then, after a heated discussion, they agreed that in the near future she should be married to one of the little cupid boys riding on the lions of Timna.

There were many unusual qualities about Miriam, the chief being that she possessed almost complete plaster curls hanging down in Egyptian fashion at the back of her head. Although a small piece of her nose was missing, she was indeed a beauty, with her dimpled chin and her creamy white complexion. Her ears were pierced for earrings, and there was a small opening around her neck, under her curls, for a necklace. One of the most remarkable things about Miriam was her eyes, which still retained some of the blue lapis lazuli commonly used for the eyes of ancient statues and well known to us from the tombs of the ancient pharaohs of Egypt.

On either cheek there was a rather odd deformity in the shape of an incision made between the eye and the ear, where a strip of the original alabaster had been carved out and a small strip of different alabaster inserted. This was obviously in imitation of the cautery or incision marks that must have been as customary among the ancient Qatabanians as among the Arabs of today. The incisions may have been made to effect a cure of some ailment, or they may have been the mark of some group or tribe.

Miriam brought luck to the workers at the graveyard, for that site began to yield more finds than had been expected. The day after Miriam's rebirth from a two-thousand-year burial, the workmen found some oxidized cloth and wood, fragments of pottery, and chips of alabaster. Then a Rubeidi tribesman from the little-known Wadi Merkha drew Professor Honeyman's attention to a small yellow object glistening through the sand. A few minutes of careful work proved enough to clean and restore it to its original condition, as it had been buried two millenniums ago.

It was a beautiful gold necklace, pendant and chain. In the

center was an upturned crescent moon bordered above and below
by gold filigree. On it there ran a legend in Qatabanian letters
mentioning two names, one a female personal name "HGRLT"
or Hagarlat, and the other a rather curious name, the equivalent
of 'Alay Fari'at which is not known elsewhere. It would have been
nice, everyone agreed, if the lovely necklace had belonged to the
beautiful Miriam, but it is reasonable to assume that the lucky
girl, Hagarlat, did her hair in the Egyptian fashion, as Miriam did,
and painted her eyebrows, darkened her eyes, and perhaps had
slashes on her cheeks, even though she may not have had the ele-
gant nose and saucy dimpled chin of our alabaster lady.

More important if not so aesthetically satisfying were the discoveries Professor Honeyman made that enabled him to reconstruct tentatively the ancient Qatabanian burial habits. Their
tombs were elaborate and well constructed, with two to four chambers opening off an entrance corridor. Each chamber was two or
three tiers deep, the tiers being separated by large paving stones
built into the sides of the chamber for strong support. Within the
tiered chambers Professor Honeyman found many human bones
but never a complete skeleton. Many of the bones were charred
and burned and were mixed with broken vases, portions of stelae,
and beads. In almost every instance the objects had been broken.

Most of the worthwhile art objects were discovered outside the
burial chambers in the entrance passages—inscribed stelae, sometimes complete pottery vessels, but only one intact alabaster head,
Miriam.

Professor Honeyman believes that these chambers were not the
places in which bodies were actually buried but that they served
as ossuaries into which the bones of the dead were piled. The
entrance passages contained indications that they may have served
some way in religious rites connected with the deceased. Professor
Albright pointed out that the contents of these graves were considerably different from those of ancient Egypt, Palestine, Syria,
and Mesopotamia. In these countries to the north, tombs reveal
intact burials, with complete jars, jewelry, furniture, and other
belongings. At Haid bin Aqil, however, most of the articles in the
graves were broken and the bones were strewn in complete dis-

Alabaster reliefs on funerary steles from the Timna cemetery, which may date back to the sixth century B.C. or even a little earlier. The bull was connected with South Arabian belief in the afterlife.

Alabaster statue of Gaba'um of the family of Han'amat from the Timna cemetery. From the first or second century B.C.

order. This was the case even in several burial chambers unearthed which had obviously not been disturbed in recent times.

It is possible, of course, that the objects were actually broken by the ancient Qatabanians themselves in connection with their burial rites. They may have taken new objects and broken them when they buried someone. Or they may have used only broken objects in connection with the burial. Both procedures were followed in different places in the world in ancient times.

The objects in the graves may have been broken during looting in ancient days, shortly after the destruction of Timna and during the following centuries, although there is some doubt about this in view of the breakage everywhere, even in graves that may not have been disturbed. The looting was so extensive, especially during the Middle Ages, because of the many references, in ancient inscriptions, to gold, silver, and other valuable offerings to the gods. Early Arab historians also made frequent references to the wealth and glory of the ancient kingdoms of South Arabia—incentive enough to send hundreds of men to cemeteries for grave robbing.

Aside from the gold necklace, we found no riches in the ordinary sense, but our archaeological treasures no doubt outweighed in value all the gold and silver that had been stolen from Timna in older times. These treasures had to be handled carefully, and we had a well-established procedure to be followed in every case of an important find. In the first place, Dick Bowen had mapped the city of Timna, Haid bin Aqil, and Hajar bin Humeid, with additions made whenever a new landmark was unearthed. Thus it was possible to indicate accurately, on this map, the exact position in which each specimen was found. In most cases, photographs were then taken of the object *in situ* from all angles.

When a specimen was brought to headquarters, it was then numbered, catalogued, described, and sent to the photographic laboratory. This was originally a small room with mud floor, walls, and ceiling, located next to the servants' quarters and directly under the main passageway to the second floor. This meant that almost every time someone walked upstairs, small or large chunks of mud dropped down, into photographic solutions or onto Ocky. Despite these difficulties, we were comfortably settled by this time. The eight upstairs rooms were whitewashed, and that's where the staff lived. Downstairs there was a hall, kitchen in which we installed our refrigerator and primus stoves, dining room, photo lab, and servants' quarters. Toilet facilities made us feel like American pioneers, only here the outhouse was made of mud.

When the photo laboratory proved too small, we appropriated half the dining room for it, and work went more smoothly. Here each specimen was photographed again from all angles with our Graphic View camera to bring out every possible feature. If the object was of special importance or had points of interest not adequately brought out through the medium of a photograph, it was drawn either by Professor Albright or by our Swahili assistant, Mohammed Hadi.

Finally, specimens were carried by the household and kitchen staff to the packing department, which consisted of Charlie McCollum and George Farrier, who seemed to be the only ones with the right combination of patience and skill required to put together boxes and pack the specimens with sufficient care for shipment to Aden.

One item that could not be packed and shipped was my obelisk, which Dr. Jamme thinks is not quite large enough to be dignified by that name but should be called a monolith. It was inscribed on four sides and was tall enough to stick out of the sands of two thousand years almost in the center of the mound that had been Timna.

With a few workmen, I had started digging around the obelisk, excavating an area about ten yards long and six wide. Everything progressed satisfactorily for some time, with several new fragmentary inscriptions turning up and a few metal objects, in addition to the writings on the obelisk itself.

Suddenly I was worried that we might reach the bottom of the obelisk without realizing it and that it would topple over. So I began to sink a test pit along one side, going down about three feet through clear sand. I breathed a bit easier, as there was obviously a fair margin of safety and the pillar seemed to go down indefinitely. But at this point I was called away on other duties and

Sandy Honeyman took over the operation for a while. Within a few hours he reported that his workmen had struck bottom only three or four inches below the end of my test pit.

The surprising discovery was that this big obelisk apparently rested in pure sand, without any elaborately carved, lion-studded base that we had expected. Only a few stones on two sides gave any support at all. One thing was certain—my precious obelisk was not the architectural highlight of the city square, as had been supposed. It was simply an official decree of about 300 B.C. set up in what now appeared to have been the chief market area of the city.

All inscriptions on the obelisk, and everywhere else, were preserved in latex squeezes. The old-fashioned method of transcribing these carvings had been to use a specially made coarse paper. Recently, however, Professor George Cameron of the University of Michigan had met with great success using rubber latex to record the famous Behistun inscriptions of Darius I in Persia. We followed his general procedure, first thinning down the latex by adding concentrated ammonia and water. This solution was applied to the face of the stone where it dried in a few minutes. A slightly thicker application was then brushed on, followed by a covering of cheesecloth and a third application of latex. After three or four hours we added a thicker solution of latex, a cloth covering, and a final coat of latex. When it was all dry, it was carefully pulled away from the stone, giving us an enduring and very accurate reproduction of the inscription.

12

PROFESSOR ALBRIGHT

The digging at Hajar bin Humeid was slow and difficult, and worst of all, there was a shortage of pottery fragments in the very spot that had been attacked for the sake of pottery.

The more difficult and discouraging the work became, the harder the Professor labored. Under the best of circumstances, he was a tireless dynamo of energy, and when challenged by a tempting mound like Hajar bin Humeid he tried to double his labor output. Professor Albright's reputation was such that Bedu traveled from miles around to marvel at the elderly Sahib without hair who never ceased working from morn till night. Now, as the season neared its end, the Professor would have worked through the night as well if he could have seen, and found human beings capable of matching his efforts, even in two shifts.

I became worried about his health, and one of my major expedition problems was to keep the Professor from killing himself at Hajar bin Humeid. For expeditions come and expeditions go, potsherds are found or they remain in the ground, but there is only one Professor Albright and there will never be another.

During the African expedition two and a half years before we had worked out an infallible system for dealing with the Professor's worries. If we were nearly out of water, one of us would mention the possibility of immediate rain, and the Professor would look up into a cloudless sky and embark on a long story of how people were drowned like rats when rain caught them in wadis such as ours. If clouds should happen to gather overhead, we would mention our acute water shortage, and then relax to an interesting discourse on how camels die in the desert, their parched noses pointing in the direction of water, with a postscript to the effect that the content of a dead camel's stomach, although somewhat greenish, is drinkable.

To cope with the Professor's present worry about his pottery sequence, I tried to reason with him, suggesting that since he had uncovered three major strata, the work at Hajar bin Humeid might be closed down for the season and continued the next year. I tried to point out how much the mound had actually yielded— structures of hand-carved stones, flights of stone stairs, plaster-lined baths, and many valuable inscriptions. He had gone down fifteen feet of the mound's total of about fifty. In Stratum A he had un- covered three occupation levels that yielded significant informa- tion about the little-known medieval Arabs of the region. Profes- sor Albright agreed, but pointed out that we had come to Beihan to study ancient Qatabanians, not medieval Arabs.

Stratum B contained several occupation levels of the period we were interested in, from the fourth or fifth century A.D. to the first century B.C. We had encountered Byzantine corrugated ware from the fourth century. We had learned that the people who lived at Hajar bin Humeid about the time of the destruction of Timna had grown lazy—one reason they were overcome by an enemy, per- haps—as shown by the fact that they sometimes used old stones from earlier buildings in making their own houses. One stone with an inscription was placed upside down in a house wall.

The two occupation levels of Stratum C had carried us back to the third century B.C. with complete details about the type of masonry work and house construction of the Qatabanians during that era. I pointed out all these achievements to Professor Al- bright, who had also been supervising the work at the South Gate and inspiring and helping all of us at all our varied tasks.

The Professor solemnly agreed with all I said, then came back to the one point that bothered him—he had established no pot- tery sequence for ancient South Arabia, and Hajar bin Humeid had to give him that sequence. In Stratum D, he felt sure, he would find the clues he had been searching for. He showed me how some of the walls of Stratum D already protruded invitingly just below the present work level in the scarp section, asking to be uncovered at once.

We finally reached a compromise, although I wonder how much of a compromise it is when the Professor manages to get his way. Still, he agreed to remain in his room for a day or two while I supervised the removal of debris that would lead us into Stratum D. He would then be able to examine the results of our work without having to spend a day in the sun.

The Professor had come to the conclusion—one that has stood up in subsequent work—that the ancient Qatabanians used far less pottery than the ancient peoples of Syria, Palestine, Egypt, and Mesopotamia. On the other hand, South Arabia yielded far more inscriptions than the Professor had found in his extensive work in Palestine.

During my work on Stratum D, however, we ran into a great deal of broken pottery, considerably more than had been found in previous levels. The Professor had been correct, as usual, in feeling that Stratum D would give him some clues, although I could hardly believe that he would learn much from the uninspiring pile of old potsherds that we accumulated.

Professor Albright came to Hajar bin Humeid after a couple of days, looking approvingly at the walls of Stratum D, then pounced eagerly on the fragments of pottery.

"Thank Heaven! We have it!" he cried happily, for many of the sherds bore inscriptions. This was the pottery he had been hoping to find, for the script gave him an accurate date in the third century B.C. It was the same as the script found in earlier tombs in our area, and nothing else had been able to give him precise dates.

The Professor was so pleased that he agreed that work at Hajar bin Humeid could be closed down for the season, although he looked longingly at the remaining thirty-five feet of the mound, containing at least seven strata that might carry us back well into the second millennium B.C.

"Next season," I said comfortingly, and the Professor nodded his head.

In all of our excavations we found no trace of manuscripts written on papyrus or leather, a surprising fact when one realizes that the Qatabanians scribbled voluminously on stones and baked mud. Beihan is very dry, so papyrus would not rot, but it also has an active and varied insect population, to which Professor Albright ascribed the destruction of all papyri. "You cannot lay a book down here," he said, "without its being cut full of holes in a few days. That may be the answer."

After our last day at Hajar bin Humeid, I returned to my room and threw myself on the bed for a few minutes' rest. Instead, I had a few seconds' unconsciousness, for my head hit something far harder than my pillow had been the night before. When I came to, I lifted the pillow and found beneath it a superb relief in alabaster portraying the head and upper torso of an ancient Qatabanian. Sandy Honeyman had recovered this beautiful object from the graveyard and, being unable to locate me at the time, had left it—as he said later—where I would be sure to find it first.

The next day I went for a complete inspection of Dick Bowen's work on the little mounds near Hajar bin Humeid. It was from one of these that he had been called away by the Arab who showed him Graffito Valley. Dick had been working quietly for some time at a most interesting piece of archaeological detective work.

One day while working at Hajar bin Humeid, Dick happened to notice what looked like the remnants of an old stone sluice or water channel. It was located on the side of the mound some distance from the scarp section, where a closer inspection revealed several more sluices of the same type. As soon as he could find time from his other duties, he cleared away the sand and found a sluice that stood fifteen to twenty feet above the present level of a small neighboring wadi which led into the Wadi Beihan.

Eventually, Dick traced a main canal which extended in Qatabanian times from the village of Beihan al-Qasab to a point about five miles north of Hajar bin Humeid, covering an approximate distance of fifteen miles. This was only one of several ancient canal systems utilizing the flow of water from tributary wadis after heavy rains. He also uncovered masonry reservoirs with waterproof cement between the stones, cleverly contrived stone gates for controlling the flow of water, and sluices branching off in many directions to carry water to the fields.

At the peak of Qatabanian civilization, the Wadi Beihan must have been a great garden, producing an abundance of grain, vegetables, and fruit, for the irrigation system uncovered was extensive, carefully planned, and engineered with great skill. We can date the time of this system with accuracy, for an inscription discovered on one of the oldest sluices came from about the fifth century B.C. Another, found on the latest phase of sluice construction, was dated about the first century A.D.

This last date indicates that even after the Kingdom of Qataban came to an end with the destruction of Timna, after 25 B.C., the irrigation works of the Wadi Beihan must have been carried on by the rulers of successor kingdoms, those of Hadhramaut, Saba, and Dhu-Raidan. But when the last of the South Arabian kingdoms collapsed, the great irrigation installations fell into disuse. In the 1,800 or 1,900 years since that time, erosion has made grotesque patterns in the silt, so that now the most distinctive feature of the Beihan landscape is a result not so much of nature's work as of ancient Qatabanian agriculture.

13

SALAAMS TO THE PRESIDENT

During the last two weeks of the first season's work there was a burst of speed at the South Gate site, which had now moved considerably inside the gate itself. After discovery of the bronze lions, Kenny Brown and his crew continued excavating in the square, and from this great storehouse of debris salvaged many beads, bronze ornaments, cooking pots, and vases, some of which were complete, as well as numerous tables of offering, alabaster reliefs, tablets, and fragments of inscribed bronze.

Some of the staff thought we had too little time to move further inside the city, but Kenny had his eye on a high sand dune beyond the square that seemed to command both the square and the gate. Suspecting that there might be a building beneath that pile of sand, he carried out a little private reconnaissance with a few workmen. Within fifteen minutes they uncovered the top of a very imposing wall. The perfectly cut blocks were fully four times as large as those of the other buildings we had unearthed, and the masonry was flawless. This must be, we all felt, a most important public building. Its discovery settled the problem for us, even with so little time left.

Most of our labor force was shifted to this site and concentrated on digging a trench eight feet wide northward along the west wall of House Yafash, which would connect the square and South Gate with the beautiful new building, which we temporarily christened Building C. Some of the men were set to removing the sand which had protected our new building for so many centuries from wind, rain, and, we hoped, looters.

Our enthusiasm for the new project must have been catching, for our diggers worked with new vigor, making it possible not only to link Building C with the square and South Gate, but also to clear the south face of the building itself. Here the mute but powerful story of the violence of war unfolded itself before us. Great blocks of stone, once part of an imposing façade, now lay buried helter-skelter in a deep mass of earth, burned timbers, smashed tables of offering, and formless lumps of bronze which had once expressed the artistic spirit of an almost forgotten people.

In front of Building C lay a ruined portico with a beautiful pavement of rose-colored flagstones containing sockets for tall columns. Along the outer edge of this portico ran a row of stone benches which, although knocked over at the time the city fell, could be completely reconstructed. In searching for the south edge of this pavement we came to another wall running from east to west. This wall was followed westward for fifteen feet and then south around the corner for another ten feet, where an inscription was found in place, giving the name and owner of the house. Someone, probably a personal enemy of the home owner, had tried very hard to erase this inscription, but we could still decipher it. Thus we had a name for Building D—House Hadath. Its masonry was of an earlier type than that found in the beautiful Building C across the way.

By the season's end Professor Albright was able to correlate the various types of masonry and script so well that he could give approximate dates to new buildings and inscriptions as fast as they appeared. The pecked Sabean masonry found at Sirwah in Yemen goes back at least to the first king of Sheba in the fifth century B.C. This is the earliest kind of masonry that Miss Caton Thompson found in her excavation at Hureidha, in Hadhramaut. The Kingdom of Qataban has yielded similar masonry, also dating from between 500 and 300 B.C. Still earlier are the massive hammer-dressed stones found in the oldest part of the South Gate and in Dick Bowen's oldest sluices. Even older than this is the oldest masonry from our Timna temples. There is some indication, however, that such masonry might be found beneath the South Gate. Settling of the pavement and of some benches between the piers of the South Gate suggests a massive structure beneath.

As the season's work drew to a close, we laid off most of the local workers, keeping only a few to help us assemble archaeological objects for shipment and put things in order for the intermission in our excavations. Fortunately, Charlie McCollum and Jama were going to stay in Beihan, and they would be able to see that certain Beihanis did not carry off half of the stones that we had exposed to view.

We gave a farewell dinner for Sherifs Hussein, Awad, and Saleh bin Naser. Our most elaborate meal of the campaign featured a combination of Arab and American blue-plate specials, through which we introduced our hungry guests to various American delicacies. After dinner we moved upstairs to the chamber normally occupied by Kenny, Charlie, and George. The room was now so clean as to be hardly recognizable, and the floor was completely covered with Arab rugs, with pillows piled generously around the edges.

At the appropriate time, I made a long and dignified speech —the occasion was such that Arab etiquette called for length and dignity—expressing our deep appreciation for the wonderful hospitality Sherif Hussein had afforded the expedition during its stay in his land. The Sherif replied that, although he was quite unprepared, he felt that he should say a few words. Rising to his feet, he dramatically drew from his breast pocket a two-page document which he read with great expression—a beautiful farewell speech composed in the Sherif's usual flowery Arabic.

When the speechmaking was over the gift-giving began. I presented to Sherif Hussein a Fairbanks Morse 1,500 K.W. generator, together with a Deep Freeze, wiring and electric light bulbs, from the generous supply given us by International General Electric's President W. R. Herod. The Sherif had long wished to have electric lights in his palace at Beihan al-Qasab, so he was overjoyed. Next I presented several cases of Coca-Cola and Colgate products, a Zenith Portable Overseas radio, a beautiful Marlin 30.30 rifle with Griffin and Howe mount and one of Henry Lyman's Alaskan telescopic sights. I wound things up with a Colt .38 Police Positive and a quantity of Winchester and Western ammunition. By this time I was so astounded at my generosity that I could hardly go on.

For Sherif Awad and Sherif Saleh bin Naser and the young Emir, who was regrettably absent on a visit to Aden, we had rifles and revolvers, with appropriate quantities of ammunition. I felt sure that nothing would please them more than fine weapons, but it is always hard to tell just how pleased a Beihani sherif is about anything because he is always so polite. John Allen, Deputy British Agent, who was also present at the festivities, assured me later that they were all genuinely delighted with their gifts and that American prestige could not be higher in Beihan.

On the morning of April 19, George Farrier and I flew to Aden to make final arrangements for the expedition's departure from South Arabia. Bills had to be paid, shipping arrangements completed, and courtesy calls made on the various officials who had helped make our first season possible. When we flew back to Beihan to pick up the rest of the expedition, young Emir Saleh was at the Aden airport to give us a royal farewell, along with Charlie McCollum and Jama, who were planning on returning to Beihan with him a few days later.

We had to circle the Beihan airstrip for a while to allow four camels to finish eating their breakfast. When they finally moved out of the way, our Dakota came in for a landing. The rest of the expedition members climbed aboard, waving final good-bys to Sherif Hussein and Sherif Awad. As we started to close the door, Sherif Awad suddenly remembered that he had forgotten something. He handed me a letter, which read as follows:

From Beihan in the Empty Quarter to the American City of Washington. 22 April 1950, corresponding to 5 Rajab 1369. From Sherif Awad bin Ahmed to His Excellency the President of the United States.

Your Excellency:
    May God perpetuate your glory and your life to serve justice and liberty.

I have seized this opportunity to send my cordial and friendly greetings to you with my friend Wendell Phillips and his honorable colleagues.

We thank God who has enabled them to come to our country and see for themselves the sad and miserable lot of our country which has kept the ancient customs from which no good can be expected. Further, we are presenting to Your Excellency some gifts consisting of a lantern, a sickle, an ink-pot and a pen, which represent the highest progress attained by us.

We hope indeed that these will secure some measure of your kindness and mercy. We also enclose herewith a poem addressed to Your Excellency.

In conclusion, I beg Your Excellency to accept my highest respects. May God preserve you.

Sherif Awad

Along with the letter and poem, Sherif Awad handed me the package containing the sickle and other items for the President. Then Sherif Hussein suddenly produced a good-by present, two lovely silver bracelets that belonged to his favorite wife. He asked me to present them to my sister Merilyn when I arrived home in California.

As the plane took off the Sherifs fired salutes in the air, and I could imagine them trying to see how close they could come to the plane as a special mark of their esteem. We had final glimpses of our mud palace, of Hajar bin Humeid with its inviting thirty-five feet of unexcavated walls and potsherds and—most important—unknown objects that would unveil Qataban for us. That same powerful lure of the unknown lay in the sands that still remained around our beautiful Building C north of Timna's South Gate, and in the cemetery of Haid bin Aqil. We looked down at the sands we would be digging through again in a few months, dreaming of finer alabaster figures, magnificent bronze statues, unlooted buildings, and piles of inscribed potsherds, yards of ancient inscriptions.

Our plane flew across Yemen, stopped briefly at Kamaran Island, refueled at Port Sudan, and landed us at Cairo's Almaza Airport, just at sunset. Gladys Terry and the noted Egyptian scholar, Professor Aziz S. Atiya, were on hand to welcome us. With Professor Atiya as guide, we slipped rapidly through Egyptian customs and went to our Cairo headquarters, maintained on behalf of the Mount Sinai expedition. Since that operation was still in progress, although nearing the completion of its work, George Farrier, Ocky Romaine, and I planned to go there to help for the last months. The rest of the expedition were leaving for the four corners of the earth, so we had a farewell dinner together on the roof of the Semiramis Hotel, overlooking the Nile.

Throughout the campaign, we always managed to get together at mealtime, no matter how busy we were or how hectic the problems. We had fun, but there was something of a cloud over the gaiety that night. For Professor Albright and Dr. McNinch were off to Baltimore, Dick Bowen to Rhode Island, Sandy Honeyman to Scotland, Albert Jamme to Belgium, Friso Heybroek to Holland, and Kenny Brown to California. We knew that Professor Albright and Dr. Jamme would be with us in Beihan for the second season's work, but the others could borrow no more time from their normal duties. New men would take their places.

No one, however, would ever take the places of Bill and Gladys Terry, as we all knew. After the completion of the work at Sinai, Bill and Gladys were going to Baltimore, and for the first time in four years, since the start of the African expedition, they would not be part of us and our work in the field. Bill had decided at last to fulfill a dream of many years and enter Johns Hopkins University to study medicine. Gladys had decided to make a dream come true, too—a big dream soon to be fulfilled in a small image.

Professor W. F. Albright directing Arab workmen at his excavation of the stratified mound of Hajar bin Humeid

The Monastery of St. Catherine, said to have been built in the fourth century A.D. by Queen Helena, mother of Constantine the Great, over the legendary site of the burning bush. Near the monastery is Biblical Mount Sinai, where Moses received the Ten Commandments.

14

MOUNT SINAI

For more than fifty years Father Pachomius has lived and worked in the Monastery of St. Catherine at the foot of Biblical Mount Sinai. So isolated is this ancient sanctuary that the good Father was considerably surprised, a few years ago, when one of the rare visitors told him about World War II—but not nearly so surprised as the visitor, who presently discovered that the monk had never heard about World War I.

At this monastery, we had been conducting a pioneering microfilm project in association with the Library of Congress and Alexandria University, with a staff of eighteen scholars and scientists from America, Europe, and the Near East. The story of this expedition is a book in itself. In time, hundreds of books will no doubt be written and published as a result of the work done there, for the expedition made available the largest and most important body of research material ever revealed in a single operation. Three thousand four hundred ancient manuscripts, written in eleven languages, were organized, studied, catalogued, and microfilmed. The treasures from this scholarly gold mine will for years to come shed light on the early history of three religions and the peoples of the Middle East, for few spots in the world are of such importance to Christians, Jews, and Moslems alike. The monastery was started, according to tradition, in A.D. 337 by Queen Helena, mother of Constantine the Great. It was built over the legendary site of the burning bush from which God spoke to

Moses, and towering above the monastery is Gebel Musa, the Mount of Moses, which Moses climbed to receive the Ten Commandments.

Here I felt as if I were in the world of the Old Testament. I was shown the sacred tree which, according to tradition, sprang from Aaron's rod. Halfway up the Mount, I saw a small chapel commemorating the spot where the ravens fed Elijah. It is supposedly built over the cave where the prophet hid from Jezebel.

On top of the mountain, after climbing 3,500 stone steps, I felt the very presence of the great Lawgiver himself, for I truly seemed to be on top of the world. To the south lay Ras Muhammed, the tip of the Sinai Peninsula. To the east across the mountains lay the Gulf of Aqaba where Solomon once sailed his trading ships. To the north was the Biblical Wilderness of Zin, and to the west the land of the Pharaohs from which Moses led the Israelites out of bondage.

On the summit stands the Chapel of Moses and a Moslem mosque. Moses' cave, where he is said to have lived alone for forty days and nights, is close to the mosque, which is still a place of pilgrimage for Moslems. Tradition tells that the Prophet Mohammed visited the Monastery of St. Catherine before the Arab conquest of Egypt in A.D. 640. He is said to have granted the Christian monks a covenant whereby their lives and property were secure under Moslem rule. There is even a mosque next to the basilica inside the walls of the monastery itself. A Kufic inscription from the pulpit records that it was built during the Caliphate of Al-Amr in A.D. 1103.

Throughout the centuries the benefactors of the monastery have included numerous emperors, kings, and popes. Pope Gregory the Great (592-604) was one of its early supporters in Rome, while Charles VI of France sent a chalice in 1411, and other French, German, and Spanish rulers made contributions and gifts to the monastery. Even Spain's Queen Isabella found time to support the monastery in addition to sending Columbus across the ocean sea. The monastery was completely dependent upon the support of the tsars of Russia during the seventeenth, eighteenth, and nineteenth centuries, although Napoleon, on his expedition to Egypt in 1798, gave his blessing to the monks and ordered the walls to be repaired in certain places.

St. Catherine's name was not given to the monastery until some centuries after its foundation. According to legend, St. Catherine was put to death in Alexandria during the persecution of the Christians by Emperor Maximinus II. The story goes that she was about to be broken on the wheel when the wheel itself was miraculously broken. She was later beheaded and as she died prayed that her body might not be found. In answer to her prayer, angels transported her to Mount Sinai. Several centuries later, Egyptian Christians found the remains of a body on a mountain slope to the southwest of Gebel Musa. They brought it to the monastery, where it was immediately proclaimed to be that of St. Catherine and has been venerated as such by the monks ever since. Her skull and hand, which is covered with rings containing precious jewels, are displayed in two small silver boxes upon very special occasions.

During the last fourteen centuries thousands of pilgrims have made the difficult and dangerous journey to the monastery, where they left innumerable inscriptions in Arabic, Greek, Latin, and Russian. Evidence of the Crusaders may be seen on all sides, for they covered many sections of the stone masonry with their arms and symbols.

The monastery reminded me of medieval establishments I had seen in other parts of the world, with every foot of space utilized to its fullest capacity. Until recently, visitors were drawn up into the monastery about thirty feet through the air in a bucket-like affair, but we entered through the large gates which lead to the courtyard and passed through a narrow, low-roofed passage protected at the end by three thick doors covered with iron plates and studded with spikes.

Next to the courtyard and inside the gardens are fruit trees, olives, vines, and other vegetable products that look strangely out of place in the middle of the Sinai desert. I visited the small plot of land nearby which the monks use as their burial ground. Since there is room for only six at a time in this graveyard, one who has already had his turn must be dug up when a new death occurs.

The bones are then taken to the bone room, where the skulls are stacked in neat piles on one side and the remaining skeletal pieces are arranged on the other side of the room like cordwood. Archbishops and special personalities have their remains kept separately in small wooden caskets or niches in the walls.

Long ago two brothers from Provence in France yielded to passion and murdered their uncle. As penance they traveled to Sinai after first visiting Rome and Jerusalem. Here they spent the rest of their days as hermits in two small adjoining mountain caves, tied together by chains. Their two skeletons still chained together lay side by side in a large double coffin.

The most famous skeleton is that of St. Stephanos, who guarded the way up the Mount during his lifetime and who said as he lay dying that he wished he could guard his beloved monastery forever. This was in A.D. 580, but to this day St. Stephanos sits dressed in his robes, with purple skull cap, rosary, and staff, guarding the entrance to the house of the dead. I never quite got over the startling effect of coming upon St. Stephanos still on guard, dimly seen by the light of candles in an atmosphere heavy with incense.

For many centuries the monastery required constant guarding, for time and again it faced attack and destruction by savage Bedouin tribes. Ammonius, a monk of Canopus, was an eyewitness to the terrible assault of the Saracens in A.D. 373. The story goes that when hope was gone and the holy men were about to fall into the hands of their enemies, the top of Gebel Musa became wrapped in flames and the Saracens fled in terror.

The number of monks at the monastery has varied greatly from century to century. In the fourteenth century, for instance, there were more than four hundred, while today there are less than twenty. They lead lives of extreme poverty and austerity, dividing their time between prayer and labor. Each morning at 3:45 the large bell rings thirty-three times, one stroke for each year of the life of Christ. This is the call to communal prayer, held in one of the fifteen chapels of the monastery.

While we were there my old cook, Gomar, although sixty-six and a grandfather many times over, received an attractive mar-

Father Pachomius, master icon painter, who has not left the Monastery of St. Catherine for over fifty years

Over the centuries it has been the rule after a short burial to dig up and stack the bones and skulls of the monks in the house of the dead.

Saint Stephanos, who in the year of our Lord 580 died at the Monastery of St. Catherine. To this day he sits dressed in his robes, purple skull cap, rosary, and staff, guarding the entrance to the house of the dead.

riage proposal. The price was a mere two pounds with no strings attached to the prospective bride. Now enters the dilemma! For this was Ramadan, the month of fasting, when all extracurricular activities are forbidden between sunrise and sunset. Poor Gomar had really had it in a big way, for at *sunset* the great doors of the monastery are bolted by the monks, keeping all outsiders out and all insiders in, and his lady-to-be was definitely an outsider. Gomar felt a little better when he learned that in Sinai the day after a wedding the bride goes off to tend sheep in the mountains, remaining forty days and nights while the new husband recuperates at home. The rest of us were more than relieved when it was found that this readily available female had already given birth to seven children and boasted that she had never washed, let alone taken a bath, in her entire life.

The library was opened for our staff at eight each morning by Father Joachim, keeper of the treasures at the monastery and its librarian for the past twenty-eight years. He prepared the various volumes, codices, and manuscripts to be filmed each day, and then, under the direction of young Wallace Wade of the Library of Congress, work began. With two cameras running eight hours a day, it was possible to microfilm an average of five thousand folios a day, a folio representing two pages of manuscripts opened before the camera. Many manuscripts were composite in contents and required page by page exploration. Others were found in disorder or had fallen in disorder when their bindings became loose. Each manuscript received a series of folio numbers to provide adequate reference for future scholars using the film.

The monastery library was the original home of the famous Codex Sinaiticus, a fourth-century Greek manuscript of the Bible. It was discovered in 1844 by L. F. K. von Tischendorf, a German Biblical scholar, who in time persuaded the monks to lend him the remaining sheets of this manuscript—many had been destroyed. He then presented his sheets to the Tsar of Russia, which infuriated the monks at the monastery because they insisted the manuscript had simply been on loan. They still speak bitterly of Tischendorf as "the Thief." They finally had to accept a price which the Tsar of Russia agreed to pay them, along with a silver shrine for the beloved bones of St. Catherine. At the time of the Russian Revolution, the British Museum purchased the manuscript for a hundred thousand pounds, where it remains to this day.

Since Tischendorf's time, the monks never leave their library unguarded, for they are determined not to lose other treasures, the chief of which is the Codex Syriacus. This manuscript is a palimpsest, or writing on parchment that contained other writing previously, which was incompletely erased and can be detected. The layer beneath the clearly visible writing is in Syriac and tells of the lives of martyred women saints. It was written in A.D. 778. There is a lower layer which is a fourth-century version, with a possible earlier unstudied Syriac palimpsest underneath. On some pages there is an extremely rare palimpsest in Greek of a portion of the Gospel of John dating from the fourth century. A number of Syriac versions of portions of the scriptures are in existence today, but this Codex Syriacus is the oldest and brings us closer than any other to the thought and speech of the time of Jesus.

Although the chief purpose of our expedition was to make accessible to the world's scholars the unworked resources of this inaccessible library, we naturally hoped to make new discoveries, too. The most important came on June 12, 1950, when Professor Atiya burst into my cell, where I was working, and urged me to come to the workroom and see what he had found. It was a codex of lives of the saints, written by a contemporary of Charlemagne, in Middle Kufic of the eighth century A.D. In addition to new material on early saints and martyrs, it contained what may be the most ancient Arabic translation of Job.

Beneath the Middle Kufic was visible on the margins and between the lines, a more archaic Kufic, probably dating from the first century of the Hejira, corresponding to the seventh-eighth century A.D. On some leaves, below this script, Greek letters could be seen, which were identified as a lectionary of the Pauline Epistles. This text is believed to be of the early seventh century and contains a number of interesting variants from the authorized Greek version.

Finally, a bottom layer of Syriac in two columns may be seen

Father Joachim, for twenty-eight years librarian and keeper of treasures at the Monastery of St. Catherine, standing before the altar dressed in his official robes

Two pages of the palimpsest "Codex Arabicus" found by Professor A. S. Atiya in St. Catherine's library. Several lines of older Syriac writing, partly erased, are seen in the central margins. An older Arabic hand appears under the extant Arabic text.

throughout the codex. In some places one can easily distinguish even two layers of Syriac, and the more ancient contains one of the oldest Gospel translations in existence. Preliminary investigation reveals remarkable variations in the text of the Gospel of Mark as compared with the fifth-century Peshitta text. It may therefore be based on an earlier second- or third-century translation, which would carry our Bible studies a step further back into antiquity. The Syriac text is certainly older than that of the Codex Syriacus, which had previously been the library's greatest treasure. Thus this text probably takes us closer to the age of Christ and His disciples than any other known version of the Bible. In any case, this new discovery, christened by Professor Atiya "Codex Arabicus," must be recognized as among the rarest of specimens in the history of manuscripts.

The Mount Sinai expedition ended with a good deal of satisfaction all around, for it accomplished not only its basic objectives satisfactorily but in such discoveries as that of the Codex Arabicus went beyond expectations. On our way home to the United States, in Cairo, Bill Terry and I were honored by Porphyrios III, Archbishop of Sinai, who bestowed on us the rare eleventh-century Order of the Knights of St. Catherine. A note from Dr. Luther Evans, then Librarian of Congress and now head of UNESCO, to whom we were deeply grateful, gave me a laugh as well as satisfaction:

Dear Wendell:

It was a remarkable success, and all bargains have been well kept. When you set up a Foundation for the Study of Women, we might be prepared to make an even bigger investment.

Back in New York, I found that the new Korean War had imposed many changes on the America I knew. My three months allotted to restaffing, financing, and equipping our second season's program in Beihan stretched into a long six months. I had the help, however, of a new secretary, twenty-year-old Eileen Salama, whom I had first met in Cairo and who had been working with the Mount Sinai expedition. Raven-haired Eileen had been born in Egypt of French parents. She was so young and attractive that

it was not easy to believe that she could be such a competent
secretary and accomplished linguist, speaking English, French,
Italian, and various dialects of Arabic. She had been a great help
at Mount Sinai, while standing the somewhat difficult life there
easily and cheerfully. As it turned out, her knowledge of Arabic
and her common sense were both lifesavers for the expedition in
the months that lay ahead.

George Farrier, who held the post of Administrative Assistant
on the second campaign in Beihan, sailed on the SS *Steel Chemist*
with new supplies and equipment, among which there was no
steam-roller for the Sultan of Mukalla but something even better
—a Le Tourneau road scraper worth around $25,000. I knew that
this would satisfy completely the customs officials of Mukalla, but
I did not anticipate that it would cause trouble in other circles.
The trouble confronted me almost immediately after landing by
plane at Beihan, so I had to fly immediately to Aden to see Sherif
Hussein, who was visiting that fair city.

Sherif Hussein was the last person I expected to cause the expedition any difficulties, since he had been so very helpful during our first season and had become a warm friend. But it seems
that the Sherif had heard about the Le Tourneau road scraper
presented to the Mukalla government. He reasoned that, American good will or no American good will, here was a country get-
ing a $25,000 scraper merely for allowing our expedition to pass
through it. How much more should *his* government receive for
allowing us to work there?

When I spoke to the Sherif it became obvious to me that some
adviser had put him up to this act of being tough and making big
demands upon us. He handed me an ultimatum of fifteen points
that asked for everything. All our vehicles were to be turned over
to Sherif Hussein at the conclusion of our work in Beihan. All
gold and silver unearthed by the expedition was to go to Sherif
Hussein. And the rest of the demands were comparable—and un-
acceptable.

The Sherif really did not have much heart for his demanding
role, and I decided that he planned to be as difficult as possible
the first day, asking for everything under the sun, so that on the

second day he could turn on the charm—as only he could do it—
and graciously withdraw several demands, winding up perhaps
with more than he might have obtained otherwise. Actually, there
was no trouble about dropping the more ridiculous of the fifteen
points. As to a division of archaeological specimens, we agreed to
a fifty-fifty split. And in true Arab fashion we left for a later date
the difficult question of the gold and silver. We parted the best
of friends and I flew back to Beihan, picking up in Aden three of
our staff members who had just arrived there—Dr. Jamme, Girair
Palamoudian, our Armenian artist and draftsman, and Gus Van
Beek, pottery specialist and a graduate of Professor Albright's
courses at Johns Hopkins. Finally, in the middle of February,
1951, I was back at our mud palace overlooking ancient Timna,
ready to start work.

15

EILEEN

Within a few days we were comfortably settled and welcomed a visit from Emir Saleh, son of Sherif Hussein, who joined us for dinner. We almost lost Eileen on this happy occasion which was the first time the Emir had laid eyes on her. It was also his first experience at our table, and he seemed to enjoy himself as one of the expedition. After dinner, we went upstairs to my room where he listened with expressions of joy and rapture to my collection of the latest Krupa, Goodman, and Lionel Hampton recordings, as well as the ukulele playing of Ellis Burcaw, one of our new young archaeologists, associated with the Smithsonian Institution, and formerly from Maryville College, Tennessee.

The next day Eileen returned the visit with a courtesy call on the Emir's wife in the village of Nuqub. She was young and attractive, but as shy before strangers as all upper-class Arab women. She was probably struck dumb with wonder, too, at the sight of another young girl speaking Arabic who was free, independent, and unafraid. The most striking thing about her, Eileen reported, was a unique design painted on her forehead, consisting of a green crescent surrounded by white stars. Eileen was very much intrigued by her personal maid, an eighteen-year-old slave girl who was vividly beautiful, like a wild desert creature. The grace of her slender body had been enhanced by a lifetime of balancing water jugs on her head, and her high spirits and happy nature revealed themselves in her movements as well as in her quick eyes and ready smile.

Eileen Salama, the expedition's lovely secretary and interpreter, with Sheikh Abdullah Bahri, at the main Bal Harith tribal encampment

Dodge Power Wagons winching ashore boxed Le Tourneau road scraper, expedition's good-will gift to the Sultan of Shihr and Mukalla

This attractive slave girl was the personal maid of the wife of the Emir of Beihan and had already been married and divorced three times at the age of eighteen

Eileen, always on the alert for colorful material for the movies of our expedition, knew that she had found an excellent subject. Since the girl was a slave, she could allow herself to be seen and filmed, as custom did not require her to hide her face or herself. The Emir's young wife said it would be agreeable to her if we took pictures, so the next day several of us paid a visit with Eileen. At that point, the slave girl became shy and coy, but happily flattered by the attention she was receiving. We got a wonderful shot of Eileen bringing the girl from the door of the house, of the girl grinning, laughing, and trying to turn away from the camera. I don't know what Eileen finally said to her in Arabic to keep her in a good pose, but suddenly she stopped retreating and smiled engagingly into the camera, her excitement showing in every look and movement.

From Eileen's visits to harems and her conversations with Arab wives as well as husbands, she gained a knowledge of marriage customs in that part of the world that the rest of us would have been denied.

An Arabian girl's wishes are not often consulted as to the man she marries. Her father's choice is law, though in some cases a mother may have a strong influence on her husband's decision. There is no courtship between a girl and her husband-to-be, and she may know nothing about his character or feelings until after she is married. Often she knows little even then, for an Arab does not look upon his wife as an equal nor consider marriage a fifty-fifty partnership. He seldom discusses affairs with his wife—business, politics, feelings, or aspirations—and rarely consults her even when an important decision concerning the entire family is to be made. The husband is complete boss. What he says is law in his family, not to be questioned.

You might wonder if a wife can possibly be happy in the Arab world. Most of them seem to be as happy as wives in the Western world. They have never heard of other ways of arranging things and have been brought up to expect and fulfill the role of wife as conceived by Arab men. Everyone has long accepted as fact here that men are superior to women, and fathers are deliriously proud when a son is born, especially if it is the firstborn. Arab men are ashamed to have only daughters and a wife who bears no children or only girls soon loses favor.

The prospective husband must pay to the girl's father a *mehr* or dowry, which varies widely according to the man's financial position, the girl's age and beauty, and her father's financial position. In other words, the younger and more beautiful the girl, the more a father can get for her. The dowry also differs in different sections of Arabia, running sometimes as low as ten M.T. dollars or as high as a thousand M.T. dollars. The girl furnishes her own trousseau, whose beauty and size are in proportion to the dowry and her position. A wealthy girl's trousseau is extremely elaborate and quite breathtaking—lovely silk gowns, embroidered lingerie, and costly jewels. The new husband must supply the house and furnishings, although in some cases the bride furnishes linens, silver, and such.

Since the father arranges marriages it is not uncommon for an eighty-year-old man to marry a sixteen-year-old girl, and quite usual for an Arab man to marry a girl half his age. Sometimes a girl may be only ten years old when she marries, though theoretically her husband is not supposed to have intimate relations with her until she has matured, at about fourteen years. The bride absolutely *must* be a virgin, and that fact must be proved not only to her husband but to all the family after the first night. The bedding is actually displayed early the first morning, and everyone is quite happy and satisfied if bloodstains are found. If they are not, bride and groom, and the girl's family, are in disgrace. The husband has only one course to follow in such a case, if he is not to lose face—divorce his bride. Some men do it immediately, others may wait for a week or two before returning the girl to her parents. If he loves her and would really like to keep her, it is very difficult.

Sometimes there is considerable violence when a girl cannot show the blood proof of her virginity. If the husband, who feels cheated and disgraced, does not beat the girl, her parents are likely to—and sometimes both. A girl may be thrown out of her parents' home and disowned.

According to the Moslem religion, a man may have as many as

four wives at a time. Divorce is easy for the husband; he need have no complaint or grounds of any kind. All he must do is to say aloud three times, in the name of Allah, that he divorces his wife, giving her name. Then he tells a judge or other official that he has done so and receives a document the equivalent of our divorce papers. A wife in most instances can only get a divorce from her husband on grounds of nonsupport.

If a man has four wives, he provides for them according to his financial resources. If he has plenty of money, he establishes each wife in a separate home, and he spends a night or two in each home in rotation. This kind of plural marriage works out very well, since the wives are not in immediate contact with each other and cannot develop jealousies and quarrels.

If a man hasn't enough money, all the wives live in the same house, each wife having her own room, sometimes rather small. The wives share the housework, cooking, and other duties, and each wife looks after her own children. There is bound to be friction in such cases, especially if the husband favors one wife more than the others, which often happens. There is always a "number-one wife," usually the one he married first, who has more influence and power than the others. But if the first wife does not bear a son, the wife who does so may become dominant. Sometimes a man gives the number-one position to another wife for other reasons, maybe because she is more beautiful, fun to be with, or more appealing sexually. The husband's decision is law, it is true, but he cannot eliminate friction when wives all live together.

Actually when a man has limited means, he usually just marries one wife, or sometimes two. In the case of two wives some friction may arise, but not as much as if he had four. If one wife dies, then the other wives take care of her children, and this is another source of friction—a wife will be inclined to favor her own children over those of even a dead rival.

"One Arab wife once told me," Eileen reported, "that unless a man can do justice to each wife equally, he should marry only one woman. As she said, 'He should feel equally, sleep equally, and laugh equally, with each wife.' She also said a man should go to one wife a night, never to two different wives in the same night."

"I have never heard of an old maid in Arabia," Eileen also told us, "and in that respect I believe Arab women are happier and less frustrated than some of their European sisters."

I had been a little concerned about Eileen's comfort in the mud palace. Being a veteran of the Mount Sinai expedition, she could, I knew, accommodate herself to a good deal of the unusual and unconventional in the way of living quarters. But staying for four or five months in a mud palace in southern Arabia is a different matter. Brought up in a well-to-do home with many servants to make life easy, she had never before even done her own laundry, which she now did with great enthusiasm. We brought with us, of course, numerous conveniences of Western civilization, such as an electric lighting system, canned and frozen food, refrigerators and deep freezes. Still, a building made of mud, straw, and dung is a building of mud, straw, and dung, even when covered with whitewash. And it was still a favorite rendezvous for Beihani spiders, who seemed to have grown a little larger in eight months —as poor Eileen found out. One evening before retiring, she removed her bedspread only to discover with horror a big spider spread comfortably in the middle of her bed.

Fortunately, however, Eileen was delighted with the mud palace and found it quite comfortable. By the time she had finished hanging curtains she had made out of mosquito nets, her room looked beautiful. Its prize piece of furniture was a real bed, in place of the army cots used by everyone else. This convenience came to her as a result of Jama's concern and generosity. Feeling that no lady should be expected to sleep on a cot, he had brought his own bed from his home in Aden for her use.

Eileen was particularly fond of our unusual bathroom—the only one she had ever heard of, she said, that was open-air and enabled one to take a shower while looking at beautiful scenery. This room was on the top floor and had been added over an extending roof of the floor below. Since there was nothing above this level, it was not necessary to put a ceiling on it. One wall, looking out over the Wadi Beihan, was just about shoulder high.

Thus the bather had complete privacy, a sun bath, and a lovely view all at once.

The only threat to privacy came when the Arab water boy filled the tank on the roof with water for the shower. This he did once a day, carrying goatskin after goatskin filled with water up through the house. The tact and diplomacy of this boy amazed us all. Without anyone saying a word to him, he adopted the practice of knocking at Eileen's door when he began his water-carrying chore. If she happened to be in her room, he knew that she was not in the bathroom, so he proceeded with his work. If he found her room empty and the bathroom door locked, he assumed that she might be there and waited in the hall until she appeared. Then, when there was no danger of his seeing her in her bath, he filled the tank. Under the circumstances, it is not surprising that Eileen looks upon the South Arabians as the most courteous and considerate men in the world.

16

THE SCAIFES

With our labor force assembled, the digging, hauling, and dumping of sand began. We lost four of our workers a couple of days later when I received a note from Sherif Abdullah, Governor of Aseilan. It asked if we would mind greatly if four little boys currently employed at the South Gate might be returned home to continue their studies in school. They were later seen with their legs chained together, clanking their way to higher learning. One small Bal Harith boy could not be persuaded however; though only seven years old, his indignation was no less than that of his adult brothers. "I am one of the birds of the desert," he protested, "I must fly over the wide spaces. If you cage me I shall pine away and die."

Only the boys go to school in Beihan, where they study the Koran and learn how to read and write. Girls stay at home, where they learn how to sew, cook, and perform other domestic duties.

Another boy was greeted with open arms and much attention. He was the boy whose face had been eaten away by yaws. I recalled my promise to Dr. McNinch to give him a report on the boy, and I remembered, too, how many medical men in the United States had said, after looking at his picture, "He simply hasn't a fighting chance to survive." But here he was—alive and apparently well. Major portions of his face were missing, as the parts which had been eaten away completely did not grow back. But the eating away had stopped at almost the point it was when Dr. Mac treated the boy. Our new medical man, Dr. Valentin de Mignard, examined the boy carefully and pronounced him completely cured—a report I happily wrote to Dr. McNinch at once.

Our hospital was going full blast even before we could start excavating again, with Dr. de Mignard continually being amazed at the same things that had amazed Dr. McNinch the first season. We had borrowed the good doctor from the Hollywood Presbyterian Hospital for our second campaign. Born in Russia thirty years before of French and Russian parents, he had lost his wife and two small children when the Americans bombed his European home during the war. Later, as a displaced person, he had entered the United States, where his medical degree and knowledge of sixteen languages enabled him to obtain a position as orange picker in Southern California. It was some time before he was able to establish himself as a physician and surgeon. Despite his many languages, English was the one he knew the least about, but his facial expressions usually made up for what his vocabulary and grammar lacked. I remember his complaining, "These Arabs don't know absolutely nothing about time. Women she just lives day from day and finally comes in dispensary with swelled tummy complaining she been pregnant for over three years too many!"

About a week after my arrival in Beihan, Charlie McCollum returned from a rush trip to Mukalla, where he had picked up the last members of the expedition—Wallace Wade, who had been director of photography at Mount Sinai and occupied the same post for our second Beihan campaign; Robert Carmean, motor transport specialist and student at the University of Redlands; and John Simpson, assistant archaeologist from the Carnegie Museum. In addition, they brought our new G.E. deep-freeze unit and a good supply of food to put in it. The next Sunday evening Professor Albright and I initiated the first of our Beihani church services, with the Reverend Gus Van Beek presiding.

Full-time excavation was now going on at four sites. The most important archaeological project of the second campaign was certainly the continuation and completion of the cross section at Hajar bin Humeid, which would provide us with the chronology of ancient South Arabian history to which all other work must be referred. Professor Albright selected Donald Dragoo, twenty-five-year-old archaeologist from the University of Indiana, to carry on the work at Hajar bin Humeid, in association with Gus Van Beek, who would record the pottery levels and dates.

The graveyard at Haid bin Aqil was put under the direction of Robert Shalkop of the Smithsonian Institution. Unfortunately, some of the graves that Sandy Honeyman had so carefully excavated the previous year had been badly smashed during our absence, doubtless by Bedu treasure hunters who found nothing of value to them and destroyed things valuable to us.

Our most impressive site was the South Gate with its courtyard and neighboring buildings. With dreams of more bronze lions and such, Professor Albright assigned Ellis Burcaw to this dig.

The fourth site was that which, from the air, proved itself to be Timna's largest unexcavated area, in the city's center. Here huge blocks of stone pushed their corners through the smothering sand, but enough of them were seen to indicate that this must have been the city's most imposing structure. I started fresh excavations here, with James Swauger, Curator of Man from the Carnegie Museum, to direct operations. We hoped that we might find a temple or possibly a royal palace.

I was happy to have the work at all four sites start off smoothly, with the promise of many more finds during this second season, especially since I wanted two important visitors to see our expedition in full operation, for without them we might not have been able to continue work at all. They were Alan and Sarah Scaife, of Pittsburgh, whose support, direct and indirect, had been in large measure responsible for our financial security during a second campaign in Beihan. Actually, Pittsburgh, leading industrial city, owes much of its own financial reality to the genius of Sarah Scaife's father, Richard B. Mellon, and her famed uncle, Andrew W. Mellon.

There was a flurry of preparations for several days before their arrival, not only on our part but in the entire domain of Sherif Hussein, who decided to give a royal welcome to such distinguished visitors. I went to Aden the day before their expected arrival there, only to learn that they would land within a few hours instead of the next day. I rushed an urgent message to Sherif Hussein to speed up the ceremonies he planned, hoping that for once the uncertain wireless was really operating.

After the Scaifes' arrival in Aden, we decided to fly to Beihan in their chartered British Dakota, since they wanted to do a little sight-seeing in southern Arabia after visiting our excavations. On the way to Timna, our pilot circled around the unique fortress of Qara, built high on top of a huge, truncated mountain. Suddenly Alan Scaife said, "What are those flashes directly below us?"

The flashes turned out to be unfriendly rifle fire from one corner of the fortress, aimed at us, so we hurriedly paid our respects to Qara by dipping our wings and flew on. A few minutes later we landed at Jaw al Milah, seven miles from Timna.

After a quick visit to our headquarters, we headed for Sherif Hussein's capital, where the ruler of Beihan put on a spectacular show. Three thousand tribesmen of different colors and allegiances had responded to his call and were lined up in massed rows on one side of a large field. We stood on the other side, where we had stopped our trucks to be greeted by Sherif Hussein—Sarah and Alan Scaife, Sherif Hussein, Emir Saleh, several members of the expedition, and Major Basil Seager, British Agent. On top of one of our trucks, Wallace Wade was busy with his Ciné camera, aided by Chester Stevens, assistant photographer during the second season.

At a signal, a company of the Sherif's finest horsemen performed for us, charging down the field toward us at a dead run, shooting their rifles in the air and whooping at the top of their lungs. Just before reaching us they swerved to one side in a cloud of dust. Next came large groups of indigo-painted tribesmen of the Musabein, walking forward hand in hand with a peculiar dancing step and chanting weirdly at the top of their lungs. Other groups dashed forward between them, firing rifles in the air, shouting and leaping, while still more wielded their naked jambiyas as if slicing up their enemies, cutting the air in front of them with a strange rotating motion.

Across the field they came, closer and closer, until they began to press near to our group. They were curious to see the visitors for whom Sherif Hussein had summoned them, and they were giving a warm greeting in that old Arab fashion of firing rifles as close to their friends as possible. But I was a little uneasy, wondering if Sherif Hussein could be sure that every one of three thousand tribesmen felt so friendly. George Farrier and I climbed on top of another truck, figuring that from this elevated position we could at least cover our guests.

My peace of mind received a further jolt when I saw Major Seager standing next to Sarah and Alan Scaife and I recalled that some wild tribes of southwest Arabia had put a high price on his head. This moment would give an excellent opportunity for someone to collect it.

A few months before, on Christmas Eve, Major Seager had been out for a late stroll in Dhala, accompanied by Mrs. Seager. He happened to notice, walking nearby with some companions, an Arab from a different locality. Major Seager stopped and asked him where he came from, and the man replied that Dhala was his home. When the Major pointed out that this could not be so, the man drew his jambiya, slashing the famous British Agent from eye to cheek and then plunging the knife in his chest. Miraculously, the blade entered near one side of the heart and pushed it aside instead of piercing it.

Major Seager grabbed his assailant and in the fight the Arab fell on his own jambiya and cut off four fingers on one hand. At that moment, government guards coming up from behind killed the would-be assassin and in the resulting battle there were several fatalities among the guards and the companions of the slain Arab. Throughout the battle, Mrs. Seager calmly stood over her husband and threw rocks at the Arabs. It was two o'clock in the morning before a doctor reached the Major's side, and only a man of his stamina could have survived.

The assassin, named Sayed Abdu Daim, had come to Dhala specifically to kill Major Seager, planning to do the job later in the evening. When he met his victim unexpectedly he had to advance his time schedule on the spur of the moment.

I felt a peculiar satisfaction when I noted that Major Seager now carried a revolver. When I first arrived in South Arabia,

Left, Wallace Wade, expedition director of photography from the Library of Congress, feeding pet gazelle; *right,* Charles McCollum, field director and chief of motor transport, mounted on his favorite Arab stallion in Beihan

Beihani tribesmen assembled by Sherif Hussein at his capital, Beihan al-Qasab, to honor the 1951 visit of Alan and Sarah Scaife of Pittsburgh

many conservative British officials had smiled with condescending amusement at my low-slung Colt, making humorous references to "Cowboy Phillips" and "Billy the Kid." Now the Britishers' number-one authority on life and security in the Protectorate had also become a "cowboy" and carried at his hip his most valuable insurance policy.

Perhaps that was one reason no one tried to collect the price on Major Seager's head that day. In any event, the noisy and colorful outdoor welcoming ceremonies finally ended without accident or fatality, and Sherif Hussein ushered us all into a long room covered with carpets and pillows. After a series of elaborate speeches, Alan Scaife presented a Polaroid camera to Sherif Hussein, who in turn presented him with a gold-inlaid jambiya. During the speeches, Sarah Scaife and Eileen were entertained in much better fashion by visiting the harem upstairs. When they returned, Sarah showed us a lovely silver belt presented by Sherif Hussein's daughter, who, she reported, was a beauty. After dinner, I presented two De Luxe Model 70 Winchesters to Sherif Hussein and the Emir, and we departed for Timna, dead tired.

The next day I took the Scaifes on a detailed tour of our four excavation sites, and then we took off in their plane for the Hadhramaut. Charlie McCollum and Bob Carmean had already preceded us with trucks and camping equipment for a stay of a few days. After the plane took off I managed to persuade our navigator to make a slight detour so that we could fly over forbidden Marib. Planes violate the Yemen frontier repeatedly— especially since its location is disputed—without anyone's knowing whether he has violated it or not. In the back of my head there was still that old dream of excavating at the Queen of Sheba's capital, unlikely as it seemed. I knew, too, that the Scaifes would be thrilled to see this most fabulous of the ancient cities of South Arabia. The pilot circled the ruins several times, and Wallace Wade shot movies of the old city and the famous dam.

Turning toward the Hadhramaut, we decided to fly over another city that we had been unable to visit by land—forbidden Shabwa. Thus we saw within a few hours, three capitals of ancient

South Arabian kingdoms—Timna, capital of Qataban, Marib, capital of Sheba, and Shabwa, capital of Hadhramaut.

Our navigator had some difficulty in locating Shabwa, which is not at all pretentious or imposing. Sarah, looking through her window, inquired in a puzzled tone what there was about this unimpressive view below to cause so much excitement. I explained that Shabwa, the mysterious "Sabota" of sixty temples mentioned by Pliny, had been the secret objective of almost every explorer to penetrate South Arabia. Traditions of sand-covered temples, palaces, and buried treasures have made this one of the best-known and most sought-after spots. We were the first Americans to see the old ruins, even from the air.

Our plane landed at Qatn, and Charlie and Bob drove us from there to Seiyun, where we had tea with Saiyid Abu Bakr, at whose palace we had stayed on our first trip to Beihan. After tea, I suddenly became quite ill with a bad case of chills, and by the next morning I was very weak. This did not improve my appearance for our 9:30 A.M. audience with the Sultan of Seiyun, ruling chieftain of the Kathiri state. Once seated inside his snow-white palace, which is undoubtedly the most impressive structure in the Hadhramaut, I turned to Eileen, who was busily talking to a mild-looking little man in his late twenties, sitting cross-legged on the floor.

"The Sultan must be lost!" I exclaimed in a fairly loud voice.

Eileen gave me a pitying look and went on talking to her little friend. Then the dawn broke, and I bowed meekly to His Highness.

Outside, while Wally Wade posed the Sultan for pictures, Sarah pointed out the women of the harem, who were peering down at us through binoculars from an upper balcony.

The next day, Sarah and Alan Scaife took off for Beirut with the words, "Count us in for a visit next season, inshallah."

17

CITIES OF THE DEAD

✳

During our first season's campaign at the huge cemetery of Haid bin Aqil, we had all commented upon the evidence of a fairly large structure at the foot of the mound's west slope. Bob Shalkop and his crew of workmen started removing the accumulated debris of two thousand years at this spot and soon uncovered a huge stone enclosure, roughly oblong in shape and with many recessed niches or panels formed by alternate projections and indentations of the building stones. Professor Albright said that this style was probably an imitation of the late Babylonian, and that the structure—a kind of mortuary chapel—may originally have been built in the form of a pyramid. After a few days' digging to clear out the interior, the walls were seen to be lined with sun-dried mud brick.

The most significant discovery in this building led to a tremendous digging operation. In one of the rooms, Bob Shalkop found a hole in the floor—a carefully constructed stone shaft rectangular in shape. It was filled with stones, sand, and debris, so Bob erected a scaffolding on top, with rope and pulley for hauling up the large stones. Down into the shaft he went, while we all hazarded guesses as to what the shaft might lead us to. Our hope was for a large and important burial chamber that had, because of its depth, been overlooked by the many grave robbers of the past. It was not a strong hope, however, for we had encountered no other evidence of deep and elaborate burial in South Arabia.

At a depth of nine feet, an archaic inscription was found on a plaster overlay of the stone. Running from right to left, the words mentioned a mukarrib who ruled about the sixth century B.C. This confirmed the opinion already formed from other evidence, that this mausoleum and shaft belonged to the period of the mukarribs, or priestly rulers, of Qataban before kings were the rulers of the nation.

At a depth of twenty feet the shaft changed its shape, becoming round instead of rectangular, and a good deal smaller in size. The digging was harder, but the men kept at it, wondering occasionally if they had encountered an old well, although a well in a mortuary chapel seemed out of place.

While excavators kept on going deeper into the narrowing shaft, others were working on the slope above, where they uncovered a second mausoleum, older than the first but without a deep hole in the ground. Inside they found a series of mud-brick benches which were probably designed to receive offerings to the dead. There were indications, too, that after this mausoleum had fallen into disuse, the spot had been occupied at three different times, very likely by people who used the foundations of the mausoleum on which to build mud-brick dwellings.

A third mortuary building was then discovered up the slope from the second, with one of its walls actually adjoining that of the next one below. The masonry of this structure was even older than that of the others, and here Bob Shalkop's Egyptian foreman, Ahmed Mohammed Ali, one of our six newly acquired Guftis, uncovered a room with paving stones, its interior walls covered with plaster. The room even had cut-stone drains and a stairway —all dating back to the seventh or eighth century B.C.

About a hundred and fifty feet up the slope of Haid bin Aqil, Bob Shalkop's men uncovered and cleared eleven multiple-roomed family tombs. They were rectangular and built against each other, one rough stone wall often serving two buildings. Each tomb contained a central aisle, with eight to ten chambers on either side, divided vertically into individual graves about thirty inches wide and six and a half feet long.

With all this excavation in a graveyard—usually the richest

Eleven alabaster objects standing exactly as they were before excavation in the antechamber to a tomb at the Timna cemetery. A few minutes before this picture was taken these unsuspected objects were completely covered by the debris of two thousand years.

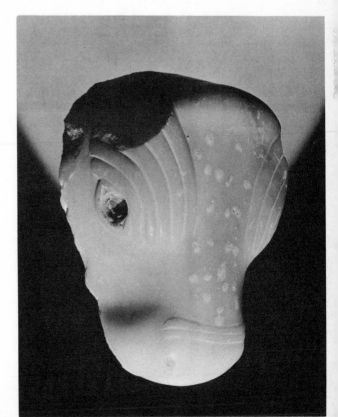

Broken alabaster bull's head from the Timna cemetery

Alabaster statues of the Hellenistic period from the Timna cemetery. Note the archaic fringe on the fat lady's garment

source of archaeological prizes—very few spectacular finds were made. By far the most exciting was a group of eleven alabaster objects from the antechamber to a tomb, only a few feet from the spot at which Professor Honeyman had stopped digging the first season. There were carved human heads and figures, bulls' heads, and inscribed votive tablets, all standing patiently in a row, waiting to be discovered.

As the stone shaft went deeper and deeper, we found more and more ancient inscriptions among the debris hauled out of it, and one bit of statuary that must be recognized as among the oldest so far found in South Arabia. The eyes were carved in a characteristic Egypto-Phoenician style which cannot possibly be later than the fourth century B.C.

Finally, as the season wore on, the bottom of the shaft was reached—sixty feet below the surface. Its last few feet were carved roughly out of bed rock, which must have been a terribly difficult task for the ancient Qatabanians who fashioned it. There was obviously no fine burial chamber leading from the shaft. It was no well, for the bottom of the shaft was still far above the underground water level. The only possible conclusion was that the important occupant of the mausoleum above was supposed to use the shaft as a method by which his spirit could travel to the world of the dead. Certainly the shaft has a religious significance in connection with burial and death.

A few days later we visited another city of the dead on the occasion of a trip to Mablaqa Pass, a narrow and difficult cut through the mountains leading to the present-day Yemeni village of Harib. Just beyond the pass, and very close to the ill-defined border between Yemen and the Western Aden Protectorate lay the ruins of the ancient city of Hajar Henu ez-Zurir, which we wanted to have a look at.

Since Sherif Hussein was leaving for Mukalla for a visit, his son Emir Saleh agreed to accompany us and arrange for our horses and camels. Armed with a sketch map, we set off at four o'clock one morning. Since we were moving so close to the Yemen border, our trip was labeled top secret for security purposes, but word about it leaked out and no one was at all surprised at our departure. There is no such thing as a secret in Arabia.

At the village of Nuqub we stopped for Emir Saleh and a picked crew of Beihani tribal guards, then drove south as far as Hajar bin Humeid. Here we turned abruptly west up the Wadi Mablaqa, and after three frightful miles left our trucks under guard at the little village of Bir Hegera. Here reinforcements joined us in the form of Rais Tabet with seven government guards, Abdrubbuh Ali with eight tribal guards, five Ashraf from the Wadi Harib to the north, and two donkey men, nine horses, four donkeys, and three camels. With these added to my sturdy group, which included Charlie McCollum, Dr. Jamme, Wallace Wade, Dr. de Mignard, Chester Stevens, and Jama, we felt ready and willing for almost anything.

Sometimes riding and sometimes walking, we started ascending the pass, which amazed us more and more the farther we went. Here was an artificial, man-made road which in antiquity served to join the Wadi Beihan and the Wadi Harib. In its length of three miles, it rose and descended about a thousand feet by a series of hairpin turns, built up on terraces which had low protective walls on the outer edges. The road itself, between twelve and fifteen feet wide, was paved with huge flagstones, some of them formed into steps in the steepest sections. As we labored up the slope and around the sharp turns, we looked down at the worn, rough stones with the realization that where our feet stepped the padded hoofs of incense-laden camels had trod, by the thousands, twenty-five centuries before. Mablaqa Pass had been a crucial link in the ancient incense route, one of the main highways by which the wealth of the East had reached the markets of the West.

As we approached the top of the pass, the incline became so steep that the ancient builders of the road had been unable to construct more terraces with hairpin turns by which to reach the summit. So they had just cut the road straight through the solid rock at the top—fifteen to twenty feet wide, forty feet deep, and a hundred feet long. With the most primitive tools, it must have been a tremendous undertaking—like cutting a tunnel with an ice pick.

As we stood in this rock-walled pass, we wondered exactly why the Qatabanians had struggled so hard to construct a road here when, only a few miles to the north, the flat plain west of Timna offered an easy route to the Wadi Harib and Marib—easy, at least, for the camel caravans of those days. The answer obviously lay in Qatabanian control of the incense trade that passed through its territory. The kingdom grew rich on taxes levied upon caravans, and would naturally go to almost any length to keep those taxes and allow no loopholes.

Dropping down on the other side by another remarkable series of paved turns, we stopped at length at the village of Bir Guwainha. Just as we mounted to go on, my horse, an especially vicious creature, jumped Dr. Jamme's mount, and the doctor took a nose dive, with me on top. I decided to stop trying to be a cowboy and mounted the nearest camel, but once again I found that, for me at least, there is no such thing as a comfortable position on this beast.

Our route led to the north of a saucer-shaped mountain called Jebel Qarn Obeid, down to the Wadi el Ain, a tributary of the Wadi Harib, and on to the high mound and ruins of Hajar Henu ez-Zurir.

This ancient Qatabanian city was unusual in that many of its buildings had remained intact without the protective covering of layers of sand. Somehow, the winds blew through the wadi in such a way that sand did not drift deep around the old walls and columns, but on the other hand they had been exposed to the wear and tear of wind, rain, and human beings for many centuries.

Dr. Jamme got busy at once, as might have been expected, copying inscriptions. Wallace Wade and Chester Stevens were occupied photographing the ruins. After a look around, the rest of the expedition staff went exploring, accompanied by a few government guards who had obviously been instructed not to let us out of their sight. In the distance, I saw a huge mound that looked so much like a buried town that I wanted to investigate it. We walked ahead, despite the mutterings of some of the guards who suddenly stood still and would go no further. Taking careful note of this new development, the rest of us fixed our eyes on the mound and slowly walked ahead.

When we reached it we found old ruins, broken votive offerings, and other indications which showed us that we had found another cemetery, another city of the dead—undoubtedly the cemetery for the city of Henu ez-Zurir. As we puttered about picking up old pieces of stone, bits of pottery, and other objects in the fashion of detectives, several Arabs with rifles appeared from the opposite side of the mound. They did not look at all friendly, as they held their guns ready in hands all too nervous for my comfort. They began to speak, and with a rather threatening politeness, inquired just how long we intended to visit in Yemen. We smiled, waved a cheery good-by, and retreated from the city of the dead.

18

LADY BAR'AT

"Wendell, I consider this our most important find to date—even more important than the lions."

It was Professor Albright speaking, after our small group returned from Mablaqa Pass. He was obviously quite excited and elated over a discovery made during our absence. So excited that he neglected to tell us what had been found and where.

"It will also add a great deal to our knowledge of mortuary practices and offerings to the dead," he announced triumphantly.

"Wonderful!" I said. "But, Professor, even though I do not want to appear unduly impatient, can you tell me what you have found?"

"Oh, yes, of course," the Professor replied. "Well, you will recall that we found no objects of major importance in the upper two strata of House Yafash."

I nodded. By this time the House Yafash had been unearthed. We had been delighted to find three rooms along its east side completely intact—the first such instance in South Arabian excavations, giving us an excellent idea of the inside appearance of an ancient Qatabanian house. Many objects had been found—bronze mirrors and incense boxes—which were very revealing and instructive, but nothing of significance comparable to the lions of Timna. All I could do was to let the Professor tell the story in his own way.

"You will also recall," he continued, "that when we began clear-

ing House Hadath, I suggested that we carefully check the strat-
ification for comparison with that of House Yafash, across the
street."

I nodded again. House Hadath was Building D, discovered near
the end of the first season, whose outer wall only had been exposed to view. For some time the work of clearing the interior
had been going on.

"Well," Professor Albright went on, "yesterday morning at
11:30 I was below the wall of House Hadath taking notes from
the street when Rais Gilani"—he was our chief Egyptian foreman, an expert who had been in archaeological work forty-six
years—"called me, saying 'Etla,' or 'Come up.' I went to him and
looked at the object he pointed out. There, to my astonishment,
I saw the back of a bronze statue seated on a stone pedestal. It
was lying face down on the floor of the cellar room of House
Hadath. I saw in one corner that some of the original plaster
floor had been preserved by surrounding mud. It was obvious,
upon closer examination, that this statue had fallen from an upper story during the destruction of Timna. Since the weight of
the statue and stone pedestal was so great, the pedestal which
landed on the mud floor adjacent to the original plaster sank into
it several centimeters, whereas the face was left without serious
damage just above the level of the plaster, without striking or
penetrating it.

"We devoted the next hour and a half to removing and cleaning the statue, using knives and then soft brushes to clear away
the earth and corrosion. One arm had fallen off when the statue
originally fell, but it was lying nearby. The other came off when
we first touched it, but the figure is easily restored and is complete. Come and see it."

This is what I had wanted to do at once, so I eagerly followed
the Professor. As we walked toward the storeroom to view the
new statue, he recalled another recent discovery.

"Oh, yes, one of the Guftis found two important pieces of pottery near our statue," he said. "One of them bore the stamp of
the Greek potter Leontes. Since this pottery is *terra sigillata,* it is

Exploratory party from the expedition ascending part of the ancient incense route through Mablaqa Pass. Twenty to thirty centuries ago thousands of spice-laden camel caravans traversed these flagstones en route to the Mediterranean world. Today this region is the scene of almost constant tribal warfare between Beihan and Yemen.

The Lady Bar'at in bronze, excavated from the cellar of House Hadath, which with inscription aided in fixing the date of Timna's destruction just before the time of Christ. Hellenistic influence shows throughout her figure and flowing garments, while her coiffure is typically Greek for the period.

of the greatest significance and will enable us to date the destruction of Timna with great accuracy."

I examined the bronze statue which the Professor pronounced our most important find. It was the figure of a lady, seated upon a stone, altogether about three feet high. She was not as lovely as Miriam, by any means, but perhaps that resulted from the difference between alabaster and bronze. Our lady possessed an aristocratic dignity that was impressive, and one felt right away that she was of high birth in ancient Qataban.

The Hellenistic influence was apparent not only in the statue but in the lady herself, for her coiffure was an elaborate coiled and braided affair popular in the Greek world in the first century B.C. The cut of her flowing garments also was Greek in style, and the modeling of the entire figure was clearly Hellenistic.

Most important to the Professor was the long inscription on the pedestal base which gave not only the name of the lady but the name of the king who ruled in Timna at the time the statue was made. Her name was the Lady Bar'at, and the king was Warawil Ghaylan Yuhanim, the son of Shahr Yagil Yuhargib, in whose reign the bronze lions of Timna were made. The inscription was a votive memorial to the Lady Bar'at, giving information about mortuary practices and offerings to the dead, with details as to her family relationship and the names of the gods in honor of whom the inscription was engraved in beautiful Qatabanian characters.

The Professor's first estimate of the date of Timna's destruction, around 50 B.C., was now revised to a later date and pinned down much more certainly, thanks to the Lady Bar'at and the pottery found near her. The type of pottery known as *terra sigillata* or "sealed earth" was originally Roman and was introduced in the east during the reign of Augustus, from 31 B.C. to A.D. 14. It was used for only a limited time, and the practice of stamping the potter's name died out around A.D. 70. The Professor also knew, as a result of his excavations in the north, that the same kind of *terra sigillata* was used in Palestine in the reign of Herod, King of Judea at the time of Christ.

The evidence presented by the statue of Lady Bar'at confirms that of the pottery. Since the style of her hair and clothing was that of Greece around 50 B.C. and a time lapse must be allowed for its spread to South Arabia, we are again brought to the time of Christ, or a few years before, as the date of the destruction of Timna. Professor Albright set to work at once comparing this exact evidence with all the other evidence we had gathered, and with the facts known about South Arabian history from other sources. There was considerable confirmation of the slightly later date, and many questions that had not been answered because of conflicting or inconclusive evidence now fell into their proper places. The picture of the chronology of South Arabia was fast becoming clear.

The House Hadath yielded other interesting and unique bronze pieces. One, found beneath the Lady Bar'at, was a plaque covered with an inscription and containing a small opening through which a hand projected, holding a shallow basin. The inscription made clear that this was a device for burning incense offerings, and the outstretched hand carried out the gesture of making an offering gracefully and vividly. The Guftis also found a bronze head of a bull with widespread horns. It had originally been suspended on a projection from the wall which stuck through a small hole that could be seen between the horns.

A well-built stairway still intact to a height of about four feet above the floor level proved that the House Hadath had been at least two stories in height. In two rooms, the plaster walls and floors were intact; two large holes in one of these rooms probably functioned as drains when the house was occupied.

Aside from the House Yafash and House Hadath, other important work was done at the South Gate dig during the second season. Building C, which had been found near the end of the first season, was cleared much further, and was found to be constructed on high foundations, with two stairways, one on the south and another on the east side, leading into it. In the northern part of the building the excavators came upon a series of stone shafts, some more than twenty feet deep, whose purpose is not clear. The fine masonry of Building C, its size and dominating position, in addition to the rows of benches found at the entrance during the first season, all suggested to Professor Albright that this was a Hall of Justice, police headquarters, and jail combined. There was also evidence that it had been used on two successive occasions after the fall of Timna. Even though the city was never again a place of importance after its destruction shortly before the time of Christ, some business may have been conducted there. The most logical place would have been this important building on an eminence, above the ashes and debris of the major portion of the city.

By the end of the second season, the South Gate dig covered an area, almost completely cleared, about 200 feet long and 175 feet wide. The gate itself, and adjoining walls, the entrance courtyard, two streets, and six major buildings were exposed to view and cleaned out, while several other buildings were partially uncovered.

Other incidents of a nonarchaeological nature occurred in connection with the South Gate. Rais Gilani captured the giant of giants among scorpions between two stones near the gate, and added him to our collection of specimens. Wallace Wade wanted to take movies of the spiders, but needed a human being in the pictures to show the relative size of these creatures. Wally thought that the leader of the expedition should get the benefit of this publicity, but I hurriedly remembered an appointment elsewhere. Others followed suit until young Chester Stevens stepped forward, calmly picked up one of the live monsters, and let it crawl up his arm for the movies. Also, near the South Gate one evening a small Arab boy got down on his hands and knees in the sand and with one finger printed the word "FILPS." Pointing at me, he proudly said, "Sahib Filps!" which I thought was very good indeed. It made me wonder how many of exceptional talent live and die out there in the sand, without a chance at anything more than mere existence.

The South Gate was also responsible for the agreement that was finally reached between Sherif Hussein and the expedition regarding the division of any gold that might be found in the course of excavations—a question that had been postponed at the start of the season. Although I did not know it until later, Sherif Hussein heard one day that work had ceased at the South Gate. The Beihani who informed him of this gave as the reason that "Sahib Phillips was on the verge of discovering a huge amount of gold at this point and wanted work stopped until there was an agreement regarding gold." Actually, we never expected to find gold objects of importance at the South Gate dig, even if they might have turned up elsewhere. Work had really stopped because at that time Ellis Burcaw, in charge of the dig, was ill, along with two or three others who might have taken his place to keep the work moving ahead.

In any event, the Sherif decided that he should come and see me about gold. I was glad to have the matter brought to a head because at that time Bob Shalkop was getting deeper and deeper into his shaft at Haid bin Aqil, and I wouldn't have been too surprised to find gold objects there. Trying to reach an agreement about gold *after* a good find had been made would be extremely difficult. The attitude of the expedition was quite different from that of Sherif Hussein, of course. We were interested in gold objects because of their artistic and archaeological value. The Sherif was interested in their monetary value. To date we had found nothing besides the gold necklace of the first season, which technically belonged to Sherif Hussein.

With Eileen acting as interpreter, Sherif Hussein and I discussed gold for three long hours, after which the Sherif suggested that the expedition keep 20 per cent of any gold found, while he should have the balance. I countered with the proposal that we should have a fifty-fifty partnership. Sherif Hussein found a way of agreeing while not agreeing, and Professor Albright was called to draw up a formal contract, which was signed on the spot with considerable ceremony. The expedition would receive 25 per cent gratis, with the privilege of purchasing another 25 per cent. With a broad smile, Sherif Hussein said, "So now you have your fifty per cent after all."

We might have known that after all this literary effort we should discover no more gold. The looters of many centuries had been most thorough—so thorough that we were lucky to wind up with even the gold necklace. The eventual ownership of the necklace proved, incidentally, that Sherif Hussein was actually much more warmhearted and generous than one might think in the midst of negotiations. He insisted that the expedition should keep the necklace, which he had previously loaned to us.

This generous act had an amusing aftermath, for Charles Inge, who knew nothing about the gift, had published in the Aden press a statement that the gold necklace would be exhibited in Aden. Assuming that it belonged to the Sherif, this would be natural. But when the British authorities asked Sherif Hussein about it, when the time came for the display, the Sherif just smiled and said, "I gave the Americans the necklace." And that was that.

19

BACK TO 1000 B.C.

At the mound of Hajar bin Humeid, Don Dragoo spent his first three weeks increasing his working space, for he could not excavate much deeper in the gradual steps necessary for a cross section without more room. In the course of this clearing, a large new inscription was turned up in an early level that had been reused by later Arabs. It turned out to be the most recent royal Qatabanian inscription found in our excavations, dating from just before the Christian era, almost at the time of Timna's destruction, along with its neighboring town to the south, for which we have never found an ancient name.

As workmen pushed down through Strata D, E, and F, large quantities of pottery sherds were found, all of which Gus Van Beek studied carefully and preserved. He and Professor Albright agreed that pottery from Stratum F came from the sixth and seventh centuries B.C., so they still hoped that the bottom of the mound would lead them far back into the second millennium before Christ.

At one period, all work at Hajar bin Humeid stopped because of the floods resulting from heavy rainstorms. Water rose so high in the Wadi Beihan that it was impossible to reach the mound safely. This wide flat valley that had so recently been a dry and dusty plain now resembled the Mississippi on rampage. The torrent roared and swelled for several days, rushing over rocks and carrying heavy debris at high speed. Even the oldest Beihani had

never seen so much water, and everyone talked about this phe-
nomenon.

After the waters subsided—and they disappear quickly into the
blotter-like earth—work was resumed at Hajar bin Humeid. Step
by step and layer by layer, the men dug down through their cross
section until, before the end of the season, they hit sterile soil
—the original earth on which the first town had been built so
many centuries ago. They had dug through fifty-one feet of cultural debris, containing some ten strata—A through J—with a minimum of fifteen occupation levels. In the lower levels there was
much evidence of reconstruction on top of original construction.
Whereas the building material of the top three strata was predominantly stone, the structures in lower levels had stone foundations only, with mud-brick superstructures rising from them.

Gus Van Beek found that, roughly corresponding to the strati-
fication, there were ten pottery phases, including many interesting
types. Burnished red slip, for instance, was used extensively as a
decorative device in the earlier periods. The burnishing technique
reflected the influence of, and commercial contact with, Palestine
and Syria during the late Iron I and Iron II periods, about 1000
to 600 B.C. There was also a good deal of painted pottery, mostly
reddish-brown paint on buff-colored clay, which gave clues as to
the more common artistic motifs. One of the most popular was a
perpendicular line with two to four parallel lines joining it
obliquely at much the same angle as barbs join the shaft of a
feather.

None of the pottery contained figure painting, but inscriptions
were occasionally found. Most of the letters were incised, or cut
into the clay, but on several pieces the letters were raised in relief.
One of the common pottery ornaments consisted of clay figures of
reclining bulls, usually found on lids and sometimes on chalice
rims. One interesting discovery was a clay camel head from about
the eighth century B.C., which had broken from the body of the
vase to which it had been attached.

Hajar bin Humeid established the pottery sequence that Professor Albright had hoped for, a frame of reference for all other
archaeological work in South Arabia. The earliest levels showed

that the city had probably first been established somewhere between 1100 and 900 B.C., with 1000 B.C. a reasonable estimate.
More detailed study of the pottery specimens will no doubt establish all dates more accurately.

As if to keep pace with discoveries elsewhere, Dr. Jamme found
during the second season a graffito even earlier than that of the
first season, which had up to that time been our earliest known
object from ancient Qataban. The new graffito went back to 1000
B.C. at least, or just about the time of the establishment of the
first town at Hajar bin Humeid, perhaps a bit earlier. The letters
of this graffito lay at every possible angle, some upside down, some
on their sides, others leaning to right or left. This was also a characteristic of the early Canaanite alphabet of the north, from the
twelfth century.* We had now gone back to a time earlier than
that of the Queen of Sheba of the Bible.

We continued to wonder about the Queen, always hoping to
uncover something that would bring her out of the mists. But
my chief concern was our work for the next year. In our second
season at Beihan, I knew that we would reach bottom at Hajar
bin Humeid, that we would have excavated enough at Haid bin
Aqil to tell us most of the story that the cemetery might reveal.
The mound that had once been Timna could take many years
of excavation, of course, but our digs at the South Gate and the
temple site would, by the end of our 1951 season, tell us the basic
facts of South Arabian history, the chronology through which we
could learn more about all of the ancient kingdoms of that area.

It would be time, I felt, to move on to some of those other kingdoms in an effort to bring their stories at least up to the point
we had reached in Qataban. My first goal was Sheba—Sheba the
home of the fabulous queen, Sheba the kingdom that dominated
South Arabia for many centuries. I remember standing on top of
Hajar bin Humeid one day near the end of February, looking
off to the northeast. There, barely forty miles away as the crow

---

* In 1954 Dr. Frank M. Cross, Jr., a former pupil of Professor Albright,
discovered several bronze arrowheads near Bethlehem, bearing Canaanite inscriptions with letters at various angles. These inscriptions date from the
twelfth century B.C. and confirm the view that the South Arabian alphabet
had been borrowed from the Canaanites in the preceding century.

South Gate of Timna (probably from the sixth century B.C.) after excavation. Before the expedition arrived this entire city area containing important buildings, streets, inscriptions, and art objects lay buried under the sand.

The stratified mound of Hajar bin Humeid showing the expedition's completed cross section, cutting down through fifty-one feet of cultural debris, containing some ten strata with a minimum of fifteen occupation levels. This established a pottery time sequence back to 1000 B.C. and will serve as a frame of reference for all future archaeological work in South Arabia.

flies, lay Marib, capital of ancient Sheba. There lay the dam that was one of the wonders of the ancient world, a dam that had made a rich green garden of a desert world. But between me and that goal lay a no-man's land containing an ill-defined international boundary—the boundary between Yemen and the Western Aden Protectorate.

I wanted more than anything to have our expedition be the first to pull away the shroud of sand from the famous city. So, despite the fact that I knew it was all but hopeless, I went back to my room and wrote a letter to H.R.H. Prince Abdullah, Foreign Minister of Yemen, at his palace in Sana. I didn't say anything to others on the expedition because it was probably just another gesture, another expression of an old wish. "Kid Phillips" was just young enough and brash enough to write the letter, but not really foolish enough to expect an answer.

To be on the safe side, therefore, I considered other likely spots for the next year. Oman intrigued me, but Oman was a complete archaeological question mark. The Kingdom of Ma'in remained, but once before I had found it impossible to reach its ruins in present-day Saudi Arabia. It would not hurt, I decided, to try again. So I wrote more letters that would set in motion my request for permission to enter Saudi Arabia. In addition to the official letters, I also wrote once more to my friend, the eminent Mr. H. St. John B. Philby, close friend of King Ibn Saud and a resident of the political capital of Saudi Arabia, Riyadh. I sent off all my letters and promptly put them out of my mind. For I was busy working at the temple site of Timna.

20

TEMPLE OF VENUS

We had not worked long at the temple site that second season before confirming our view that here lay the largest building of ancient Timna. It was certainly the first really monumental building to be excavated in all South Arabia, for we dug in an area 160 feet long by 135 feet wide without yet reaching the end of what was a complex of buildings and courts making up the Temple of Athtar, the Arabian equivalent of our Venus.

Dramatic—and back-breaking—signs of the violence of the conflagration which doomed the ancient city were found in the center of a huge court of the temple complex. Here the heat of the fire had fused together a huge mass of rocks and debris that yielded only to sledge hammers, which finally broke up the mass sufficiently for the pieces to be hauled away by the winches on our powerful trucks. With these out of the way, the remaining sand covering the large court was carried off, revealing a spacious area paved with polished pink marble slabs. Stairways of stone leading up on all sides showed that the court had been a slightly sunken square lying in front of the temple proper, on the east. Here a marble staircase about twenty-one feet wide made an imposing entrance to the chief building. Its steps were worn deeply at the edges by the feet of the thousands upon thousands of worshippers who had in times past marched up into the temple for religious services.

The stone walls around the court showed the same niched and

recessed construction that had been found in the large mauso-
leums at Haid bin Aqil, suggesting a strong Babylonian influence
and aiding greatly in the dating of this part of the excavation.

I was particularly concerned with a sounding made along the
east face of the temple wall. While Jim Swauger and, after his departure, Jack Simpson, supervised the main temple work, I concentrated on a very small area, growing more thankful that it was
small as we went deeper and deeper into the sand and debris in
our effort to find the bottom of the foundation. Twenty feet down,
the nature of the construction changed completely, for below this
level the stones were smaller and more roughly hewn. Here, then,
were the walls of an original building upon which a second one
had been built. The weight of the newer building had even caused
the lower walls to buckle slightly at some points. We dug down
ten more feet, until our cut reached a depth of thirty feet. From
these lowest levels were retrieved many fragments of beautifully
burnished pottery in red and brown, dating back to the seventh
or eighth century B.C. and showing strong Syro-Palestinian in-
spiration.

In time we concluded that there had been four main periods of
construction of the great temple. The earliest, represented by the
lowest walls of the temple proper, was during the mukarrib
(priestly ruler) period of Timna, around the seventh or eighth
centuries B.C. During the second building period the niched and
recessed walls of massive masonry were erected, at a later mukarrib
time around the sixth century B.C. The court itself, and the steps
leading from it into the temple, date from the third period when
kings reigned in Timna and the influence was strongly Persian,
probably in the latter part of the fourth century. The last period
showed Hellenistic influence and came during the time of the
greatest known builder of Timna, King Shahr Yagil Yuhargib,
of the bronze lions. This was during the first century B.C., just
before Timna's fall. Many broken inscriptions from this time were
found inside and outside the temple area.

A series of rooms from this same age were excavated along the
western side of the pink-marble court, and were found to be in
much better condition than the temple itself, which had been de-

stroyed to ground level. The large quantity of sherds found in these rooms indicated that they may have been used as storage rooms for the temple during its last period.

In the case of two stairways, the existence of two stages of construction was vividly revealed, showing that the ancient Qatabanians remodeled and enlarged old buildings just as we do today. A stairway leading to the court from the south was made of small well-cut blocks of drafted masonry of the Persian period, but it was placed in one of the niches from the earlier temple construction of more massive stones. Shortly before the end of the season another stairway was found, on the north side of the temple, so wide and imposing that it was undoubtedly the main entrance during the time of King Shahr Yagil Yuhargib. Here the masonry was not only different, but the staircase had actually pulled away somewhat from the older building, when its foundations had settled. Beyond this stairway lay another courtyard, which was excavated to a distance of twenty-five feet from the steps. Here it disappeared under the sands, and we never learned how far it extended, for we had to call a halt some time, at some place.

The temple must have been a beautiful and imposing structure, for we found a central nave and foundations for four or five rows of gigantic pillars, with five pillars to a row. What an awe-inspiring spectacle this great Temple of Venus must have been to the weary traveler from Shabwa or farther east as he gazed upward through its forty to fifty columns!

Even if we were deprived of that sight and could learn nothing here of the religious practices of the Qatabanians, the western courtyard gave us an unexpected discovery. It happened during a visit of the acting governor of Aden, W. A. C. Goode, with Mrs. Goode. Sherif Hussein put on a fine welcome, as only he can do it, with lots of shooting, speechmaking, singing, and dancing. Then, while Eileen conducted Mrs. Goode through the Sherif's harem, the rest of us left for an inspection of our archaeological sites.

As we were looking at the temple site, the Governor called Professor Albright's attention to numerous mason's marks found on the face of some paving slabs in the northeast corner of the colonnade running around three sides of the low central court. Although such marks had been recorded by the score from detached facing slabs, this was the first time they had been noted on slabs in place.

The next day Professor Albright and Dr. Jamme set to work. They saw that the marked stones were laid in regular rows, each containing an inscription of a South Arabian letter. Professor Albright looked at once to see if there was any significance in the order of the letters in each row, and immediately discovered two groups in the first and second rows which exhibited exactly the same order of letters as in the Ethiopic alphabet.

This was a discovery of the first importance. The ancient Qatabanians who had paved this court inscribed their alphabet around it. We had never known before the proper order of the ancient South Semitic alphabet, but now it had been discovered. It would be comparable with the discovery, some millenniums hence, of the order of our alphabet by scientists who had figured out how to read our words but were handicapped by being uncertain of the order in which letters were arranged.

Apparently the South Semitic alphabet was arranged in an order like that of the much later Ethiopic alphabet. Actually, the earliest-known evidence for the order of that alphabet is a good 1,500 years later than these mason's marks in the temple courtyard of Timna.

While work on the temple site was going on, I received late in March a letter from St. John Philby, in response to my inquiry about the possibility of working in Saudi Arabia, at the site of the ancient Ma'in civilization. I hardly expected a favorable reply, because I had been able to get nowhere through our own State Department. Although I have always had excellent relations with most agencies of the United States Government, and have received from various branches major support in the form of funds, equipment, personnel, and encouragement, certain State Department officials in the field did not seem to recognize or understand the importance of the work in which our expeditions were engaged, either scientifically or as a matter of American prestige. It is a long way from the office of a friendly assistant secretary of state in Washington to a lonely consulate in South

Arabia. It was a long way, not only in distance but in the co-operation our expeditions received.

I firmly believed that American good will was a commodity that had to be actively demonstrated by the way Americans lived and acted from day to day in foreign countries, not something to be measured or bought merely by loans or gifts of American dollars. I had a habit, also, that was unforgivable in certain American diplomatic circles, one that I learned from our British cousins. This was always to put my country's interests first. Yes, I was pro-Beihani, pro-Yemeni, and pro-Omani, but never at the expense of being pro-American.

In the case of a projected visit to Saudi Arabia, I had been forestalled two years before for rather vague reasons that did not hold water. Now I was being discouraged again, without my understanding why. Mr. Philby's letter confirmed my feeling that something was lacking in the State Department's efforts on my behalf. He wrote, in part:

My dear Phillips:

I have been away on a long trip in the Midian area since the middle of November, and only got back here on March 2nd, when I found your letter. I am delighted to hear that the expedition is in full swing, and I feel confident that this season's work will produce results which should finally settle all the outstanding chronological issues regarding South Arabian History. I have also received Professor Albright's interim report on the first season's work, and studied it with the deepest interest.

Now I come to the matter of your desire to visit Jidda and/or Najran. I saw the new American Ambassador the other day at Jidda, and I gathered from him that he had had no instructions to apply for permission for you to visit Saudi Arabia. On the contrary, I have since been told confidentially that the authorities here have been warned that you have returned to these parts and may try to enter Saudi Arabia informally! I cannot fathom the meaning of this hole and corner attitude on the part of the State Department; but it is definitely interpreted in official circles here as indicating a desire of the State Department that you should not be allowed to come to Saudi Arabia. You will realize that this makes it virtually impossible for me to do anything to further your plan. I think it is fair to say that the

Saudi authorities themselves would have no objection to your coming here (some of them, interested in archaeological matters, would certainly welcome your visit in view of possible arrangements for a dig), but they cannot very well invite or permit you to do so against what appears to be a specific demand from the American authorities that your visit should be discouraged. In the circumstances it would seem that there is no alternative but that you should tackle the State Department again and endeavour to get its attitude to you modified. Otherwise the proposition seems quite hopeless; and it is particularly annoying to realise that almost anyone else in the world could come and visit me at Jidda or even here, while you alone are barred from entry into the country owing to your own country's objections to your coming here. It is not difficult for those who are not your friends to put about stories of your being hand in glove with the Jews, etc. etc., which they seem to be doing. Yet within the last three months an English Jew has been allowed to travel freely in this country in search of birds, etc., being received by the King and entertained at the places he passed through. The British government supported his application for a visit, and he got the necessary permission. That shows up in a nutshell the difference between the two cases; and I have no doubt whatever that if the State Department had supported you, you would have been perfectly free to come and wander about here.

Until your difficulties with the State Department are settled it is no good thinking of the Nejran project at all, while I doubt if your Embassy would be prepared to secure a visa for you to visit even Jidda on your way to Cairo.

I do hope I have made things clear to you, and all I can do now is to wish you luck in your efforts to convert the State Department from their present unfriendly attitude. I also send you all my best wishes for a most successful season at Beihan.

Yours sincerely,
H. St. J. B. Philby

The master explorer Philby had written a masterful letter and had in one small sentence given the key to the entire situation, the key to America's position in the Middle East today: "The British government supported his application for a visit, and he got the necessary permission." American support of Americans—that was the key, the key that was missing.

What a situation! By now I knew personally more Arab rulers than almost any other American. I had traveled freely, explored and excavated in major areas of the Arab world, and was welcome to return everywhere. Yet here I was excluded from the one Arab country I had as yet never set foot in. Because of my own State Department's lack of support, I was black-listed by the Saudis, despite the fact that two years before, the acting Saudi minister of foreign affairs, Sheikh Yousef Yassim, had appeared most cordial and receptive when the late prime minister of Egypt, Nokrashi Pasha, had introduced me as his "American son."

As I went back to work at the temple site, I kept asking myself one question: what interests could possibly be served by keeping my American expedition out of Saudi Arabia?

It was a month later before I heard anything more about possible sites for the next year. One day in April, while I was in bed with a fever, a large quantity of mail was forwarded from Aden. One letter in Arabic was written on official-looking stationery, but I couldn't make it out. No one was available at the moment who could read Arabic, so I casually set it aside. It was a few days before I noticed it again, and handed it to Eileen with the almost cynical remark, "Wouldn't it be nice if this were an invitation to Marib?"

She took the letter and went to her room, but returned in a few minutes, obviously very excited.

"How could you possibly have known?" she asked.

"Known what?"

"That this was a reply from His Royal Highness Prince Abdullah, Yemen minister of foreign affairs, inviting you to visit Taiz for an audience with the King to discuss Marib!"

I grabbed the letter and tried to read what I could not read but wanted to look at—in black and white. I made Eileen promise solemnly that she was not kidding me, but it was some time before I calmed down enough to believe that there was really a slight chance of excavating at the greatest remaining archaeological site known in the ancient world. No American explorer, no English explorer, had ever visited the city of the Queen of Sheba. No real excavation had ever taken place. Marib was a closed area within a forbidden land. So far as I knew, no one had ever been able to talk to the present King about Marib.

Quickly I reminded myself that all I was invited to do was talk. But I vowed that if ever in my life I had done a good job of selling, I would have to do it now.

I had been ordered to bed by Dr. de Mignard with a high fever, yet here I was out of bed and ready to go, although my legs felt a little shaky. In less than a week we had arranged for a chartered plane to fly us to Aden, where expedition trucks were available to drive us from that city to Taiz. Although Professor Albright was scheduled to return to Baltimore, I hoped that he might make this trip with us. Much as he was tempted, however, he decided that there were too many chances of his being delayed, and he went on to the States after going with the rest of us as far as Aden. I was sad to see him leave and to know that he would miss this important event of our expedition. The Yemen party that finally made the trip consisted of Eileen, Charlie McCollum, Wallace Wade, Dr. de Mignard, Bob Carmean, Jama, and myself.

As we set off, I tried to act like the dignified leader of a scientific expedition, but inside I felt like a little boy who has just discovered a whole mountain of ice cream—and his favorite flavor at that!

21

INTO FORBIDDEN YEMEN

Leaving Aden on April 10th, we passed through the barrier gate at Sheikh Othman, and drove across the flat, dusty Sultanate of Lahej. Although the so-called road was washed out in several places, our trucks had little difficulty in getting through and fortunately we had a Yemeni guide who knew the route well.

We welcomed a hilly country covered with green foliage and blessed with many streams. Along the way we passed several large wells, at one of which there was a big crowd of women and girls, gathering water in large earthen jars. They all wore long blue pants fastened around the ankles, and were quite pretty. Dr. de Mignard kept pointing to their cute little yellow-painted faces and exclaiming, "Beihan was never like this!"

At the customs post of Raidha, about sixty miles from Aden, we were delayed for an ostensible ten minutes, which in Yemen means "Prepare to spend the night." After two hours our host, Sheikh Ali Mohammed Ruhbaiti, informed us that he had just telegraphed the Imam and that permission had been granted for our entrance into Yemen. This was the first occasion on which we learned that in Yemen all officials seem to double- and triple-check. In Yemen, visas mean nothing; official documents mean nothing. Even with all the necessary papers, no one crosses the border into that country without specific on-the-spot telegraphic instructions from the King. By the time we were okayed at Raidha, it was almost dark, so we decided to remain where we were for the night.

Our host brought us something we had not seen for months— fresh tomatoes, oranges, onions, and potatoes, delicacies we proceeded to enjoy immensely. Sheikh Ali declined our invitation to eat with us because he was chewing qat and he never ate a meal and chewed qat at the same time.

While Jama prepared dinner, Eileen retired to a special bathroom far more air-conditioned than the bath at our headquarters in Beihan. Finding it had a large picture window with no shade or covering, she hung her dress over the opening, only to discover later to her dismay rows of small boys gathered in quiet attendance outside so as not to miss anything.

These same boys, apparently curious about everything, watched us eat our dinner and were on hand to witness our departure the next morning.

As we climbed into the mountains we all marveled at the wonderful terracing of the steep slopes, where every foot of even the highest mountains was used for agriculture, demonstrating human energy and industry beyond compare. In heavy rains some of the terraces were washed away, only to be built up again quickly. Less energy was exerted when the road washed out, as ours had. We finally had to detour around a couple of mountains and approach Taiz from a route that hid the city from view until we were almost there.

Taiz is not the capital of Yemen, but it is the present home of the King. This queen city of South Yemen lies at an altitude of 4,500 feet, with its back against the massive mount, Jebel Sabir, on the south. On top of the precipitous cliff is a romantic-looking medieval citadel commanding the entire town. On the other three sides the mountains are farther away, so walls have been built for the protection of the city.

At the gate we were greeted by Amir Galib Jarmoussi, who divides his talents as director of aviation and director of the guest house. At the moment we were interested in his latter capacity. He led us up narrow, winding, cobblestoned streets while all the citizens stared at us as though we were a circus parade. People from the world of Europe and America are a rarer sight in this important city than in the wastes of Beihan. All the buildings, we noticed, were built of stone—which was plentiful in the mountains. Our quarters were very comfortable—with fresh sheets, electric lights, hot and cold running water, food, cooks, and servants, all generously provided as a courtesy by His Majesty the King.

The next morning at ten o'clock we were visited by Sami Manna, an assistant in the Ministry of Foreign Affairs, and a half-hour later by a senior official in the Royal Cabinet, Abdul Malek Al Amri, who was accompanied by Dr. Adnan Tarcici, a delightful Lebanese who also serves in the Ministry of Foreign Affairs. Dr. Tarcici spoke a little English, and with Eileen to back me up with her fast-flowing French and Arabic, we got along quite well.

Dr. Tarcici tried to point out how difficult it would be to reach Marib and work there. Wouldn't we be just as happy, he wondered, to study some of the remarkable archaeological sites around the city of Sana?

"We certainly want to see these other ruins," I replied, "but I would not consider moving the expedition and spending money except to excavate at Marib."

Dr. Tarcici quietly digested this information, then took leave of us to consult His Majesty. This left us sitting and twiddling our thumbs for some hours, so I asked and gained permission to take some movies of the city that afternoon. We climbed the high cliff immediately behind Taiz and saw Yemen, Arabia Felix, spread out before us—mountainous, green, and fertile. The word "Yemen" itself means "on the right" and since the Semitic tribes have always oriented themselves facing east, the right hand pointed to the bright and happy south, as opposed to the dark and forbidding north.

At the summit of the cliff we saw at close hand the citadel, where the King keeps hostages from the various tribes of his realm. Over the entrance I noticed what looked like Christian crosses, but no one could tell me what they were or what they meant. At the foot of the citadel's wall lay the ruins of a Jewish synagogue, dating back to the fourth century when Jewish kings ruled Yemen.

At six o'clock that evening, Talaat Ghussein, Director of the Yemen Press Division and one of five members of the Yemen delegation to the United Nations, called upon us and said that in ten

Excavation in progress at the Temple of Athtar (the planet Venus-in-the-Morning), largest building inside ancient Timna. This wide flight of steps formed the main entrance in the early first century B.C. during the reign of King Shahr Yagil Yuhargib; they were probably built two or three centuries earlier, and the temple itself seems to go back to the eighth century B.C.

En route to Taiz in southern Yemen the expedition stopped to be entertained by a dancing girl and musician. *Left to right:* Wendell Phillips, Charles McCollum, Eileen Salama, Dr. Valentin de Mignard (*standing*), Yemeni guide, and Robert Carmean

minutes we were to visit the palace and sign the royal register. After a mad scramble for somewhat whiter shirts, we were rushed through the streets by two qat-chewing maniacal drivers and out beyond the city walls to the palace.

Standing at attention before the impressive reddish stone building were three askaris, beautifully dressed in white flowing robes, with decorated jambiyas and crossed cartridge belts. Inside, we were served the finest coffee in the world—Yemeni Mocha—before signing our names to the royal register, first in English, then in Arabic.

Then came another day of waiting—a favorite pastime in all the Arab world but carried to an extreme in Yemen. We took movies in the city, but at one place the police stepped in to prevent our taking pictures of a large crowd of tribesmen from the hills. At this, a very important-looking official ran from a nearby building and in no uncertain terms ordered the police away. While Wallace Wade went ahead with his movie, I learned that the Imam himself was inside the building and had personally sent this man to see that we were not disturbed.

At 10:15 that evening, I received a very simple note:

Dear Mr. Phillips:
  Good evening to all. H.M. the King will receive you tomorrow. The cars will pick you up about nine.
                                        Yours,
                                          Talaat Ghussein

So the big moment had arrived! Then I wondered if the King was to receive me or the entire party, and I sent Jama to get the details. He returned with the message, "All but Miss Eileen. His Majesty never receives women."

The chief sufferer from this custom, I concluded, was His Majesty. Then I set about reviewing my presentation for the next day, for everything depended upon it. I was being given a chance that no explorer had obtained and that dozens had hoped for. But for the first time in my career of asking important people for concessions, funds, supplies, permissions, and favors, I was not sure how to proceed. I was dealing here with one of the most absolute rulers in the world, who could and would decide yes or no without the necessity of consulting anyone. On the other hand, he was—like his country—isolated in many ways from the rest of the world, cut off by his own choice from the ideas and currents of modern times. Even the other Arab nations looked upon Yemen as a country still living in the Dark Ages.

Although the King was an absolute dictator, he suffered restrictions perhaps greater than any he imposed on his own subjects. Since the assassination of his father three years before he had not visited—some said he had not dared visit—the capital of his country, Sana. Prince Hassan, one of his brothers, was viceroy in Sana and virtual ruler of northern and eastern Yemen. Many people said that he coveted the throne himself. In any event, the memory of his eighty-four-year-old father's death was still vivid enough to make King Ahmed wonder at all times about his own security.

One February morning in 1948, His Majesty Imam Yahya was seated outside his Sana palace from nine o'clock until eleven thirty, receiving his people's petitions, according to custom. As he rose to leave, Prime Minister Qadi Abdullah Al Amri returned from inspecting some land recently purchased by the Imam, and reported that the new pumps were functioning well and would supply water for about ten kilometers of land.

Imam Yahya was pleased and decided to see his new fields. With his Prime Minister he set out at once. Rounding a bend, the driver of the car found the road blocked and a covered lorry parked nearby. Masked assassins from the truck opened fire, and nine bullets struck the Imam and his two-year-old grandson, while the Prime Minister, the driver, and one guard died where they sat.

Back in Sana, Abdullah al Wazir, first secretary to the Imam and instigator of the murder plot, was standing on the roof of his house, waiting for the signal from his paid accomplices. When the signal came that the King was dead, he immediately rushed to the Qasr, the military barracks and armory, where all arms and ammunition were stored. There he told the soldiers that the Imam Yahya had gone to Taiz to meet his son Crown Prince Ahmed and that he, Abdullah Wazir, had been left in charge. His first order was for the gates of the city to be closed. Then he dispatched an Iraqi artillery specialist, Captain Jamil Jemal, to surround the royal palace and trap the princes.

News of the Imam's assassination traveled like wildfire, and within a short time, the royal princes, Hussein, Yahya, and Mohsen set out on foot for the military barracks, only to collide with Jamil Jemal and his soldiers at the bottom of the palace stairs. Although they drew their jambiyas to defend the palace, the princes did not have a chance and fell under the fire of the soldiers. Princes Hussein and Mohsen were killed on the spot. Prince Yahya was wounded and lay as if dead, but he was later imprisoned in the palace.

Crown Prince Ahmed was serving as governor of Taiz at the time news of his father's death reached him. Although he knew he was next on the assassin's list, he set out by jeep for Hajja, some distance from Sana. Here he assembled about 13,000 loyal tribesmen. After four days of siege, Sana surrendered to these Bedu hordes. Twelve hours later the *suk,* or market place, was a complete wreck, its hundreds of little shops destroyed. At the end of four days there was hardly a house which had not been systematically looted. Close to two hundred inhabitants lost their lives.

On the day the Bedu tribes entered Sana commanded by His Royal Highness Prince Seif Al Islam Abbas, Prince Yahya convinced his guards in the palace to free him, and together they captured Abdullah Wazir. This man, who had been the so-called Imam of Yemen for twenty-four days, kept insisting, "But you can't do this to me. I am Abdullah Wazir, your King." Covered with chains he was still repeating this six days later while being driven in an open car to Hajja. These may have been his last words as his head parted company from his body at Cairo Palace, along with the accumulated heads of his associates—about thirty-five in all. Eileen was told that Abdullah Wazir's head was fastened to a pole and exhibited outside the Ministry of Health for several days, for all to see and appreciate the reward for over-ambition in Yemen.

Thus Crown Prince Ahmed became undisputed ruler, His Majesty Imam Ahmed, King of Yemen. He was also the spiritual leader of the Zeidi sect of Moslems, since he traced his descent from the

Prophet Mohammed through the Prophet's son-in-law Ali and daughter Fatima. The ruling family of Yemen also claims descent from the pre-Islamic Himyarite rulers of Yemen.

This was the man I was to meet the next day in an effort to gain permission to excavate the city once ruled by the Queen of Sheba.

22

AUDIENCE WITH THE IMAM

As might have been expected in Yemen, it was ten-thirty rather than nine o'clock when cars came for us, under the guidance of Sami Ezzedin, Foreign Affairs Officer. After leaving the guest house, we stopped to pick up Dr. Tarcici, and then drove not to the palace as I expected but to the building in the city outside of which the police had tried to stop our picture-taking.

We were ushered into a rather plain room and there had our first sight of His Majesty, the King of Yemen. He was sitting on an ornate chair, holding a small boy on his lap. The boy was playfully kicking the leg of a table which stood in front of the King.

The ruler of Yemen was a heavy-set man in his middle fifties, striking in looks because of his black beard and very large eyes which seemed to take in everything before him at a glance. He was beautifully dressed in a white silk robe, with a jeweled jambiya thrust into a green and gold sash. On his head he wore a gold brocaded turban. Behind his chair, on lovely Persian rugs, stood his advisers and a group of white-robed guards holding rifles.

The King greeted us with a friendly smile and shook hands all around. As Jama bent low to kiss his hand, His Majesty remembered that he had first met our chief Somali during his visit with entomologist Hugh Scott in 1938, and inquired, "How are my favorite people, the Somalis?"

I was seated on the King's left, whereupon he leaned forward and put one hand on my knee as he asked, "Takallam Arabi?"

(Do you speak Arabic?) I replied in my best Arabic that my best was not very good. He seemed to be convinced of the truth of this statement, so Dr. Tarcici acted as chief interpreter from that point on.

We fell into a rather easy conversation about general subjects. The King seemed to be in an excellent humor, laughing and joking a good deal. I was so pleased to find him in this receptive mood that I smiled and laughed a good deal myself. In these interviews, so much depends upon the general atmosphere. Even a king can get out of the wrong side of the royal bed some mornings.

In answer to his question, I was describing our work in Beihan when the Imam interrupted to say that as a young man he had himself collected numerous inscriptions and that consequently he was keenly interested in our work. Somehow, this seemed to be a cue to Jama, who caught my eye and gave me a meaningful look. I stood up and motioned for the presentation of our good-will gifts, which included assorted Colgate products, cases of Coca-Cola, Square D binoculars, Marlins, Colts, Western ammunition, a General Electric fan, a Hallicrafter radio, a Royal typewriter, and a Polaroid camera that had been left with me by Alan Scaife. When I apologized for not having more to give, the King replied, "The Prophet Mohammed accepted gifts, whether they were large or small, for it is the spirit behind the gift, not the gift itself, that matters."

Next I presented the King with a copy of Friso Heybroek's map of South Arabia made during our first season. He looked carefully at the border between the Aden Protectorates and Yemen, marked with a series of dashes and question marks, and I wondered if he might be annoyed that our geologist had not put the boundary where the King thought it ought to be. But he smiled and said, "Next time, please remove the dashes and leave only question marks."

Finally we began to come closer to the project at hand. I tried to lead from our work in Beihan to the work we would like to do in Marib when the King interrupted with a question.

"Have you been to Shabwa?" I knew, of course, that Yemen claimed this ancient city and the territory around it.

"I have seen Shabwa only from the air," I replied. "Charlie McCollum, who became lost on his way to Beihan once, saw it from the ground."

"How much meat did he give to a Shabwa man?" the King asked pointedly.

I was startled, for I had heard nothing about any such incident. Turning to Charlie, I looked questioningly at him, and he answered that he had given some gazelle meat to an old man who was hungry. The King seemed satisfied with the reply, while I was lost in admiration of his intelligence system, wishing that Washington might have one like it.

Finally I brought up the crucial question—"How about Marib?"

The King just looked thoughtful, so I launched into a discourse on the relative merits of the great Sabean capital and our Timna. The Imam interrupted me with a bombshell.

"Were you responsible for the plane that circled low over Marib without permission, and did you take any pictures?"

Without waiting for a reply, the King unrolled an official note from the Aden authorities, written no doubt in reply to his protest. It definitely pointed the finger of guilt at me, and stated that the plane had been a privately owned American aircraft. Now this last was not so, and I was upset. I was prepared to take full responsibility for anything I had done, but the plane had been chartered; it had an excellent British captain and crew, and a huge Union Jack was painted across its tail. The British authorities knew all this, for they had checked the plane and received landing fees at Aden.

I admitted being in the plane and taking pictures, but pointed out that the aircraft itself had been British.

His Majesty replied, "Hamdulillah." (Praise be to God.)

Finally I reached the point of asking specifically for permission to excavate at Marib, and the King replied, "Inshallah." This word, which literally means "God willing," can actually mean anything in the Arab world, from "Maybe so," to "I'm just trying to say no politely."

That ended the subject of Marib, for the King announced that he was placing his royal airplane at our disposal for a visit to

Sana, the capital. "When during the next few days would you like to leave?" he asked.

"This afternoon, inshallah," I replied, still so excited, so hopeful that in this case the King's "inshallah" meant "perhaps," that I forgot all about pictures which I had learned in advance we would be permitted to take. The King himself reminded me, and kindly suggested that we stand next to him for the picture, which should of course be taken with the new camera we had given him. We took our places and Wallace Wade took up the camera. Then we stood there and fidgeted while Wally tried to fit the film into the camera. It didn't go right, and we all broke out into a nervous sweat—except the King, who seemed to be amused at our embarrassment.

Finally the film was in place, pictures were taken, and with a final "hamdulillah," from the Imam, our audience was ended. It had lasted two hours and forty minutes, and we were told later that it was the longest interview he had ever granted.

This was encouraging but we all fought hard to keep from counting chickens that might never be hatched. Luckily, we were able to keep busy, for that afternoon we climbed into the royal DC-3, manned exclusively for some strange reason by Swedish pilots, and took off for Sana.

Even from the air the size and importance of this capital city was apparent, and we were all anxious to see it, for Jama had told us a good deal about it. Surrounded by mountains, the city lies at an elevation of over 8,000 feet and enjoys an ideal climate. We landed at its airfield, some distance away, and entered a blue 1946 Chrysler, escorted by Sami Ezzedin, who had been commissioned by the King to serve as our guide. On the way into the city we saw extensive wheat fields and beautifully cultivated orchards, with orange, banana, and peach trees. The city itself was large, with a population of more than 60,000. Inside the walls we saw the former Imam's palace of seven stories, and many mosques and public buildings showing strong Turkish influence.

The Sana rest house was even more comfortable than the guest house in Taiz. After a dinner that boasted four desserts, we were entertained by the local merchants who spread before us lovely rugs, jewelry, jambiyas, fezzes, kaffiyas, and cut stones.

The next morning we visited the so-called Sana Museum, which is actually just a storeroom in the basement of the rest house. Here lay a magnificent jumble of Sabean inscriptions and small statues. One statue attracted our immediate attention and admiration. It was a seven-foot bronze warrior in the Greek style, standing upright and dominating the far end of the room. It was made of the same material as our bronze lions, and had been dug up some years before from the bottom of a deep well about fifty miles from Sana.

I found it difficult to keep my mind from rushing back to Taiz and the deliberations of the Imam as to our request to work in Marib. But we greatly enjoyed a delightful audience with the Yemen minister of foreign affairs, Prince Seif Al Islam Abdullah. This handsome Prince is one of the few Yemenis who is well traveled, having spent several months in the United States, England, and France. Before we left, the Prince presented me with Arabic copies of two books on the history of Yemen, written more than a thousand years ago.

The return trip to Taiz was uneventful except for Wallace Wade's near disappearance through an escape hatch which he removed to take better pictures. Immediately after landing, Eileen and I went at once to see Dr. Tarcici to learn if the King had an answer to our request. We found him in an agony of composition, and the document he was trying to write was an agreement concerning excavations at Marib to be undertaken by the American Foundation for the Study of Man.

I was speechless with joy. We were going to excavate the Queen of Sheba's capital!

When I calmed down somewhat I realized that problems could conceivably arise in connection with details of the agreement that might upset the apple cart. But I was determined to see that nothing of the sort should happen. I vowed to cause no difficulties, to smooth all obstacles, while at the same time making certain that the agreement was fair and covered all essential points. The time to settle all differences is at the beginning, when everyone is in harmony, enthusiastic about the work to be done in the future. Half an expedition's success depends upon the terms and conditions agreed upon in advance. Our work and responsibilities had to be defined clearly. The King's responsibilities had to be put down plainly in black and white. Methods of handling finances, getting in equipment and supplies, had to be settled. Establishment of proper living quarters and storage facilities had to be decided. We had to make sure that our trucks could move where needed, that roads would exist over which they could travel, that an airfield might be cleared at Marib for planes to land. And as always, the most ticklish problem of all was the division of archaeological finds during the course of excavation.

Some of these matters could not be settled in detail until after I had inspected the site at Marib, so I suggested that one provision of the agreement be that with a small party I should be allowed to investigate the ancient city, after which an additional agreement could be reached about roads, living quarters, et cetera. This solved part of the problem that Dr. Tarcici wrestled with but not all. He sat down to draft a new tentative agreement, while Eileen and I returned to the guest house.

At hourly intervals Dr. Tarcici came with new drafts for my approval. Sometimes queries were brought up by me, and sometimes new ideas were injected by Dr. Tarcici or other advisers of the King, whom he must have been consulting.

At three-thirty in the morning I was asked to prove that I was actually the president of the American Foundation for the Study of Man. By this time I had to look at our stationery and documents to find out for sure if the Foundation even had a president. Finally, at 4:00 A.M. an agreement was produced that met everyone's approval, and it was signed by me and by Crown Prince Seif Al Islam Mohammed Ahmed Al Badr, officially representing His Majesty the King.

It began, "In the Name of God, the Compassionate, the Merciful—By God's permission, agreement has been reached between His Majesty's Government the Imam of the Mutawakilite Kingdom of the Yemen, referred to hereafter as the first party, and The American Foundation for the Study of Man. . . ."

For the first time in history the King of Yemen had granted a foreign concession for scientific research, exploration, and excavation in one of the world's greatest archaeological treasure houses—Marib, capital city of the Biblical Queen of Sheba.

My dream had come true!

23

ACROSS UNEXPLORED LAND

Our return trip to Beihan was made, it seemed to me, on a beautiful cloud, and I set to work at once preparing for the first exploratory party to investigate Marib. This ancient city was only forty miles from our headquarters at Timna, as the crow flies. We knew that it was considerably farther by any ground route, but we had to go by truck. According to our agreement, I cabled the King the expected day of our arrival in Marib.

Charlie McCollum and I spent several hours over maps, selecting the best route. One possibility was around and over Jaw al Kudeif, but although this was the safest way, it was by far the longest. The only other alternative was to skirt along the mountains past Nejd Mergat and then cut straight across the open dunes. This was the shortest route, but the loose sand of the dunes might be impassable except by camel. Charlie finally settled the question by exclaiming, "When K. T. Keller gave us these Dodge Power Wagons, he meant us to use them. Let's do it."

So across the dunes it was, though every map marked this entire area "Unexplored."

We finally found that we could be ready one day ahead of schedule and decided to move ahead. Eileen dispatched a runner, the day before we left, to Saiyid Al Kohlani, Governor of Harib and Marib, with greetings and the good word that we were leaving for Marib one day before our scheduled departure, as cabled to the King. By the time the runner returned with a reply, we were already on our way, so we did not learn for two days that Kohlani had said he could not permit us to travel to Marib until he received personal notification from the Imam, and he had not received such notification. When Eileen received this, she sent back the cheerful reply that "the matter was now in the hands of Allah, for the party had already departed."

And departed we had, with such feelings of elation and excitement as I have never had in my life, before or since. The agreement was one thing, yes, but here we were on our way to the Queen of Sheba's city! We were going to see it with our own eyes, plan the work of excavation we would do there. Unless you have had a deep dream of several years come true you cannot possibly imagine my feelings.

It was a difficult trip, to say the least, and something of a gamble, so I took only those I considered absolutely essential—Charlie McCollum to drive and keep the Power Wagons moving, aided by George Farrier, who would also serve as still photographer, Dr. Jamme to evaluate the inscriptions and help plan later work, Dr. de Mignard to keep us alive and bring us good will with his medical chest, Wallace Wade for movies, Ibrahim to cook, and Jama to interpret and take care of a thousand other things. We had difficulty finding a guide, for no one wanted to lead us into this forbidden region. Finally we had a volunteer in the form of a small boy from our graveyard site, whose parents lived in Marib.

Keeping close to the mountains while skirting north to Nejd Mergat, we crossed Wadi Harib on our left by eight o'clock in the morning. At Jebel Henu, Charlie faced an insurmountable barrier and reluctantly turned north into the great sea of parallel dunes, as high as small mountains. Our wheels spun in the loose sand as we laboriously climbed to the top of a dune, only to find a sheer drop on the other side. Then we would turn back, travel further, and try to cross the dune at another point. Again and again we were forced back miles out of our way, searching for passable spots. In each case we finally made our way over, although some of the slopes we descended were so abrupt that any other trucks would, I am sure, have turned over. Off in the distance, through the haze, I was finally able to make out an impressive mountain which I recalled from my previous flight over Marib. I knew that our city lay beyond and to the right of this mountain.

By this time our young guide was unbelievably frightened and kept assuring us, from wishful thinking, that there was just one more row of dunes ahead. Actually, there was a total of seven ranges of huge dunes to cross, and it was noon before we topped the last one. The speedometer had clocked over seventy-five miles while we crossed some twenty miles of sand.

I could understand the plight of Aelius Gallus, the Roman general who had tried to conquer the spice lands in 24 B.C. Misled by his Nabatean guides, he had met some resistance in the fertile Nejran, but pressed on toward Marib. Before reaching it he encountered the forces of the Sabeans, which defeated him after a week-long battle. And on the return journey, the great general lost most of his army in the never-ending sand dunes.

At about one o'clock we came upon a fairly smooth plain where we stopped for lunch under a giant elb tree. Our guide had regained some of his equilibrium and his sense of direction, for when we started on he motioned us down the Wadi Misela between two large mountains. After a short while, Dr. Jamme let out a yell and sprang from his seat to gaze at the first series of Sabean inscriptions we had seen—lying tumbled about on the ground. After stopping, we looked ahead and there, rising out of the plain in the distance was MARIB.

Directly in front of us were the ruins of an ancient building, with huge stones lying haphazardly on the ground, literally covered with Sabean inscriptions. In the distance, the town and part of the ruins of the old city perched atop a high mound, looking like the mirage of an American skyscraper metropolis. Off to the left a line of beautifully constructed columns jutted up out of the sand. We learned later that this was a temple dedicated to the moon god. To the right we could see the remains of the magnificent circular Temple of Bilqis (Mahram Bilqis). Moslems have always referred to the Queen of Sheba as Bilqis, a name of unknown origin.

This temple was too much for us, and we dashed across the plain for a closer look. We wandered among its well-preserved

His Majesty Imam Ahmed, King of Yemen, on the occasion of the expedition's first audience to discuss excavating Marib, Sheba's ancient capital

The present-day Yemeni town of Marib standing on a high mound of stratified archaeological deposits with a very small part of the unexcavated ruins of Sheba's ancient capital appearing in the foreground

round walls for about half an hour, with Dr. Jamme furiously
deciphering inscriptions. Finally, we decided that we had better
head for the town. No welcoming committee had come to greet
us, and I thought this was ominous.

It was.

As we pulled up at the foot of the present-day village of Marib,
we were immediately surrounded by a mob of silent, tough-looking
tribesmen and soldiers, covering us with their rifles. They were an
ugly-looking lot, dressed in blue robes, their faces painted with
indigo. There was no way out. We were surrounded and outnum-
bered, so there was no use making any strange motions. Their bel-
ligerence was somewhat tempered by their curiosity, for they had
never before seen Europeans or motor vehicles. One man stepped
forward for a better look at our trucks, but as he did so the leader
of the askaris viciously swung his rifle butt against the man's skull.
The others fell back, and Jama, obviously worried, asked the
askari, "Weren't you expecting us? Didn't the King send word
that we were coming?"

The askari's face remained expressionless. "No," he replied.
"When we heard the motors we kept looking into the sky for airplanes. We had orders to open fire with machine guns. You are
our prisoners."

Jama and I were finally taken away, while the others remained
under guard. We were led up a steep trail into an ominous fortress
a little apart from the rest of the city. Here a black-bearded man
sat on a pile of rugs, and we both started in surprise as we looked
at each other. I knew him at once, for he had come to our base
camp at Timna for medical treatment the year before and I had
talked with him. His name was Qadi Ahmed Bakr, and he was
the local *hakem* or judge. From his expression, I realized that he
could not treat me with extra kindness because of our previous
acquaintance.

"What are you doing here?" he asked.

"We have permission from the King to come and excavate in
Marib," I replied.

He looked at me incredulously, so I handed him a copy of my
agreement with the King. He read it as if he could not believe

the words, then shook his head. "I cannot believe it," he said. "You are my prisoners!"

We were all herded together into a small room with stone walls a foot and a half thick, while a dozen askaris stood guard over us. Hours later Jama informed me in a whisper that the outlying Obidi tribes were at that moment assembling around Marib, having heard that I had an army of trucks only a short distance away, coming to rescue us and invade Marib. As I couldn't do anything about this mistaken notion, we finally turned in.

It was not easy to sleep, for apart from our uneasiness, the guards had a nerve-racking system of relay signals consisting of screams intermixed with off-key bugle calls. When I finally drifted off to sleep, I was awakened by a soldier who was peeking under my mosquito net. Suddenly, out of nowhere, came a large hand to yank the intruder away, and I relaxed, knowing that guardian Jama had everything under control.

The next morning I sensed a change in the atmosphere when Qadi Ahmed Bakr came in looking worried. He earnestly inquired after our well-being and said he hoped that we had had a good night's sleep. Then came the explanation of his change. A runner had just dashed into town announcing the approach of the King's special representative on horseback. The courier was the King's own brother-in-law, Saiyid Ahmed Ibn Hussein Al Kibsi, who arrived from Sana with the news that we were coming to Marib.

We were immediately released and, at Qadi Ahmed's suggestion, went out to meet the distinguished visitor in one of our Power Wagons. He was mounted on a beautiful white horse, surrounded by guards. He had learned of our plight from the desert grapevine and had ridden most of the night.

In front of the tower fortress, the soldiers lined up singing while three trumpets blew a screaming salute. During this ceremony, Wally Wade took me aside to tell me that after we had gone to meet the royal visitor, one of the soldiers had grabbed for his revolver. Fortunately the grab missed, and George Farrier accidentally tripped, falling against the soldier and sending him backward into a bucket of garbage.

Saiyid Ahmed next made public announcement that we were

to be allowed a free hand in Marib on orders from the Imam. At this moment, Saiyid Al Kohlani, Governor of Harib and Marib, arrived with his armed camel corps and a large band of soldiers. His one objective was to arrest us and carry us off to Harib in chains. Now, with the heaven-sent presence of Saiyid Ahmed, everyone had a good laugh at the perspiring Kohlani, which did not improve his sense of humor or his fondness for us. A few minutes later, I was amazed when a tiny message was slipped me by one of Sherif Hussein's spies from Beihan, warning me of Kohlani's departure from Harib and of his intentions toward us. This little "intelligence boy," by his obvious exhausted state, must have run most of the way from Beihan. What a friend we had back there!

Despite the ominous difficulties of our arrival at Marib, I felt that all would be smooth from now on, and I could not wait for our first inspection of the ancient ruins.

24

THE QUEEN'S CITY

We were standing where no American or Englishman had ever stood and where no non-Moslem had been, to our knowledge, since 1889. We looked at the buried ruins of what had once been the largest and richest of the ancient cities of South Arabia, the center of a great culture almost three thousand years ago. And we were going to dig away the sand that covered it, push aside the veil of secrecy that had for so long hidden most knowledge of that civilization. We were going to excavate at this prize site where no scientific excavation had ever taken place. If you had told me that the mound in front of us contained a gold mine at which I could help myself, I could not have been as excited, as deeply moved, as I was by the prospect before us. In my mind I tried to picture the sand and debris removed and to look at the many streets, the houses, the temples, and statues that we would, *inshallah,* soon see. I tried to imagine what volumes of information would come to us from the thousands of inscriptions on buried stones in and near the mound. Timna had told us a great deal, but Marib could reasonably be expected to tell us many times as much.

At our first inspection it seemed to us that ten Timnas might easily fit into the area of Marib. The present Arab village occupied only a small portion of the ancient city area. Columns, walls, and pillars extended everywhere as far as our eyes could see, in an endless crescent. At one point, present-day Yemenis had already

The expedition visits for the first time the great walled enclosure of Mahram Bilqis, the ancient Temple of Awwam, dedicated to the moon god Ilumquh

The Hakem of Marib, Qadi Ahmed Bakr, in center next to exposed ruins of what was a beautiful ancient Sabean building until it was destroyed by the Yemenis to provide building stones for their fortress seen in the background

The first American exploratory party ever to reach Marib dam (April 15, 1951). In the center, Dr. Albert Jamme points to a fragmentary Sabean inscription mentioning two names "'Il'azz and Halak'amar." *Left to right:* Dr. Valentin de Mignard, Wallace Wade, Wendell Phillips, Dr. Albert Jamme, Charles McCollum, Jama Ismail with two Yemeni askaris. George Farrier served as photographer.

dug deep for the beautifully cut Sabean stones from which they had built their ugly fortress and portions of their houses. They had gone down about seventy feet through one stratified layer after another. This depth, when compared with our cut of fifty-one feet at Hajar bin Humeid, suggested that Marib was considerably older than the Qatabanian cities in Beihan. Inscriptions had already been found carrying the city back to the eighth century B.C., but there could be little doubt that it had originally been built some time in the second millennium B.C., when cities first arose in that part of the world. And it must have been occupied continuously for more than 1,500 years, or until about the early seventh century A.D.

The first explorer to visit Marib was the French pharmacist, Thomas Arnaud, in 1843. Then came another Frenchman, Joseph Halévy in 1870, followed by the amazing Austrian, Edward Glaser, who in 1889 sent natives far and wide searching for inscriptions. Early in 1936, the former king, Imam Yahya, allowed a Syrian traveler, M. Nahib Moayyad el 'Azm, to copy some inscriptions at Marib. In 1947 the noted Egyptian archaeologist, Dr. Ahmed Fakhry, who had been associated with our African expedition, carried out valuable studies and observations during a brief visit to Marib. And that was the story, before we came.

The most famous ruin at Marib is the dam, which was considered one of the wonders of the ancient world. It was probably constructed as Sheba approached its most powerful period, around the eighth century B.C. Lying a few miles from the old city it is really a series of dams, sections of which are still standing. Even today, after centuries of lying in ruins, it is a spectacle beyond belief. As we climbed over the first major section, Charlie Mc-Collum asked if this was what we had seen from the air with the Scaifes, but I could not be sure. In the distance, Dr. de Mignard pointed to another far more impressive section of the dam on the far side of the wadi. This spot was especially attractive, for at the base of the structure a fair-sized river was flowing.

We saw where whole sections of mountainside had been carved away alongside the dam to form spillways to irrigate the adjacent fields. The dam had served as the central control for the mass of waters pouring down from the mountains of Yemen, the spot from which it was distributed to create mile upon mile of green fields.

Most amazing was the way the great stone walls had been put together. Huge boulders were so perfectly dressed that they fitted into each other like pieces in a jigsaw puzzle. We saw no trace of mortar of any kind, yet we looked at portions of the wall that were more than fifty feet high, standing as they had when Sheba's great artisans built them about 2,700 years ago.

Other sections of the vast structure were missing, washed away no doubt by the great sixth-century cloudburst during Abyssinian rule, a catastrophe about which the *Encyclopedia of Islam* says, "There is hardly any historical event in pre-Islamic history that has become embellished with so much that is fanciful, and related in so many versions, as the bursting of the Marib dam—Sudd al Arim." The Koran, for example, tells of how "the people of Sheba had beautiful gardens with good fruit. Then the people turned away from God, and to punish them, He burst the dam, turning the good gardens into gardens bearing bitter fruit." Another old Moslem story tells of a King Amr of Sheba, who was informed by a soothsayer that if he saw a mouse digging into the dam, that would be a sign from God that the huge structure was about to give way. The King then went to the dam and saw a mouse which moved, with its tiny feet, a great stone that could not be budged by fifty men. And the next day the dam burst.

Many Arab historians have attempted to explain the downfall of all the South Arabian kingdoms as the result of the bursting of the Marib dam. It seems more likely, however, that the great days of these kingdoms had long since passed, and that the changing of the spice route from land to sea was the most decisive factor in their decline. There are records of leaks and repairs in the dam in earlier centuries of the Christian era. It may well have been neglected by a people already on the way out, so that a great storm or flood or earthquake could destroy it.

After wandering about the ruins for part of the day, Saiyid Ahmed offered our party a temporary dwelling in a stone fortress outside the city, which would serve until a satisfactory new headquarters could be constructed for us, according to our understand-

A section of the great Marib dam, one of the wonders of the ancient world. Original construction was begun about 2,700 years ago as the Kingdom of Sheba approached its most powerful period. The dam burst in the sixth century A.D. during Abyssinian rule.

Near these thirty-foot Marib pillars, called by the Arabs *el-amayid* (the pillars), a broken inscription was discovered giving the name of this temple as "Bara'am, dedicated to the god Ilumquh," the moon.

ing with the Imam. As we entered our building, we noticed that on the roof there was a well-oiled Model 1895 Colt machine gun, ready for immediate service. Elsewhere in the world, such a relic would be featured in a museum.

At nine o'clock, Saiyid Al Kohlani joined us, with his pock-marked son, who seemed to be quite an agreeable lad. Our initial bad impression of Kohlani was confirmed by his babbling about how "the Imam must be trying to impress America by allowing us in Marib." He was obviously part of the very strong group in Yemen that we had heard about, violently opposed to all foreigners and foreign influence. This group was made up of many of the saiyids, who looked to Prince Hassan, brother of the Imam and ruler of eastern Yemen, for leadership.

Kohlani seemed eager to speak to Dr. de Mignard, and after a little hesitation, asked the doctor for some potent medicine. He finally explained that he had three wives and his manly powers had been slipping a bit lately. Dr. de Mignard sighed and explained that unfortunately scientists had been as unsuccessful in searching for the Elixir of Youth as explorers.

Early the next morning we were taken on a guided tour of the Marib fortress. After we passed inside and through two heavy doors that were unlocked for us, we could hardly believe our eyes. For there, in a large room, stood at least six hundred ancient alabaster statues, standing in neat rows. Dr. Jamme almost trampled over the rest of us to get close enough to read the many inscriptions on them. These statues were entirely different from anything we had found at Timna. In the main, each one consisted of a large stone slab with two square holes cut deep into the center. Inside each hole an alabaster face peered out—some with plain eyes, others with eyes that had been painted black. This treasure house of ancient sculpture had resulted from superficial and casual digging carried out by the local Yemenis in search primarily of building stones. It gave us a hint of the tremendous quantities of valuable material we could expect to find with detailed excavation.

In the afternoon we drove out about two miles to revisit the Temple of Bilqis, and later examined the site of the high square stone pillars which we had seen jutting above the sand as we approached Marib.

These shafts of Jurassic limestone, though partially buried in the sand, towered above us at least thirty feet. Even if they did not go very far down—and they probably did—we knew that the moon god in Marib had been worshipped in a temple of real magnificence. Nearby Dr. Jamme discovered a broken inscription giving the name of this temple as "Bara'an, dedicated to the god Ilumquh," the moon.

As if this were not provocative enough, a blue-painted warrior pointed to a huge sand dune in the distance and said, "It has been told us from generation to generation that once a beautiful alabaster city stood there, only to be buried in one night by the worst sandstorm that Allah ever visited upon the world." If true, what a Sabean Pompeii awaits some future archaeologist!

About an hour later, Charlie parked the "reconn" car near the spot where Dr. Jamme had first examined the tumbled Sabean inscriptions the day of our arrival. Climbing up the steep mountain, which borders the pass on the left as one enters the Marib district, we came upon one ruin after another. The high crest of land on either side of the pass was lined with small circular tombs, similar to some I had examined four years before in Sinai.

Wallace Wade, who was feeling under the weather, fell near the summit, cutting himself badly while trying to save his Speed Graphic. I stayed with him while Charlie and Dr. de Mignard went on ahead to investigate a thin shaft of stone protruding from the sand about half a mile away. In about fifteen minutes I heard two shots, then a space followed by two more shots. This signal meant that they had found something well worth another climb and a walk. I told Wally to sit this one out while I went to have a look.

One glance and I fanned off my shots signaling for Wally, for he wouldn't want to miss this no matter how badly he felt. Near the top of the delicate stone shaft was a beautifully carved circular sun with a crescent moon, while below was a long Sabean inscription in perfectly chiseled characters. For some twenty-five hundred years this graceful stone pillar had stood guard above

the sands near Marib as a kind of memorial of the many other
columns and walls that lay buried below.

That evening was spent in talk and plans and dreams about
Marib. We who had seen many an imposing ancient site were
somewhat awed by the Queen of Sheba's city. The obvious wealth
of inscriptions made us hope that we would learn a great deal
about the habits and customs and daily lives of the people of
ancient Sheba. We knew a little about them already, but just
enough to make us want to know more. From our work at Timna
and other studies, we knew that the Queen of Sheba's people were
of medium build, with fair complexions and short straight noses
like the Yemenis of today. They were exceptional artisans and true
engineering geniuses, going so far as to build not only the great
dam but to quarry translucent alabaster in thin sheets for windows in their multi-storied houses. The spice route riches brought
them a standard of luxurious living inconceivable to the poverty-
stricken South Arabian Bedouins of today. Like nearly all Semitic peoples they worshipped the moon, the sun, and the morning star. The chief god, the moon, was a male deity symbolized
by the bull, and we found many carved bulls' heads, with drains
for the blood of sacrificed animals. We even knew from ancient
writers some of the social customs of Sheba's people—that, for instance, a man's wife was made available to her husband's father,
brothers, uncles, and all men of that particular family.

All this had been learned from work and studies that had only
scratched the surface because no one had ever been allowed to
do more than that before. We hoped to reconstruct an entire
civilization and perhaps bring to light the story of the Queen
whose visit to Solomon had made her famous for many centuries.
That was the burden of our talk after our first brief inspection
of Marib, although I had also learned just what the situation was
so that I could take up business matters with the Imam and his
advisers. Something would have to be done about a road, or
enough of a road for our Power Wagons to bring all our heavy
equipment from Beihan. Another track across the deserts and
mountains would have to be laid out from Sana to Marib, for
bringing in new supplies and equipment from the Red Sea port

of Hodeida, once we got started. Somewhere near the city a field
would have to be cleared for landing airplanes. Most important
was the construction of a proper headquarters building, for living, storing, and studying; this had already been agreed to by the
King's representatives. It did not seem to me that there should be
any insurmountable difficulties, however, so I went to sleep content.

Jama called us at four o'clock the next morning, so that we
could get an early start for the return trip to Beihan. We had
passengers, too, for Saiyid Ahmed was coming to Beihan for a
visit as our guest, and Kohlani was hitching a ride back to his
city of Harib. At first, we had thought of leaving Dr. Jamme behind for a few weeks so that he could start making latex squeezes
of the thousands of inscriptions available at Marib even before
excavations started. We could either send a car to pick him up
after two or three weeks or he could come to Timna by camel.
At the last minute, however, Saiyid Ahmed decided that it wasn't
a good idea. In view of Kohlani's unfriendly attitude toward the
whole expedition, and the number of his followers around Marib, Dr. Jamme might not be entirely safe. As Saiyid Ahmed himself said, anything can happen at Marib, and we agreed that it
must not happen to our Belgian epigrapher.

While everyone was getting into the trucks, a young Beihani
boy ran up and begged, with tears streaming down his cheeks, to
be taken back to Timna. I recognized him, and learned that he
had just been sent over by Sherif Awad to check up on us and
see if we were all right. He was appalled at the prospect of returning to Beihan on foot, so we took him along.

The trip back over the sand was simpler than when we came
because we kept the mountains close on our right all the time and
did not go so far afield into the high dunes. At any rate we now
had a pretty good idea of the route the road should follow from
Timna to Marib. Kohlani, in his efforts to impress Saiyid Ahmed,
insisted that we all have lunch with him at Harib. In that city I
realized that if I wanted, I could see the ruins near Henu ez-
Zurir, where I had first been warned out of Yemen territory into

which I had wandered a few feet. At that time I certainly never dreamed that I would be having lunch with the local Yemen governor at Harib so soon.

Part way up the Wadi Harib we stopped at a very high city mound that looked typically Qatabanian. We knew about the existence of this town, where King Warawil Ghaylan struck gold coins around 50 B.C., as described in inscriptions from Timna. To the best of my knowledge we were the first ever to examine or photograph this imposing ruin.

At Harib we were forced to waste three hours on lunch with Kohlani, despite my insistence that we must be moving along. When we finally started on our way again, free of the unpleasant Kohlani, Charlie decided that perhaps he could save time and many miles by going up the east flank of the Wadi Harib to a point where there is a natural pass over the mountains between the wadi and the Ramlet Sabatein. This pass, called Nejd Mergat, was once an important link in the ancient spice route similar to Mablaqa, with the ruins of a flagstone pavement between two walls that are still standing. Two years before, during my first visit to Beihan, three hundred tribesmen fought for possession of this vital pass and the customs post at this summit.

Part way up, Charlie climbed out of his lead truck and ran ahead to see if we could make it. Evidently he thought we could, for he came back and we started up. I was sitting on the outside at the time and not paying particular attention until I happened to look down off the right fender and saw nothing there—absolutely nothing. At that instant we began to slide sideways. I yelled at Charlie, "Jam on the brakes" and jumped clear, followed by Saiyid Ahmed and the rest.

The "reconn" car hung there, half on and half off the crest. While Wally Wade covered him with the movie camera, George Farrier attached the winch cable from the Dodge behind and slowly, ever so slowly, began rescue operations. Charlie insisted on pushing fate by taking the wheel again and guiding the "reconn" back to safety.

Then we had to retrace our route around the mountains the

long way. Thus we approached Timna from a different angle.
There, within sight of our mud palace, we came upon a high,
dune-protected mound covered with ruins—a site none of us had
ever seen before in all our months in Beihan. By that time, however, we were too tired to do more than wave as we went by, for
this had been a trip to remember.

25

FAREWELL TO BEIHAN

Eileen was out to meet us even before the engines were shut off, and there was no mistaking the relief in her eyes as she counted noses and found the full complement present. After we had caught our breath and a cold Coca-Cola, she told us how at 9:30 in the evening of the day we left, Emir Saleh had arrived. Eileen asked if he brought good news, and he said, "I am afraid not. A spy has informed Sherif Hussein that your party has all been captured and placed in underground dungeons."

Poor Eileen was shocked and immediately went to Beihan al-Qasab to confer with Sherif Hussein, who was extremely concerned over our predicament. He did not ease Eileen's mind by describing in graphic detail the usual fate of those interned in Yemen. He inquired if Eileen was going to notify the press, and she assured him absolutely not, and he assured her that he had already done so by cable to Aden. Sherif Hussein then introduced Eileen to a visiting Yemeni sheikh from Beidha, with the somewhat amusing suggestion that he should be held as hostage in Beihan until our party had been released.

While the rest of the expedition gathered around to hear our story, our artist, Girair Palamoudian, started to draw up plans for our Marib headquarters, to be submitted to the Imam for approval. Sherif Hussein and Saiyid Ahmed left for a dinner party at Beihan al-Qasab.

With hardly a moment's rest, Dr. Jamme was back at work on

his beloved inscriptions. Early in the second campaign, he had traveled seventy miles south to Mukeiras to record over a thousand new inscriptions from this edge of the Qatabanian kingdom, bringing his total for both campaigns to well over five thousand. It was the Queen's own city that was now his great goal.

I wrote a report for the Imam on my conclusions and suggestions after my inspection of Marib, and the next morning took an R.A.F. plane to Aden with Saiyid Ahmed, who was returning to his home in Sana. From Aden I flew to Cairo to meet my mother and my sister, Merilyn, who were on a minimum-budget tour of the Mediterranean and were adding Beihan to their itinerary. It was a pleasant surprise to find Karl Twitchell seated next to me, for this noted engineer-explorer probably knows more about Arabia in general than any other American. More than anyone else, he had been responsible for attracting the major American oil companies to Saudi Arabia.

While in Cairo I held a press conference at which I announced the signing of the agreement for excavations at Marib. This was an important part of my Cairo visit, for it enabled me to express before the whole world my appreciation to His Majesty, the King of Yemen, for granting us this concession.

Back in Beihan with my mother and sister, I found that everything had been running smoothly, archaeologically speaking, as the end of our second season's work approached. Socially and perhaps morally, there had been some difficulties. Eileen reported to me that a few nights before, Sherif Awad had come to her room very excited about something. But he began his complaint with a long and flowery compliment about the irreproachable conduct of all members of the expedition. Then he added that the Somalis were "disgraceful." He explained that he had just learned that Jama was keeping a woman in his house, had sent a soldier to investigate, and had found a young girl there.

"This is a very serious offense in my country," Sherif Awad said. "I want Jama sent away immediately."

The next morning Charlie got the full story from Jama, who was very upset, since he is the proud husband of two wives and the father of nine children and wanted nothing to endanger his sterling reputation.

"A local Bedu wanted to marry this girl," Jama explained, "but both her mother and the girl ignored the man's proposal because he is no good. So to ruin the girl's reputation, the suitor went to Sherif Awad and told him these vicious lies."

At Eileen's request, Sherif Hussein came to our mud palace that afternoon and listened gravely to the whole story. "I am very sorry," he said, "that you have had all this trouble while Mr. Phillips is in Cairo. I will stand by the expedition twice as strongly while he is away, for without Wendell, I regard the expedition as children without a father. Anyway, Sherif Awad should not have made such a fuss. Even if it were true—so what? Why are women put in this world if not for that purpose?"

Despite this rather cynical comment, Sherif Hussein's attitude toward women was as gallant and chivalrous as anyone could wish. My mother and sister got along famously with him, and the Sherif was in the habit of stopping by almost every day for English lessons from "Professor Merilyn." He had progressed far since the time when I met him, at nine-thirty in the morning, and in reply to my "Good morning" he had said in his best English, "Good night"!

As the time for departure and packing of all our specimens drew near, we planned a party for Sherif Hussein, Sherif Awad, Sheikh Ali, and a few other notables. But as with everything out here, good or bad, we got more than we bargained for and wound up with forty guests and an assortment of slaves none of us had ever seen before. Since I knew that nothing would please him more, I presented Sherif Hussein with one of our precious Power Wagons, with a supply of Goodyear sand tires, and his gratitude was overwhelming. After dinner we showed our movie from the first season, a big success and for most of those present their first cinema experience.

Five minutes after our guests had departed we were almost completely flooded out by a terrific hail and rain storm. Our chief concern was for the many cardboard cases of specimens piled high in the courtyard, ready for shipment to Aden. All of

us had been involved in the thankless task of packing the hundreds of items as soon as they were photographed by Chester
Stevens—a long and arduous task involving marking the cases on
the outside to correspond to packing lists, as well as careful packing of each individual item. We managed to cover the containers
and save them from the storm.

The next day Eileen, George, Jama, and I took off for Aden
and a quick trip to Taiz. I had to discuss and settle with the
Imam the points brought up in my written report. There, the
deputy minister of foreign affairs, Qadi Mohammed Al Amri,
thanked me for the Cairo press release, which, he said, had reflected great credit on Yemen. He also told me that several letters had been received from Washington and elsewhere warning
His Majesty about my activities, whatever that meant. I recalled
the letter from Philby and wondered once more why anyone
should try so hard to hamstring the work of the American Foundation for the Study of Man. Wondering if they could really
cause serious difficulties in Yemen, I must have looked disturbed,
for Qadi Al Amri smiled, waved his hand as if brushing away
something inconsequential, and said, "How can a stone thrown
at a mountain hurt the mountain? A little sand will blow off,
but the mountain will still stand." It took Eileen some minutes
of retranslating and explaining for me to understand that I had
been paid a high compliment. I still did not like the idea of
someone trying to influence the King against me. One stone might
not do much, but what if the stone throwers, whoever they might
be, kept at it?

The King was gracious, however, the next morning at eleven,
when I explained to him in detail the wonders of Marib, as well
as the best way of handling certain problems in connection with
implementing our agreement. He seemed agreeable to our suggestions, and we were able to come to an understanding about the
handling of money, which was always one of the difficulties in
countries using different currencies and with restrictions on the
flow of any currencies. As in Beihan, the workers around Marib
would expect to be paid in Maria Theresa dollars. I suggested
that, since the government of Yemen might like to possess Amer-

ican dollars, all monies we paid out in Marib should be advanced to us by the Yemen government or its officials and we would in turn give to the Yemeni legation in Washington the equivalent in American dollars. This idea was accepted with approval.

At the end of our interview, the King smiled and said, "Hamdulillah!" (Praise be to God!) When I learned, a few minutes later, that he had replaced the unfriendly Kohlani as governor with a member of the Imam's own family, Saiyid Abdul-Rahman, I too said, "Hamdulillah!"

That night at a special dinner party the power failed, and while Jama lit a lantern Qadi Al Amri, his eyes on Eileen, commented, "Even if we were in complete darkness, there would still be light in the room."

At five the next morning we left by truck for Yemen's chief seaport, Hodeida, accompanied by the new Marib governor, or *amel*. For several hours we drove through high mountains and deep, palm-filled valleys, cool and lovely. At several points, Jama pointed out extensive slopes covered with "hashish."

By noon the mountains were behind us and we spent eight hours crossing the deadly hot, dusty, and monotonous coastal Tahama plain. We finally reached Hodeida at eight in the evening, and never in my life have I been as uncomfortable from heat and high humidity, not even on the island of Zanzibar. We saw a bit of Hodeida the next morning but were not attracted sufficiently to explore it thoroughly. The city is made up of a conglomeration of mixed buildings including everything from ornamented stone houses to straw huts surrounding the inner walled city. The market place or *suk* reminded me of Damascus, with its long narrow streets covered over above to shut out the sun.

At four in the afternoon we were received by His Royal Highness Crown Prince Seif Al Islam Mohammed Ahmed Al Badr, Viceroy of Tahama. The Imam's son was about twenty-five years old and greeted us as old friends, smilingly reminding me that in Taiz he had been kept up until four o'clock in the morning to sign the agreement for excavating at Marib.

All at once the royal band, assembled in front of the palace, broke into the French national anthem for Eileen, followed by the "Star-Spangled Banner" for George and me. Eileen never tired of reminding us that she had been honored first.

When George lined us up for pictures, Eileen, fully aware of Arab custom, diplomatically stepped to one side so as not to embarrass Prince Badr. His Royal Highness graciously objected, to the extent that picture number one included Eileen on his right.

Later we were shown through the coffee workrooms of Sheikh Saleh al Jebely, brother of the Imam's agent in Aden. We saw women and girls sorting out the famous Mocha coffee on the floor, working twelve hours a day, seven days a week, for twenty cents per day.

We were happy to leave hot, sticky Hodeida at four-thirty the next morning in an effort to drive to Sana in one day despite everyone's assurances that it was impossible. At the last moment, the new governor of Marib asked us to carry one passenger and, as might have been expected, five showed up to add to our already dangerously overloaded Power Wagons. For the first few miles we kept fairly close to the Red Sea, traveling north along the sandy coastal plain. When we turned inland and began to climb, things began to improve. The air cleared and it was worth being alive again, as we laughed and sang through the magnificent mountains, enjoying the clear rivers, the abundant vegetation, and the spectacular skyscraper fortresses on the highest ridges.

It was about five-thirty in the afternoon when, after going east up the Wadi Masna, we finally reached the top of the high plateau which levels off at an elevation of over 8,000 feet. On either side jagged mountains soared to 11,000 feet. We passed several walled towns along the plateau before starting the last ascent up to Sana. The last fifty miles were maddening because we had to stop every forty or fifty yards to ease the car over a small earth ridge running across the trail. The local farmers use this device to channel water from one field to another.

A few miles outside of Sana, Jama pointed to a monument of piled stones beside the road, marking the spot where the Imam Yahya had been assassinated in 1948. We reached the city gates at nine-thirty, completely exhausted but having accomplished the Yemeni impossible.

The next morning we were informed that His Royal Highness Prince Seif Al Islam Hassan, Viceroy of Sana, would see us at ten-thirty. This was going to be interesting, for Prince Hassan was the prime hater of all things foreign, according to reports, and a very great power in Yemen, according to facts. When we arrived at the appointed place at the appointed time, a red-faced guard said that it was all a mistake—the audience was for ten-thirty the *next* day. We heard later that those responsible for the mix-up had been promptly encased in leg irons.

The next day we had our audience with Prince Hassan, who was joined by his brother Prince Ismail, Minister of Public Health, both of whom listened gravely to our excavation plans at Marib. Although they were friendly and extremely polite, they did not seem overly enthusiastic. Prince Hassan inquired in all seriousness if it really would be necessary for us to construct new dwellings. Could we not live in the ruins we excavated at Marib?

At the close of our visit, Dr. Mamdouh Tahsin Fakir, a Syrian dentist who had joined forces with Eileen as interpreter, asked if I would like to meet his famous father-in-law.

"Certainly," I said. "Who is he?"

When I heard the name, a thrill ran through me, for His Excellency Qadi Ragheb Bey was a very great man indeed. A member of the Turkish diplomatic corps, he had first been sent to the Court of St. Petersburg at the turn of the century and had come to Yemen in 1914, where he had remained after the Turks were expelled. He had entered the service of Imam Yahya and had held the posts of governor of Taiz, Hodeida, and minister of foreign affairs.

Tall, dignified, and stately, this grand gentleman of the old school bowed low to kiss Eileen's hand in greeting. While sipping tea, he told us in delightful French how the first motorcar was introduced to Yemen. When he first arrived in the country he sent the car as a gift to Imam Yahya. Since the Imam was in Sana at the time, and passable roads were nonexistent, the car was stored for three years. One Friday morning, while the Imam was

on the way to his favorite mosque, Ragheb Bey drove up and offered him the seat of honor. A saiyid standing near by exclaimed,
"Your Majesty, are you going to ride in that Christian contraption?" The Imam slowly stepped down from the running board
and continued to the mosque by horseback.

Some time later this saiyid who had objected to the car went
on pilgrimage to Mecca. On his return via Hodeida, he became
very ill, and dispatched an urgent message to the Imam, begging
for some kind of caravan to transport him to Sana. Fortunately,
this duty was assigned to Ragheb Bey, who immediately sent the
car, which was in danger of failing through disuse. When the saiyid returned to Sana, he thanked Ragheb Bey with tears in his
eyes for saving his life. Ragheb Bey replied that he was not interested in thanks but in positive payment. The saiyid, believing
that a goodly sum of money might be involved, grew a bit pale.
But Ragheb Bey said, "Pay in this way—go and inform His Majesty how useful this Christian contraption is, and that it is something to have and to hold, not to fear." Thus the automobile came
to Yemen.

The next day we received an invitation from Saiyid Ahmed Al
Kibsi, who had saved us from prison in Marib and traveled to
Beihan with us. We visited him in his home, one of the loveliest
in all Yemen, and were served refreshments with his own hands
—a custom reflecting particular honor on guests throughout the
Arab world. We were joined there by a very agreeable young
man of nineteen, Emir Yahya, son of Prince Hussein who had
been shot after the assassination of the former king, and by
another emir of the same name, son of Prince Mutahhar.

While we sat and discussed life in California, Eileen visited the
harem, where she was presented to Saiyid Ahmed's wife, who is
the sister of the Imam. Eileen described her as "very sweet and
refined, with a lovely voice," and was most impressed by her fabulous personal jewelry, which included perfectly matched diamond
bracelets, necklaces, broaches, and rings. Even her hairpins were
tipped with tiny diamonds.

After this brief tour of Yemen's chief cities, we returned to
Beihan for the last few days of the season. I found that my mother

Rows of carved ibex heads, once probably the capital of a giant rectangular column whose location is now unknown. The ibex (*wa'al*) still inhabits South Arabia and in Sabean times represented the moon god. Dr. Albert Jamme believes it was of religious significance to the ancient Sabeans that the curved ibex horn held sideways resembled the first quarter of the moon.

Some of the approximately six hundred ancient alabaster statues stored in the Marib fortress. These specimens were uncovered by Yemeni workmen during their destruction of irreplaceable Sabean temples, palaces, and buildings to obtain building stones for modern construction.

Visitors' day at the cemetery of Timna. *From left:* Robert Shalkop, Sunshine Phillips (author's mother), Wendell Phillips, Eileen Salama, Merilyn Phillips (author's sister), and the Emir of Beihan

and sister looked as tanned as Beihanis and eager to start their trip back home by traveling with Bob Carmean on his next convoy to Mukalla, rather than going by air as I had planned. I learned later that Bob and Wally Wade had finished the trip in a state of complete exhaustion and, while they recuperated, my mother spent her time spear fishing off the treacherous coral reef.

The day before our departure from Beihan, Sherif Hussein invited all the members of the expedition down to his capital for a farewell party. We arrived during a heavy rainstorm, which soon subsided, much to our host's relief. Chairs had been arranged in a semicircle, with a glass-topped table in the middle. In the background stood a large group of tribesmen, predominantly Bal Harith.

When everyone was seated, Sherif Hussein dramatically produced a long document. Reading aloud in his beautiful Arabic, he extolled the merits of the American Foundation for the Study of Man and its Arabian expeditions. Then, while the movie camera clicked away, and George Farrier held the recording microphone close, Sherif Hussein pointed at me and continued.

"I am very grateful to you for your wonderful conduct with all of the Arabs and your friendship and assistance to everyone here in the Wadi Beihan. Because of this and because you have worked in our country, I would like to give you an Arabic name —instead of mister, sheikh; and instead of Wendell Phillips, Hussein Ali. And because you have lived with the Bal Harith and worked in their areas, you will be called Al Harithi. Thus your full name will be Sheikh Hussein Ali Al Harithi—Chief of Archaeological Works. It will be an honor and a privilege if you accept this name from me, and, to make this official . . ." Here Sherif Hussein stepped forward and placed a white headdress with a gold agal on my head and wrapped a gold-edged robe around me, while the assembled tribesmen fired in the air in noisy approval.

The first to step forward and offer congratulations was that grand old desert warrior and paramount sheikh of the Bal Harith —Sheikh Ali. He handed me a scroll which read, "Sheikh Ali bin Monassar Al Harithi, Sheikh of the Sheikhs of the Bal Harith, sends his salaams to his new son, Sheikh Hussein Ali Al Harithi, called the American Wendell Phillips."

I was so touched I could not speak. This was without doubt a very singular honor, rarely granted to an outsider. I had been given not only the title of sheikh but named Hussein Ali after the two leaders themselves—Sherif Hussein and Sheikh Ali.

Next the chairs were removed and rugs were put down on the ground for us to sit on. While Sherif Hussein and his tribesmen sat back comfortably, Ellis Burcaw gave out with some first-class cowboy songs, to the accompaniment of his ukulele. Then it was our doctor's turn, and Dr. de Mignard was the hit of the afternoon. He had once attended a magician's academy in Prague, and his deft sleight of hand brought forth cries of wonder from everyone there. Even the prisoners enjoyed the show through the barred windows across the courtyard, and jingled their chains in approval.

The next morning we all assembled at the airfield at six o'clock sharp, waiting for the plane to take us away from Beihan. There we stood for three hours in a sandstorm before learning that the plane was scheduled to arrive at six Greenwich time, not by Beihani clocks. Still, this anticlimax did not take away from the deep and conflicting emotions in all of us as we took off and flew away with a last long look at our mud palace, at the ruins of Timna we had excavated, and at the smiling faces of Sherif Hussein, Sherif Awad, and Sheikh Ali, our friends.

26

QATABAN REVEALED

We left Beihan with considerably more knowledge about ancient Qataban than we possessed on our arrival. Then we had known the names of a few kings, but even these we could not date accurately. Scraps of information from a few inscriptions were so limited that their significance had not even been agreed upon. Now we knew enough to fill the large volumes which will soon be issued by The Johns Hopkins University Press, plus numerous scientific reports written by individual members of the expedition.

We felt reasonably sure that the history of human settlement in the towns of Qataban went well back into the second millennium B.C.—perhaps as far back as the Hebrew patriarchs from Abraham to Joseph (2000-1500 B.C.). Our specific knowledge of the history of Qataban begins with Dr. Jamme's graffito inscription, carrying us to the tenth or eleventh century B.C., the oldest inscription yet found in South Arabia. Next came the period of the mukarribs, or priestly rulers, who governed Qataban for many centuries. It is difficult to say exactly what these mukarribs were, since they certainly ranked lower than kings but served as the recognized leaders of their nation. We know with certainty the names of only a few of the mukarribs, who ruled between the seventh and fifth centuries B.C.

About the end of the fifth century B.C. a mukarrib by the name of Yadiab Dhubyan was very likely the builder of our present South Gate of Timna. In any case, he was the author of the oldest inscription found there. Glaser's Arab scouts had made copies of a small portion of this inscription, while Kenny Brown discovered the remaining piece, buried outside the South Gate. His new fragment, which represents two-fifths of the entire inscription, gave the names of Yadiab Dhubyan and Timna, neither of which occurred in the previously known fragment which had, however, mentioned the sons of the god Amm—that is, the people of Qataban. It was interesting to find that this new fragment written in archaic characters also mentions the name Beihan. Yadiab Dhubyan probably made himself the first king of Qataban, or was among the first group of kings. He carried out extensive building operations and reorganized the tribal confederation.

The second group of Qatabanian kings extends roughly over the late Persian and early Hellenistic periods, from about 350 to 250 B.C. It was started by a king named Abshibam. We name the dynasty, however, in honor of his son, Shahr Ghaylan, who was the author of many known inscriptions, including several texts at the South Gate. To this dynasty belongs one of the most famous kings of Qataban, Shahr Yagil, who recorded in one of his inscriptions that he had conquered Ma'in, land of the Mineans, to the north. Professor Albright places him at the end of the fourth century B.C. This family of kings ended with Shahr Yagil's brother, Shahr Hilal Yuhanim, who erected the obelisk in the center of Timna.

There followed several kings who are not yet placed in any special dynasty. The last of these was Yadiab Ghaylan. It was in his reign that House Yafash, in which the bronze lions were found, was first built—some time late in the second century B.C.

The third main group of Qatabanian kings covered the period from about 100 to 25 B.C. Its first ruler was Haufiam Yuhanim, whose son Shahr Yagil Yuhargib rebuilt the tower at the South Gate as well as House Yafash. His son Warawil Ghaylan Yuhanim is known to us primarily because he probably struck the earliest known Qatabanian gold coins, minted at Harib. The latter's brother, Farikarib Yuhawdi, was the last king of this group. Several other kings, however, lived during the first century B.C., one of whom, Shahr Hilal Yuhaqbidh, son of Dharikarib, built House Yafaam inside the entrance to the South Gate.

The most important period in the history of Qataban fell between about 350 and 50 B.C., during the late Persian and Hellenistic ages, from which have come most of the long inscriptions and monuments. Then Qataban seems to have been, part of the time, the most important single state in South Arabia, with Ma'in and probably also Sheba subject to it.

Somewhere just before the time of Christ, the capital city of Qataban was invaded by an unknown people and destroyed by fire. Then a new kingdom appeared on the scene—the Kingdom of Saba and Dhu-Raidan, which replaced part of old Qataban as well as Sheba and Ma'in. "Dhu-Raidan" means "The One of Raidan," and may possibly refer to the god of Mount Raidan, a striking conical peak at the southern end of the Wadi Beihan.

For two and a half centuries there was the dual monarchy of Saba and Dhu-Raidan, which flourished in Yemen and had its capital at Marib. To this period belongs our Stratum B at Hajar bin Humeid.

The Kingdom of Hadhramaut absorbed part of Qataban after the fall of Timna. During the first century A.D. Hadhramaut and Saba were the most important states in South Arabia. It seems that through the Roman period, from the time of Christ to the fourth century A.D., Qataban had disappeared as an independent state.

One of the remarkable inscriptions found by Dr. Jamme reads as follows: "Yadiab Ghaylan son of Ghaylan, King of Hadhramaut, who built his city of Dhu-Ghaylan." Since it is almost impossible to imagine that this stone was brought into Wadi Beihan from Hadhramaut, we must assume the existence of a town called Dhu-Ghaylan, probably lying about ten miles north of the present Arab town of Beihan al-Qasab. We now have three inscriptions in the valley of Beihan mentioning kings of Hadhramaut after the fall of Timna. One was already known and the other two were found by our expedition.*

* An inscription studied by A. Jamme at Marib says that Nabat, King of Qataban, was contemporary with a king of Saba whom W. F. Albright would

The Greek sea captain who wrote the *Periplus,* describing a journey around Arabia to India about A.D. 50, mentioned two kings of South Arabia. One of them, Eleazus, King of the Spice Land, is identical with King Ilazz Yalit, one of several known Hadhrami kings of the first century. He also reigned over Beihan.

We know that the three kingdoms—Sheba, Ma'in, and Qataban —were all in existence at the same time. But they did not all flourish simultaneously, for the most powerful period of each came at a different time. Qataban, whose period of greatest power came last, has revealed itself to us. Ma'in, which flourished before Qataban, lies buried in the Djof of Yemen and the Nejran region of Saudi Arabia, thus outside of our present sphere of activity. Sheba, whose power and dominance came first, reigned supreme between the tenth and fifth centuries B.C., with our Biblical Queen coming near the beginning of this great era. That would be our next goal—to unveil Sheba as we had unveiled ancient Qataban.

date in the late first century A.D. This king is the same as Nabat, son of Shahr Hilal, who is mentioned with his son Marthad as king of Qataban in an inscription with late script found at Hajar bin Humeid in 1951. These Qatabanian kings reigned in Harib and the surrounding area of western Qataban after the Hadhramis had conquered eastern Qataban and had destroyed Timna between about 25 and 1 B.C.

Migration of "S" Tribes (Qatabanians, Mineans, Hadhramis) from North into Their Historical Homes	Before 1500 B.C.
Migration of "H" Tribes (Sabeans) from North	Before 1200 B.C.
Camel Caravans Begin to Be Common in Arabia	Before 1000 B.C.
Date of Biblical Queen of Sheba	About 950 B.C.
Probable Date of Earliest-Known Inscriptions from Qataban	Tenth century B.C.
Date of Earliest-Known Mukarrib of Sheba	About 800 B.C.
Yithamar Watar of Sheba Sends Tribute to Sargon of Assyria	715 B.C.
Karibil Bayyin of Sheba Sends Tribute to Sennacherib of Assyria	About 690 B.C.
Karibil Watar Establishes Monarchy in Sheba	About 450 B.C.
Sidqiil of Hadhramaut Founds Kingdom of Ma'in	About 400 B.C.
Yadiab Dhubyan Founds Monarchy in Qataban	Fourth century B.C.
Shahr Hilal Yuhanim Erects Obelisk in Timna	Third century B.C.
Yadiab Ghaylan Builds House Yafash in Timna	Late second century B.C
Shahr Yagil Yuhargib and Summit of Qatabanian Power	Early first century B.C.
Warawil Ghaylan Strikes Gold Coinage in Qataban	About 50 B.C.
Shahr Hilal Yuhaqbidh Builds House Yafaam in Timna	After 50 B.C.
Invasion of South Arabia by Aelius Gallus	24 B.C.
Destruction of Timna and End of Qataban	About the Christian Era
Description of South Arabia in the *Periplus of the Erythrean Sea*	About A.D. 50
Establishment of Dual Monarchy of Saba and Dhu-Raidan	About A.D. 70
Description of South Arabia by Ptolemy	About A.D. 150
All South Arabia United under One Ruler	About A.D. 300
Abyssinian Conquest of South Arabia	About A.D. 525
Persian Conquest of South Arabia	About A.D. 575
Latest Himyarite Inscriptions	Late sixth century A.D.
South Arabia Converted to Islam	After A.D. 630

A note of explanation with regard to "S" and "H" Tribes:

The Qatabanians, Mineans, and Hadhramis spoke dialects which were nearly the same and all shared the grammatical peculiarities of a causative and pronoun suffix of the third person in S, as in Babylonian and Egyptian, etc. The Sabeans spoke a similar dialect, but substituted H for S in these grammatical forms; the H they shared with Hebrew, Aramaic, North Arabic, etc. Their dialect is in other respects less archaic and more like that of the central Semitic peoples.

27

TROUBLES IN MARIB

Since additional funds, equipment, and personnel were required for the expedition to Marib, Eileen and I flew back to the United States to look after these essentials. Many of our staff had to return to their normal duties, since they had signed on only for the Beihan campaign and could not take additional time for the work in Yemen, much as they wanted to. Several stayed with us, however, and set to work almost immediately on the formidable task of preparing matters in Yemen. Bob Carmean became field director at Marib, and paid his first visit there as early as June 7, 1951. A bit later he was assisted by Chester Stevens, photographer, who added many other duties as circumstances required.

Charlie McCollum helped Bob Carmean get supplies and equipment moved from Beihan to Marib, then took on the task of representing the expedition at Aden, Hodeida, Taiz, and elsewhere, with occasional visits to Marib as well. He had to establish bases and ports of entry for our supplies and equipment, and arrange for ways by which they could reach Marib—no easy task in Yemen, where things enter from the outside with the greatest of difficulty and move about inside almost not at all. Until facilities were properly established, I could not very well send a major party to undertake excavations. Expecting that this should be done by late August or early September, I attacked the American end of the work as vigorously as possible.

As things turned out, I could have taken my time, although I was continually worried by the fact that things did not move as fast as I wanted them to. When Bob Carmean arrived in Marib, he found that not a step had been taken by the representatives of the King of Yemen to construct proper housing and storage facilities. But before he could tackle that problem, he had to build a road between Beihan and the ancient city of the Queen of Sheba. Our trucks could not wander about the dunes while transporting everything from Timna to our new headquarters.

Seeing that the Yemeni promises to build the road meant little, Bob finally obtained permission to do the job himself. He got together the necessary workers, equipment, and water for working in the desert and in fourteen days had laid out the best route from Beihan to Marib. Twelve hours later the first convoy of four trucks was on the way with supplies and equipment. For the month of July they were busy rolling back and forth carrying the motor maintenance equipment, food supplies, power plants, hospital units, photographic equipment, refrigerators, and other goods left in Beihan. Rains that came earlier than usual helped at first because they packed down the sand and made travel easier, keeping the dust down.

Everything was moved by the first of August, but there was still no headquarters for living or proper facilities for storage. Bob Carmean, Chet Stevens, Othman Ismail, Jama's brother, and other Somalis had to live in quarters occupied by the King's soldiers. They were cramped, filthy, and uncomfortable, and then some members of the expedition staff contracted sand-fly fever, so they moved outside and slept in tents. Eventually a house was turned over to the expedition in lieu of the new building promised. It was too small and in bad shape, and a body of soldiers lived there. But Bob installed a kitchen and a workshop, cleaned the place up as much as possible and moved the staff in. The soldiers, however, did *not* move out.

Even without proper facilities, Bob was anxious to get preliminary excavations under way as soon as possible, since our agreement with the Imam called upon us to "implement" the agreement within three months of its signing. Although moving of equipment and establishment of a small staff at Marib could properly be considered the first act of implementation, Bob felt that our position would be much more secure once digging began. Even if Yemen did not live up to its end of the contract, Bob was determined to see that we performed all that we had promised.

About the first of August, therefore, just after everything was moved from Beihan, Bob notified the new governor of Marib, Saiyid Abdul-Rahman, that he planned to start removing sand around the outside wall at the so-called Temple of Bilqis (Mahram Bilqis). He had two of our best Egyptian Guftis with him, Rais Gilani and Shater Ahmed, who could expertly direct the archaeological operations of a good-sized crew of workmen. When Bob told the governor of his intentions, Abdul-Rahman asked, "Do you have permission to excavate?" Thunderstruck at this question, Bob pointed out that the whole purpose of the agreement with the King was to excavate and that he would not be there in Marib at all if it were not to excavate. But the governor, or amel as he is called, would not grant permission without special word from the Imam. It was the old story we had already run into so often before in Yemen. Official documents, even when executed by the King himself, meant little. Local officials had to get specific permission all over again.

For three weeks Bob waited for permission to begin work at the temple. He repaired trucks, tried to improve the living quarters, explored the surrounding country while he waited and waited. Finally permission arrived from Taiz. But by that time the rains had started full force and a raging flood tore down through the wadi and around the ancient ruins of the dam. During the next forty days the water rose eight feet. Trucks and equipment were on one side of this flood and the Temple of Bilqis on the other side. Bob cabled the King this information, the first of many cables, to none of which he received any answer.

The flood could not stop Bob, however. He finally managed to tow and winch the trucks and equipment across the torrent so that excavations began at the Temple of Bilqis at the end of August. Enter, at this point, the two gentlemen who were, more than anyone else, responsible for later developments at Marib. They were Qadi Zeid Inan and his assistant, Nagib Muhsin, special representatives of Prince Hassan, Viceroy of Sana and virtual ruler of eastern Yemen. Were they the "official representatives" of the King as mentioned in the signed agreement? Or was Abdul-Rahman, the King's relative who had been appointed governor or amel of Marib shortly after the agreement? Those were questions that no one could ever answer—not even Qadi Zeid Inan or Abdul-Rahman. Since these two gentlemen rarely agreed on anything, including the extent of their authority, and each frequently countermanded the orders of the other, Bob Carmean found it difficult to take a step without breaking somebody's rules, although he exercised superhuman patience trying to keep everything going smoothly.

The Amel was, actually, comparatively friendly and co-operative. He did not see that Yemeni obligations were fulfilled, it is true, and he hesitated to move without personal word from the King at every turn. But he did seem to understand that our general purpose was to excavate ancient ruins at Marib and that the people best qualified to carry out this work were the staff of the expedition. Up to the first of September, Bob's troubles had come chiefly from inertia on the part of Yemeni officials. They didn't build roads or houses or storage buildings, but they did not interfere actively. Qadi Zeid Inan, on the other hand, could not be accused of laziness. He stepped right in and did things—the wrong things.

He started mildly enough, however. When Bob Carmean wanted to begin excavating at the Temple of Bilqis, he placed an order for local workers with Zeid Inan, as he was supposed to do; the agreement called for all negotiations between Yemeni workers and the expedition to be carried on through a representative of the King. Bob told Zeid Inan that he needed about eight men and twenty boys to get started, and that he would gradually increase the force as men were trained. The next day Zeid Inan appeared with a total of seven workers, and said that no more could be found. Bob knew this was ridiculous since there were scores of men and boys in the village eager for work to commence. He sent Othman Ismail to the village, and he had no difficulty at all in rounding up all the workers Bob needed, then or later, when they eventually had 121 men and boys, plus sixty oxen on the job at one time.

When work started, Bob found that he was also to have the King's appointed labor foreman in charge of laborers—one Abdul-Rahman Ghadi, not to be confused with the governor of similar name. This man began to change working crews around each week, thereby disrupting the work regularly and costing the expedition considerably more money with loss of effective time. Just as soon as a group of men were trained fairly well by the Egyptian archaeological specialists, Rais Gilani and Shater Ahmed, they would be switched by the foreman to a different job, and the business of training would have to start all over again. Some time later, Bob heard that if he had put the foreman, Abdul-Rahman Ghadi, on the expedition's payroll in addition to his being in the King's pay, all would have gone considerably smoother.

The labor foreman found other ways of supplementing his salary, however, when Bob failed to bribe him. He just deducted a certain amount of money from each worker's pay. If any of them objected, he had them arrested and thrown into jail, fined all they had in their pockets, and then sent back to work as prisoners in leg irons. As prison workers the foreman did not need to pay them, of course, so he could collect all their pay. Bob was unable to intervene because the agreement specified that all negotiations with workers be conducted through the King's representatives—of whom the foreman was one.

Despite these difficulties Bob was able to accomplish a great deal of important preliminary work at the site, removing tons of sand from the ancient ruins, photographing and recording every phase of the operation, turning up countless inscriptions and artifacts which he managed to store safely somewhere, despite the lack of facilities.

Zeid Inan was active and imaginative in his efforts to make work difficult. He complained to Bob one day that the workers did not have enough water at the site. Bob investigated and found that he had regularly been supplying more than twice the amount used by the men. When he reported this to Zeid Inan, that gentleman said that the water was to be used for prayer—Moslems are supposed to pray five times daily, after washing themselves—and that water for this purpose must be stored in a separate container.

Bob promptly complied. Since the expedition had been working for two years only forty miles away, and had never encountered any difficulty in religious matters, we did not anticipate any in Marib. Because of the heat, Bob had allotted the workers two hours for lunch, and had felt that this gave them sufficient time for their noon prayers. But under Zeid Inan's encouragement prayers became so lengthy, and there were so many rapid converts to this idea of zealous observance, that it was hard to get much work done in the afternoon. Bob tried to take the wind out of Zeid Inan's sails by going along with the idea instead of opposing it, as expected. He offered to build a prayer circle at the Bilqis site. Zeid Inan countered by insisting that two trucks stand ready each afternoon to carry workers into the village for prayer at the mosque. This was going too far even for the Amel, who put an end to the farce by issuing an order that all workers pray on their own time. In this instance, the governor won and Zeid Inan dropped the subject, as fast as the workers dropped prayer time.

Work finally started on the expedition's headquarters, which were to be in the form of additions to the old governor's house they occupied, late in September. At that time, Bob Carmean had to go to Mukalla on expedition business, and left Chester Stevens in charge. Zeid Inan took advantage of this situation by trying to involve Chet in a quarrel, and finally moved himself and his belongings into one of the new rooms of our long-delayed building. Chet objected, since members of the expedition were still sleeping outdoors at this time. But Zeid Inan insisted that as the King's special representative he was technically a member of the expedition. So he stayed, Chet not wishing to press the issue until a serious quarrel arose.

At this point illness struck several members of the expedition so that excavations had to be stopped temporarily at the Temple of Bilqis after going on for only about three weeks. But it was resumed again shortly and things went along for a while without any serious incidents. Work on the headquarters building progressed at a snail's pace, with many interruptions. There was no work at all on the airfield and road from Sana. Zeid Inan and the soldiers continued to occupy quarters in our building, despite Bob's efforts to have the soldiers removed. Worst of all, Bob began to feel as if he were cut off from the world, for he had received no word from me. Not until the first of November did he get a letter from me, although I had written many times, as had Eileen. He had no idea whether or not I had received his reports to me, and, as I learned later, I did not receive all of them by any means. After serious trouble started in November I heard nothing until my arrival in Taiz. Cablegrams that Bob tried to send to anyone outside Yemen were paid for but were just not transmitteed, as we found out later. Bob began to suspect this, however, and sent any really important messages during December and early January by messenger to Beihan, from which Sherif Hussein was kind enough to see that they reached their destination.

On November 2nd, Dr. Jamme, who had been in Belgium for a period between the Beihan and Yemen campaigns, arrived at Marib. That seemed to be a signal for a heavy barrage of troubles instigated by Zeid Inan. The first thing Zeid Inan did was to show Dr. Jamme a manuscript he was working on, called "A History of Yemen," with the added information that he expected the expedition's work at Marib to help him complete his book. The next day Dr. Jamme started work with his accustomed vigor, and found Zeid Inan following him everywhere he went, apparently curious about the nature of our Belgian epigrapher's work. He was impressed, obviously by Dr. Jamme's taking latex squeezes of inscriptions. He made special note of the value ascribed to these most important reproductions of ancient writings.

Members of the expedition began to see what lay behind much of the action of various Yemeni officials. Like many nonscientific people, they had the idea that archaeologists are busy looking only for gold and precious stones. They wanted to be on hand when any such things were found. When commercial valuables of this nature were not found, they could not really understand the reason for archaeological work or the motivation behind the men who did it. Seeing that latex squeezes were considered of great value by Dr. Jamme and others of our staff, they decided that latex squeezes might also be of value to them, even though they could not figure out why. Thus began the demand for latex, which became one of the great issues as the weeks passed.

Zeid Inan asked for copies of latex squeezes for the Yemeni government, and Jamme, thinking only that he wanted two or three for curiosity's sake, made copies of two he was working on at the time. Zeid Inan thereupon reported to the Imam that the expedition was going to furnish a copy of every squeeze, and the King said that was fine. Thus, when Zeid Inan the next day told Dr. Jamme that the government must be given a latex squeeze of every inscription found, he said it had the force of a command from the King. Dr. Jamme felt that he had no authority to comply with the demand, which was a decision for the leader of the expedition, but he began then his consistent method of dealing with the ridiculous, impossible orders of Zeid Inan. He did not refuse, but on the other hand he could not comply. He made every effort to avoid a fight, a showdown, and went about his business as best he could, simply ignoring Zeid Inan when possible. Our supply of latex was limited and could never begin to cover all new inscriptions, let alone duplicates. Also, in many instances it took hours of painstaking labor under the boiling sun to make even one latex copy.

In addition to his work on inscriptions, Dr. Jamme took charge of the excavations at the Temple of Bilqis until the arrival of our chief archaeologist, who was then on his way from the United States. This was Dr. Frank P. Albright, a former student of but no relation to our Professor W. F. Albright. One day at the temple, Jamme's Arab assistant, Ahmed, told the Belgian that he had seen a beautiful inscription about halfway between Marib and Bilqis. He left with the young Arab to have a look at it, but they had gone only a short distance when Zeid Inan sent a soldier after them, ordering Ahmed to return to the temple at once. There Prince Hassan's representative informed the Arab that he was forbidden to show Dr. Jamme any inscriptions, on pain of being jailed. Zeid Inan thereupon informed all soldiers and workers that they could not show inscriptions or graffiti to Dr. Jamme.

Bob Carmean and Dr. Jamme both protested vigorously to the

governor, but were unable to get him to change Zeid Inan's order. They saw that as Zeid Inan's opposition to the expedition increased, the governor showed less and less force of will in withstanding him. He just did not have the strength of character to buck a person like Zeid Inan, who was acting for Prince Hassan in territory controlled by that brother of the King rather than by the King himself.

Zeid Inan followed this triumph by making more demands: free access at all times to Dr. Jamme's decipherings of inscriptions, a copy of every inscription written down by Dr. Jamme together with a translation, a photograph of every inscription found, and to top things off instruction from Dr. Jamme in the ancient Sabean language.

Bob and Dr. Jamme turned down all these requests, but in the most diplomatic way possible. Dr. Jamme pointed out, for instance, that he had no connection with photographic work and no control over the expedition's photographs. He also explained that he had come to Marib to study inscriptions and not to teach languages. As for the copies and translations of inscriptions, Dr. Jamme did not so much turn down the demand as explain his position, which was that such material belonged to him personally as a scholar and that the results of his work belonged to the expedition which had brought him to Marib. Its disposition was therefore controlled by the head of the expedition, and he had no right to do anything with it except turn it over to me. Bob further pointed out that the agreement specified that the expedition would submit to the Yemeni government "appropriate technical reports at the end of every period of work." This obviously did not mean every time Dr. Jamme found or copied an inscription.

Charlie McCollum brought funds for the expedition from Aden, since the agreement about having the government advance Maria Theresa dollars to be repaid in American dollars to the Yemeni legation in Washington seemed not to be working very well. While in Marib, Charlie took up the matter with the Amel, who agreed to advance the money needed. Everybody thought that problem was ironed out, anyway. And it was essential because the workers at the excavation had demanded increased pay in November, instigated by Zeid Inan despite our previous arrangements in Taiz.

Near the first of December, Dr. Frank Albright arrived in Marib and took over supervision of the excavations at the temple, which had been progressing well. Dr. Jamme took up with Dr. Albright a problem that had begun to bother him—support for the tall pillars from which sand was being removed. Dr. Albright thereupon put in an official request for cement through the Amel, who after a couple of weeks said he did not have any. Bob thereupon started investigation to see how and where he could obtain some, but decided that he had better start work on the future airfield, since no motion had been made toward building it by the King's men. With a proper landing place for planes, supplies could be brought in more easily. Without the promised road from Sana, the only way to get materials was through Beihan and Aden or Mukalla—roundabout and needlessly traversing the territory of the Aden Protectorates.

At the same time, Bob tried to push construction of the expedition headquarters, which stopped and started fitfully and even when moving forward did so at such a slow pace that it would have taken years to complete it. Bob knew that I would soon be on my way to Marib with a good-sized party and there had to be some kind of accommodations for us.

With Dr. Albright working at the Temple of Bilqis, Dr. Jamme gave his full time to copying inscriptions. Remembering the hundreds of inscriptions in a storeroom at the fort, he asked permission to take latex squeezes of these. Zeid Inan agreed that it would be all right, but said that the key to the locked rooms was not available at the moment, that he would have it "tomorrow, inshallah." The next day, Dr. Jamme was told that the key was in Sana. Feeling that he was just being put off, Dr. Jamme went to see the Amel, who gave him the same answer. The governor, at least, promised to have the key sent to Marib.

At this point Bob took over the problem and in two days got the report that the key was on its way. Two more days passed by and "it was coming by small plane." A week later—"the key had left Sana, but the messenger bringing it had fallen ill on the way."

Finally Bob and Dr. Jamme called upon the Amel and pointed out to him that he, Abdul-Rahman, was the governor and as such the King's official representative. He therefore had the power to dispose of monumental problems such as a missing key. Why not break the lock and demonstrate before everyone his authority as governor?

This appealed to the governor, so he immediately wrote out an elaborate authorization in red ink and handed it to Bob, saying the door would be opened the next morning, key or no key. At nine the next morning, the Amel sent an invitation to members of the expedition to witness the opening of the locked door, which would take place when Bob presented to the governor, in front of the door, the official red-ink authorization which he had written the night before.

Dr. Jamme, Dr. Albright, Bob Carmean, and Chester Stevens, with the two Egyptian foremen, arrived at the fort to witness the ceremony. After waiting an hour, they saw the Amel approach with twenty soldiers. Even after he got there, he said they should wait a while longer to see if the key would arrive. Finally deciding that it would not come, he asked Bob to present to him the written authorization. Bob did so, and the Amel with great ceremony ordered the soldiers to break the lock on the door. Dr. Jamme and Dr. Albright stepped inside, but soldiers barred the way to Bob Carmean and Chet Stevens.

For a short time, Drs. Albright and Jamme were permitted to study the inscriptions under the watchful eyes of many soldiers. When informed that their time was up, Dr. Jamme asked permission to continue his work the next day. The Amel promised to permit it, but the next day he said that he had written the King about the matter and would have to await special permission from him. It never arrived.

Dr. Jamme, who could find work to do anywhere and was happy only when working, set about studying inscriptions on ancient stones that had been built into some of the present-day houses in the village of Marib. He found a very interesting one over the door of a house, but two small stones had been placed on either side of it in such a manner as to cover part of the inscription. Through Bob, Dr. Jamme asked the governor's permission to remove the two small stones carefully for a few minutes to photograph the inscription, after which the stones would be replaced as they had been.

The governor agreed, but before Dr. Jamme could touch the stones, Zeid Inan appeared in a fury and forbade him to do what the Amel had just ordered he could do. Dr. Jamme merely pointed out that he had the governor's permission, then walked away when he saw that it was useless to argue with Zeid Inan, who immediately cabled the King in Taiz that Dr. Jamme was "tearing down the houses of Marib." This was one of the reports that confronted me for the first time when I landed in Yemen.

Dr. Jamme then decided that he could study the inscriptions that had been exposed on some of the walls and pillars at Bilqis, so he and Chester Stevens left headquarters to walk to the temple, where they worked that day. But in the evening Bob was called before Zeid Inan and the Amel, who said that Dr. Jamme and Chet had not informed Zeid before they went to Bilqis. Bob said there was nothing in the agreement restricting their movements within the territory around Marib, but Zeid and the Amel ordered that henceforth no expedition member would leave headquarters without telling Zeid where he was going and no one could go anywhere without at least one soldier along. Bob followed his customary diplomatic tactic of welcoming what Zeid thought would make him furious, but in this instance the Yemenis must have been infuriated at the reasoning behind Bob's acceptance of the new order. He said that Zeid and the Amel had just officially confirmed reports that he had long heard throughout Arabia about lack of security in Yemen and that he was glad to have soldiers protect the lives of expedition members from the lawless Bedu around Marib.

One reason for placing such restrictions on Dr. Jamme was that Zeid Inan, who still tried to follow the Belgian everywhere, could not keep up with the vigorous epigrapher when he started to walk across the sands. Dr. Jamme was always happy when he could shake Zeid and his assistant, Nagib Muhsin, because once they had insisted on rolling over a stone with an inscription, without protecting it with the pieces of wood Dr. Jamme had brought along. Thus about twenty letters were badly scratched. Another time Jamme and his Arab assistant, with the required soldiers, went out in a truck to make latex squeezes of twenty inscriptions. After working all day in the boiling sun, they were stopped on their return by a soldier who made Dr. Jamme take out all the squeezes and unroll them in the sand for inspection.

Meanwhile Zeid had insisted that all stones and artifacts found by the expedition be put in a storeroom to which he would hold the key. Bob got out a copy of the agreement between the Imam and the Foundation and pointed out the clause requiring the Foundation to "take the necessary steps to organize and safeguard whatever is found." But Zeid would pay no attention and Bob was forced to comply. Next came the order that all of Dr. Jamme's latex squeezes be put in a case and placed in the storeroom. Dr. Jamme could hold the key to the case, Zeid said, but Bob and Dr. Jamme both pointed out that this would mean little if the case was in a storeroom whose key was held by Zeid, who also placed soldiers at the door to guard it. Two days later, on December 18, Dr. Jamme was commanded by Zeid Inan to cease all work of every kind.

Bob Carmean went to the Amel at once and the next day procured from the governor written permission for Dr. Jamme to work again. But then Bob himself got in trouble. The Arab grease boy who worked on the trucks had been arrested and fined four times by Zeid Inan for riding on the Power Wagons he helped take care of. Bob paid his fine every time and the fourth time went to see the governor about the matter. The Amel said Bob could keep the boy and he could ride on our trucks, but the next day Zeid Inan fired the boy. Bob pointed out that he had the Amel's permission, but Zeid just scoffed and went back to Marib, reporting to the governor that Bob had hit him. Bob was called up before the Amel at once, denied hitting Zeid Inan, but admitted feeling like it.

On January 3, the worst blow of all fell. The Amel refused

to advance the expedition any more money. Bob had to pay the workmen, so he drove to Beihan to borrow enough for the next payday from Sherif Hussein, who as always was most co-operative. It was the day after this that I left New York by plane, knowing almost nothing of what had been going on. So few reports had been allowed to reach me that I knew only that work promised by the Yemenis had in the main not been performed, that Bob had gone through numerous difficulties, but that excavations at the Temple of Bilqis were moving ahead very satisfactorily. Beyond that—nothing. Meanwhile, Bob and Chet and Dr. Jamme and Dr. Albright hung on in the face of hardships, insults, restrictions, antipathy, and stupidity because they felt sure that when I reached Taiz and could speak to the King, all problems would be solved. They knew that none of their side of the story had reached the Imam, but thought that when I learned the facts and presented them to His Majesty, I could probably obtain the removal of Zeid Inan, the chief source of trouble.

Neither they nor I had the faintest notion that it would be impossible for me ever to see the King again.

28

CONFUSION COMPOUNDED

Eileen and I arrived in Aden on January 15, 1952, and were met by Charlie McCollum and Jama, who had been there for some time, and by the new members of the expedition who had arrived two days before. These were Commander Charles H. Gilliland (M.C., U.S.N.), our new medical director assigned to duty with us by the Navy's Surgeon General, Admiral Lamont Pugh, who had been with me on the African expedition; John H. Scarff, architect and historian from Baltimore; James Rubright, archaeologist from Akron, Ohio, and the University of Chicago; Ralf Andrews, archaeologist from the University of Oklahoma; and Richard Bussey, administrative assistant and business manager, from my home town of Concord, California.

From Charlie I received more details about troubles in Marib, but not many because he had received few of the messages Bob Carmean tried to send him. If I had known the full story, I doubt that I would have taken the rest of the party into Yemen at all, but would instead have tried to get the others out. It's hard to tell, however. I might have thought that an audience with the King in Taiz would remove major obstacles. But, knowing only a very small part of the Marib story and expecting as friendly a reception in Taiz as before, we set out from Aden, arriving at the King's city without difficulty on January 22. All of our party, except Eileen and me, had official visas to enter Yemen, and we two did not feel they were necessary because we had always entered the country at the express invitation of the King. Charlie had taken care of the special permission he knew would be required by cabling the deputy foreign minister, Qadi Al Amri, the day before we left Aden, so we got through without long delay.

Rooms had been prepared for us at the rest house in Taiz, and we were welcomed cordially. The next day we had an interview with Qadi Al Amri which went smoothly and concluded with his wish that our stay in Marib be long and fruitful, *inshallah!* I was highly encouraged, therefore, and felt that any existing difficulties would easily be ironed out. Al Amri did mention a few points that bothered him and, I suppose, also the King. He was disappointed that I was so long in returning to Yemen, and that excavations in his opinion had proceeded too slowly at Marib. I refrained from pointing out that both these facts stemmed from his government's failure to provide facilities they had promised. There was no use, I thought, in getting into futile arguments about past events when the aim was to make the future pleasant and productive. At one point Qadi Al Amri, who is graced with a fine personality, keen intelligence, and a wonderful sense of humor, smiled and said, "I fully realize that Yemen is a backward country, but changes must be inflicted gradually. If a man swallows a big dose of poison he will have drastic results, but if he takes it a little at a time, the chances are he will survive."

I was disturbed by Qadi Al Amri's report that our friend Prince Abdullah, the foreign minister and one of the King's brothers, had visited Marib and been very displeased by the rudeness of Bob Carmean. The Prince had requested the King to expel Bob from Yemen, but the Imam had ignored this as completely as he had ignored Bob's cables. I learned later that Bob had been in Aden on business at the time of this visit and had not even seen the Prince.

Later that day I received a startling cable from Bob in Marib. After my arrival in the country, wireless officials apparently decided they had better send his messages. The cable read as follows:

YEMENI WORKER KNOCKED ASIDE PILLAR SUPPORT AT TEMPLE
CAUSING CHAIN REACTION SIX PILLARS FELL STOP OUR EGYPTIAN

FOREMAN RAIS GILANI ALMOST KILLED STOP GOVERNOR MARIB
BLAMES DR JAMME FOR INCIDENT ALTHOUGH JAMME MILES AWAY
AT TIME STOP JAMME NOW HELD VIRTUAL PRISONER MARIB STOP
CHESTER ARRESTED BY GOVERNOR FALSELY ACCUSED OF THREATENING
LIVES YEMENI WORKERS STOP PRINCE HASSANS REPRESENTATIVE QADI
ZEID INAN DEMANDS JAMMES RUBBER LATEX COPIES OF INSCRIPTIONS
STOP ALL ARCHAEOLOGICAL SPECIMENS TAKEN FROM DR ALBRIGHT
AND LOCKED UP GOVERNOR HOLDS KEY STOP SOLDIERS CONSTANTLY
STEALING FOOD ARTICLES FROM EXPEDITION HEADQUARTERS STOP
PLEASE COME URGENTLY FEAR SITUATION GETTING OUT OF HAND.

Here was the story behind this cable, as I learned it later. Dr.
Albright had become increasingly concerned about the pillars and
had stopped digging in front of them, transferring workers and
oxen inside the old temple. Unable to get cement anywhere, he
finally resorted to wood, although wood is not too satisfactory, especially the limited amount available around Marib. Bob Carmean
had got hold of the straightest and longest poles he could, and
set to work putting up braces against the pillars with poor bases.
But after one day's work, he found that servants of the Amel had
come and taken all the best of the remaining poles for use in the
Amel's own house.

Finally on January 15, the day I had arrived in Aden, a Yemeni workman backed into one of the wood supports and dislodged
it. The pillar swayed and finally fell against the next pillar, and
so on until six pillars had fallen, some of them breaking as they
landed. Rais Gilani had been standing near the first pillar that
fell. He shouted a warning, and all workers ran, but Rais Gilani
himself, in order to escape being hurt, had to jump from a high
wall. He badly sprained one ankle and hurt his side in the process.
There was only one other injury. A Yemeni boy had banged into
something while running away, and cut his head, but that was
easily fixed.

It was a most unfortunate accident which would never have occurred if the expedition had been able to bring in cement when
it was requested, or been allowed to bring it in over roads that
should have been built. As it was, however, all the pillars could
be restored, and no one was critically injured. The incident gave

Zeid Inan and the Amel a wonderful excuse to cause more trouble, and they took it. Just why they heaped all the blame on Dr. Jamme was bewildering, for he had finally been ordered to stop all work on January 12, three days before the falling of the pillars, and was confined to the headquarters building. Moreover, he had had nothing to do with the excavations at the temple since Dr. Albright arrived on December 2. Still, the blame was put upon Dr. Jamme because he had become the butt of most of the attacks of Zeid Inan, with almost as many directed at Bob Carmean. Dr. Albright had managed to escape most unpleasantness. The reasons became clear only later, when I saw that Zeid had been conducting a carefully planned campaign. He wanted to build up such a strong case against one important member of the expedition that any action against that man would later sound justifiable to the Imam. Dr. Jamme happened to be the one because he was the first prominent scholar to arrive at Marib.

As for the other items in Bob's cable, I learned that Chester's so-called threats against workers were as nonexistent as Bob's striking of Zeid Inan and his insult to Prince Abdullah by long distance. The latex problem and locking up of specimens were both old stories by this time, but new to me, as Bob realized. Apparently the stealing of supplies by Yemeni soldiers was an old story, too, which Bob had not bothered to mention because he considered it inevitable with such soldiers living in the expedition headquarters.

After receiving the cable I went at once to Qadi Al Amri and read it to him. He took rapid notes in Arabic, looked disturbed, and then with his most reassuring smile told me not to be alarmed, that everything would be all right now that we were together again.

Several days passed, however, without anything happening. I still could not gain my requested audience with the Imam, but set this down to the usual delays and my own impatience to get to Marib. I finally sent a message to the Imam saying that if it were inconvenient for him to see me at this time I might go on to Marib, with his permission, and come back later to discuss affairs with him. No answer. Meanwhile, I was somewhat disturbed by the fact that, while our members were allowed limited sight-seeing around Taiz, they were not allowed to take photographs as before.

One afternoon I received a cable from Bob in Marib requesting my permission to send an empty convoy to Aden via Beihan for urgently needed expedition supplies. He had the permission of the Amel of Marib. I checked with Qadi Al Amri, who said it was all right, so I cabled Bob, "Roll them."

Late in the day, Jama rushed up with another cable from Bob in Marib which read:

SOLDIERS ATTACKED CONVOY PREVIOUSLY INSPECTED STOP WINDOWS SMASHED BY RIFLE BUTTS RIFLE JAMMED INTO MY STOMACH STOP CONVOY RETURNED MARIB UNDER GUARD.

We were all shocked and within minutes I dictated a letter to the Imam informing him of this report and urgently requesting action on his part, as well as an audience to go over all problems at Marib. There was just one answer to this letter—an official-looking document in Arabic stating that our archaeological agreement was to be canceled in thirty days. No explanation.

None of us could say a word. We just sat and stared at each other, too bewildered by this unexpected blow to know what to do. Finally Eileen picked up the document again and began to study it carefully. Suddenly she spoke.

"This letter is already five days old and bears the seal of the Ministry of Foreign Affairs in Sana." She then noticed that it was signed by Qadi Al Amri himself, although we knew for sure that he had been in Taiz for the past week, not in Sana.

The next morning we all went to see Qadi Al Amri, who had called in as his official interpreter Mr. Husseini, a cousin of the famed Grand Mufti of Jerusalem. During the next few minutes we learned in no uncertain terms that the Imam was furious over my letter regarding the attack on Carmean and references I had made about my concern over American lives. I learned later that the attack had taken place just as Bob described it. With written permission from the governor and a cable from me that clearance was given by Qadi Al Amri, he had his trucks thoroughly inspected by soldiers, then set out. He had gone only a few miles when other soldiers stopped the trucks, broke in the windows of Bob's convoy and rammed a rifle in his stomach. The soldier in charge later denied this and insisted that a strong wind had broken the windows.

At this moment, I did not want to enter into discussions of the King's anger over my protest about the attack. Without a word, I laid before Qadi Al Amri the letter canceling our archaeological agreement. Al Amri at first appeared surprised and then pointed out for some reason which escaped us that it was dated several days earlier and postmarked Sana. No reference was made to the obvious fact that the letter bore his signature alone.

I decided it was high time for a quiet review of the situation, so I said to Qadi Al Amri, "These new expedition members have recently been granted visas by the Yemeni legation in Washington for the sole purpose of traveling to Yemen and working at Marib. A large amount of American equipment and supplies plus tens of thousands of American dollars have been spent in transporting everything and everyone to Aden, where an official invitation awaited the party to journey immediately to Taiz. Here, for five days we have been given nothing but words of encouragement regarding our long-range program of research at Marib. Then, on the fifth day, Bob Carmean's convoy is attacked and later the same evening our concession is canceled by a letter predated several days." And, I should have added, signed by himself, the very man who had been giving us every encouragement.

His Excellency was extremely gracious, as always, and told me not to worry, that everything would work out for the best. He wound up by saying, almost with a fanfare, that we all had permission to attend the "Eid El Nasar," or three-day victory celebration of Imam Ahmed, commemorating the beheading of those who had assassinated his father in 1948. While we were much more interested in getting to Marib, straightening out troubles, and getting to work, we realized that in this case "permission" meant "command."

The celebration began at sundown, with a barrage of firecrackers. The vast crowd of Yemenis seemed to derive tremendous amusement out of holding an assortment of lighted firecrackers in their hands and then tossing them at their nearest friends. When darkness fell, the entire mountainside behind the city, as well as the rooftops and minarets of Taiz, burst forth with kerosene-fed flames. These long tongues of fire, under a new moon, and with sound effects from booming cannon and the unearthly falsetto singing of thousands, created a spectacle that none of us will ever forget.

The next morning, dressed in our best *agals* and *kaffias* (head-dresses), we were seated in the special grandstand by eight-thirty, as we had been instructed. For the next two hours the wind blew a gale around us and covered everyone with thick layers of dust. It was after ten-thirty before the King finally put in an appearance and by then all of us, including the young British chargé d'affaires with his fancy "Lord Nelson" uniform, looked like something out of Kitchener's Sudan campaigns.

Before us stretched a large open square completely surrounded by a mass of Yemeni humanity, adorned in their brightest and fanciest. When the King walked into the arena, he was pic-turesquely attired in silver robes and surrounded by his picked bodyguards who wore bright blue and were armed to the teeth. A huge gold ceremonial umbrella shaded His Majesty from the sun, while in front of him and to the rear rode trucks with mounted machine guns.

After the King was seated on his throne, the program started with the Yemeni national anthem, accompanied by the waving of innumerable massed red Yemeni flags with their white scimitars and five stars. This was followed by several speeches praising the King, then gymnastics, and a foot race won by a Bal Harith tribes-man, much to the joy of a young Californian named Sheikh Hus-sein Ali Al Harithi. Although we had been told that all of us except Eileen would be allowed to shake hands with the King at the end of the ceremony, this permission was withdrawn for some reason.

Commander Gilliland, who was serving as our movie camera-man as well as our doctor, was especially disappointed when we were denied permission to take movies of any part of the victory ceremony. So we went back to the rest house after watching the

King end the performance with a ride around the square on a lovely gray stallion, with an amazing burst of speed at the end as he disappeared into the crowd. For two days more this celebration continued with slight variations on the first day's program. When it was over we were still sitting patiently in Taiz, while Bob and the others in Marib were desperately wondering what kept us.

Late one afternoon we learned that earlier in the day a large truck on its way from Taiz to Hodeida with full drums of gasoline, had turned over. This might not have been such a serious accident except for the fact that some forty Yemenis, eager for a free ride, had tied themselves on the back, many secured to the 450-pound drums. The accident took place thirty-five miles from Taiz, and the lucky ones were those killed outright. The rest were horribly mangled and broken. One man had jabbed his jambiya into his throat to stop his suffering. We got the whole story from an eyewitness.

I rushed Jama to see Qadi Al Amri with a note offering our trucks as ambulances and the expert services of Commander Gilliland. We waited all evening and received no reply. The next day I asked Qadi Al Amri and was told that we had not been needed, that everything had been taken care of satisfactorily. However, we all knew that none of the injured and dying had been brought back to the so-called hospital of Taiz, a place so primitive that foreign doctors are said never to be granted admittance. The injured could not have survived the much longer and pointless journey to Hodeida, so our only conclusion was that they must have crawled or been dragged into the brush by the side of the road— to live or die, *inshallah.*

During our enforced stay in Taiz we heard many stories from reliable sources, often from the people most concerned, about the difficulties encountered by all foreigners in Yemen. One European employee of the King had been sitting in Taiz for more than a year waiting for permission to return to his home in Sana. He wanted to leave the country, but the government owed him so many thousands of dollars that he could not afford to go.

The Imam had brought in a foreign engineer to build a radio station in Sana, but the poor man was ready to give up. For nine months much valuable equipment sat in trucks in Taiz, and every time the engineer asked about getting it moved to Sana, he received the answer, "Bokra, inshallah" (Tomorrow, God willing). When it finally reached its destination, it was almost entirely useless, from neglect.

This kind of treatment is not confined solely to non-Moslems. A Lebanese dentist and his wife came to Taiz, under contract from the King to set up an office. He was promised a house and complete equipment, but received such abominable quarters that his pregnant wife slipped and fell on the slime of the bathroom floor, where the water leaked, and injured her arm. After some time, the dentist received permission to fly with his wife to Asmara for treatment—there are only four or five doctors in all of Yemen—and I'm sure he never returned.

After several more days of waiting in vain for an audience with the King it was finally suggested by a high Yemeni official that I offer to charter one of the Imam's three royal Dakotas to fly us to Marib. I decided that was the best thing to do, get to Marib, learn all I could of the situation there, then return to settle affairs when I might be able to see the King. We agreed on the charter price of three hundred Maria Theresa dollars, and Captain Lund, the genial Swedish pilot employed by the Yemen government, estimated our total weight and luggage to fill his plane to capacity.

When this was settled, not five minutes elapsed before we were notified that five members of the King's family were to ride to Sana on our charter, and Qadi Al Amri insisted that we carry fifteen sacks of cement to repair the broken pillars. I knew then that we were approaching the end of the line. There was a small take-off area at Taiz, and Sana lay at an elevation of more than 8,000 feet, so with that load we could neither take off nor land safely, and I said so. Jarmoussi, Yemen Director of Aviation, immediately notified the Imam of our refusal to fly, and it was said the King took this as a personal insult to his family.

Early that evening a short message came from the King stating that it would now be impossible for any of us to go to Marib, and that we must all return home at once by way of Aden. This was the worst possible news, for by now my chief concern was over the safety of the expedition members in Marib. If I had to get out of Yemen, what would happen to them?

Charlie McCollum and Dick Bussey had already driven our two trucks from Taiz back to Aden to load essential supplies, including Commander Gilliland's Navy medical stores. They were going to convoy them to Marib by way of a road just opened between Aden and Beihan, which was barely passable.

I went to see Qadi Al Amri that night for a long heart-to-heart talk. He actually seemed rather disturbed by this sudden change, and at his kind suggestion I wrote an elaborate letter to the King about our cement and royal family misunderstandings, ending with an urgent request that we be allowed to reach Marib.

At five the following afternoon, Jama ran up out of breath. "Sahib, I have good news!" he said. "The Imam has just given permission for our party to fly to Marib and work for thirty days!"

Almost as interesting as this welcome news was the last part of the Imam's message. It was almost impossible to work out a meaningful translation, but it said something to the effect that reasons beyond the Imam's control had forced him to the regrettable decision of canceling our agreement. Since the King would scarcely admit that anything in Yemen is beyond his control, I had all our Arabic experts go over the words many times. Literally, the words said, ". . . the reasons were against our hope of co-operation as you know." That really meant the same thing, and made me regret all the more that I had been unable to talk to the King. I still think that he wanted us to excavate at Marib and wanted things to go well. Others in Yemen were just as determined that things should not go well and that the expedition would end, somehow, before it got anywhere. Foreign forces from Washington and Aden were at work, too, with certain advisers of the King being sympathetic, others unsympathetic.

Anyway, I felt better knowing that we could reach Marib, even if matters were worse there than in Taiz. I certainly did not give up hope of trying to smooth things over once I arrived there, with the idea that if problems could be resolved the King might extend our working period and reinstitute the agreement. In a discussion that evening, Qadi Al Amri expressed the same opinion.

Jarmoussi arrived late that night with orders to accept officially the numerous good-will gifts, gold engraved, that the expedition had brought the King from the heads of various American corporations supporting the Foundation. Thus we bid rapid good-by to the following: Gray Audograph Electronic Soundwriter, General Electric refrigerator, De Luxe Winchester Model 70 sporting rifle with Lyman Alaskan telescopic sight, V-M Tri-o-matic phonograph, Hallicrafter and Zenith overseas radios, ivory-handled Officer's Model Colt .38 revolver, Remington Rand adding machine, Brush tape recorder, Graflex camera, a case of fine Squibb medical supplies, et cetera.

Finally, on February 7, after an enforced stay of sixteen precious days in Taiz, we were ready to leave for Marib. Having been told to be packed and ready at 8:00 A.M., we were delighted that there was only a two-hour delay before a truck arrived for our luggage. At the airport, we climbed on board and so did the five royal hitchhikers, who had to come along even if the cement remained behind. But just then Ralf Andrews looked out and saw that the bags of cement *were* being loaded into the plane. So we all climbed out and sat on the ground in a large circle under the left wing. Jarmoussi ran up waving his arms and crying that he had solved the problem of the 1,400-pound overload. The expedition members would leave their luggage and personal belongings behind. They came to just the right weight, and it made everything so simple.

For the next hour cables flew back and forth between airport and palace. Finally, upon my assurance that Charlie would convoy a load of cement to Marib by truck—which Eileen had suggested days before—we were permitted to take off. As we raced down the runway, I wondered whether or not we should be grateful, but we managed to lift into the air just a few feet in front of the abrupt drop off at the end of the field.

The Dakota remained in Sana just long enough to deposit our royal companions, and less than half an hour later circled over Marib and landed at "Carmean" airport, the finest and newest airfield in all Yemen.

29

DANGER AT SHEBA

As we drew to a stop I was surprised to see wild desert tribes-men riding by at full speed. I thought we were receiving a true Beihani welcome, but Bob Carmean, who was on hand to greet us, explained that for some days a war had been going on be-tween tribes living around Marib and others living around Sirwah. The airfield was a sort of no man's land between them, and a good many wounded Bedus had been coming to expedition headquarters asking for treatment. Commander Gilliland was ob-viously going to have plenty to keep him busy whenever his main medical supplies arrived by truck from Aden.

His first patient, in fact, came to him before he had unpacked. It was the Amel himself, on whom we paid a courtesy call even before visiting our headquarters and saying hello to the other expedition members. Before the end of our visit, the governor, Sai-yid Abdul-Rahman, asked for an examination by our doctor, who happily complied the next day, giving the Amel some medicine for his preventable ailments and pointing out that he was looking forward to the arrival of his full medical equipment so that the expedition might offer its facilities to other Yemenis, as it had in Beihan.

Our first visit with the governor was, as we expected, a diplo-matic and social call devoted to coffee, compliments, and good wishes. The Amel was surprised to see with us a distinguished Abyssinian gentleman, Emir Soumsan, who at the King's order had accompanied us with the alleged purpose of seeing if he could arrange matters more smoothly at Marib. This elderly emissary had long served the late Imam Yahya and was, according to reports, close to the present Imam.

The governor introduced us to Prince Hassan's two representatives, Qadi Zeid Inan and Nagib Muhsin. We all had the definite feeling that Emir Soumsan was as little impressed with these two as we were, but we dared not put too much hope in results that might be achieved by the Emir. We had some doubt about the extent of his power and authority, above all in Prince Hassan's own territory.

Leaving Sabean archaeology and other problems for later discussions, we finally left the Amel and went to our headquarters, such as they were. Bob had had a difficult time finding room for everybody, and I could see at a glance that the preliminary group of the expedition had been working under great handicaps, without adequate living, storage, garage, or working facilities. Worst of all was the kitchen. Our Somali staff, who had never been known to complain about anything before, were on the verge of giving up. They could not even see the food they were asked to prepare in the black, filthy hole assigned to them as a kitchen by the governor. The next day, after our chief cook collapsed from breathing too much smoke, Eileen persuaded Emir Soumsan to come and see for himself. He promised to cable the King.

I was astounded to see heavily armed soldiers walking through our quarters, but Bob explained that this was normal procedure. Three nights before, he told me, some indigo-painted soldiers had entered Charlie McCollum's room, while he was in Aden, and shot his little pet Beihani dog in the stomach while she was nursing seven tiny puppies. There was no conceivable reason for such action, but the soldiers paid no attention to Bob's protests. When he went to the governor to report it, Abdul-Rahman laughed and could not see why Bob was upset.

"What is it like around here after dark?" I asked.

"We are all kept in at night," Bob said. "There are soldiers in some of the rooms, soldiers outside the doors, and a machine gun on the roof. The soldiers amuse themselves by beating drums and blowing their lungs out on screaming bugles. When they exhaust these possibilities, they resort to an elaborate system of catcalls between one another in the surrounding fortresses. In any event, we get almost no sleep."

The men looked it, too. They were drawn, tired, nervous, and worried, despite their excellent morale and courage. I was more worried at this news about the inability to sleep—which I verified myself within a few hours—than you might think. I knew from experience that good rest and good sleep are the basic requirements of an expedition in the field, as important as good food and water, and more important than good working conditions. After a sound night's sleep veterans of expeditions can face anything. Without it, the ground is cut away beneath their feet.

I was most shocked at the appearance of Dr. Jamme. He had always been our most energetic scholar, of prodigious physical strength and cheerful disposition—the kind of man I thought could never be discouraged. Now he was angry, bewildered, frustrated, and worried—and the strain was plainly visible. He had been held a virtual prisoner for twenty-eight days, after a long series of harassing actions on the part of Zeid Inan. Unable to do one stroke of work, kept from moving any distance from our headquarters, he could not understand what had happened, or why it had happened. It was Dr. Jamme who first advised me that the situation was more than just difficult—it was actually dangerous. After giving me a complete and objective report on all the incidents in which he had been involved, Dr. Jamme told me of his conviction that the lives of the expedition's members were in danger.

Things had been bad enough, he said, before the beginning of the recent tribal war, but since that time the force of soldiers around Marib, and around our headquarters, had been increased, and the soldiers themselves were highly excited, fearful of what might happen. Their fear had turned their feelings against the expedition into something approaching the violent, for they daily saw men in authority acting against expedition members. Dr. Jamme was convinced that the animosity of the soldiers had been fermented and encouraged by higher authorities, chiefly against himself as the chosen scapegoat.

I was truly amazed to hear such talk from Dr. Jamme, a man so strong and unafraid that he was inclined to minimize dangers and had never been known to exaggerate them. He gave me a recent example of the kind of incident which convinced him that the soldiers might easily get out of hand.

"A few days ago Dr. Albright asked me to accompany him to the archaeological storeroom since he wanted to show me something. At first I said no, because I did not wish to risk the slightest incident. I gave in only at Dr. Albright's insistence that I was forbidden to work, not look at something with him. He explained to the soldier on guard that I was only accompanying him, so I was permitted to go in. Dr. Albright then asked the soldier the whereabouts of a little bronze specimen recently uncovered. Zeid Inan had placed it in a special box under lock, which also contained a few other small objects and some little stones. The soldier gave the box to Dr. Albright, and we examined the bronze object. Not knowing that the stones belonged to Zeid Inan—for in that case they should not have been put in the archaeological storeroom—I took one in my hand to look at it.

"The soldier was furious," Dr. Jamme continued, "and ordered me to replace the stone in the box. While I looked at him in bewilderment he threw himself at me, with a naked look of hatred in his eyes. To avoid further action, I put the stone in the box. He then screamed at me that I had no right to be in the archaeological room at all and ordered me to leave at once. I replied, quietly, that I did not understand and that he should explain himself to our interpreter. Meanwhile, another soldier—the one who had smashed the windows of the trucks—had rushed in at the sound of his friend's screams. His eyes could not have expressed more hate. The first soldier, red with rage because of my calm attitude, asked his friend, 'Is your jambiya ready?' I just looked at them and then, without hurrying, left the room."

Dr. Jamme was most deeply insulted, however, by the recent effrontery of Zeid Inan in publicly questioning his deciphering of an inscription. I could not help laughing at the idea, but when Zeid Inan began questioning the scholarship of one of the world's

On Friday, April 9, 1954, at his capital, Beihan al-Qasab, Sherif Hussein generously presented two recently discovered Timna statuettes to the author on the occasion of a one-day visit to Beihan after an absence of over two years. *Left,* bronze statuette of winged, bearded deity of Dionysius type. An import from a Hellenistic center, possibly Alexandria (late third or early second century B.C.). No other statue in the round of this type is known, but the type occurred in relief from the time of the classical period in Greece. (Identification by Dr. Berta Segall.) *Right,* bronze statuette of a woman with a Qatabanian inscription incised across upper body. A stylistic discrepancy exists between head and body. The face and hairdo are copied from a classic Greek head. The body, flat, with only the faintest indication of detail, conforms to Near Eastern styles of the end of the first century B.C. (Identification by Dr. Berta Segall.)

Dr. Albert Jamme inspects extremely long latex squeeze of one of the eight monumental Sabean inscriptions running around the nearly thousand-foot ovoid wall of Awwam, the Temple of Ilumquh (Mahram Bilqis), the largest of ancient South Arabian temples. This inscription mentions the building and dedication to the god Ilumquh of a part of the enclosure wall.

foremost authorities on South Arabian inscriptions his aim was obviously the complete discrediting of the expedition.

After lunch, and a complete briefing on the situation in Marib from Bob, Chester, and Dr. Jamme, we drove out two miles to the temple, where Dr. Frank Albright was directing excavations. Even before I had time to greet Frank, Rais Gilani and Shater Ahmed, our two faithful Egyptian foremen, rushed up to me and pleaded to be returned to their home in Egypt immediately. It was impossible to continue working in Marib, they insisted, and increasingly dangerous to remain there. Rais Gilani told me that the week before one of the Yemeni soldiers had drawn his jambiya and threatened to take his life.

Dr. Albright's enthusiasm about the archaeological wonder before us, however, immediately cast all difficulties in the background. And I could hardly believe my eyes when I looked at what they had uncovered under thirty or more feet of sand. How they had managed to remove so much debris under trying circumstances I could not imagine, for they had used men and boys requiring much training even in the simplest tasks, along with oxen and Arabian-style scrapers. The wonderful Barber-Greene belt conveyor, which picked up vast quantities of sand and dumped it some distance away, had been in use only a short while because of the shortage of gasoline.

We saw an ovoid temple almost a thousand feet in circumference, its long diameter being about 375 feet and its short diameter about 250 feet. There was an elaborate and complicated peristyle hall and complex of buildings terminating in a row of eight tall columns. Here was the Temple of Ilumquh, not the Temple of Bilqis (Mahram Bilqis) as the Yemenis had long called it. The temple itself was called Awwam, and the god Ilumquh to whom it was dedicated was the Sabean version of the moon god common to all South Arabian religions.

The peristyle hall, measuring approximately fifty-seven by seventy-two feet, had once been covered with a flat roof surrounding a hypaethral court, with the outer side of the roof carried by a wall and the court side by thirty-two rectangular pillars. Frank pointed out an interesting series of sixty-four false windows of imitation lattice, in stone, along a section of the wall inside the hall.

All of the tall pillars were monoliths except two. In these two a taller section was placed atop a shorter one, kept in place by its weight only. No cement or clamps were used, except in later repairs and reconstructions, where a poor quality of lime cement had sometimes been employed.

Two doors led from the peristyle hall, one into the temple and the other—a large triple door with two massive pillars—to an outer court. Bronze coverings were used in several doorways elsewhere in the temple, but there had been no sign of the metal here. Dr. Albright believed that the doors themselves, and perhaps wooden door frames as well, may once have been covered with sheets of bronze.

A single entrance which was probably open at all times led into the main oval temple proper. The steps here had obviously been covered with bronze, for considerable green copper oxide had penetrated deeply into the stone in certain places. Actually the whole entrance between the massive pylons may once have been covered with a bronze floor.

A large and mysterious hole had been worn in the middle step and had been cut rather deeply in steps above and below it as well. All available evidence pointed to the fact that at one time water had fallen on the steps, like a fountain, from some place overhead. It had fallen so long and with such force that it had eventually cut through a copper or bronze basin placed there and then into the stone itself. From this point an alabaster conduit led across the court to a bronze tray bearing an inscription.

On the west and north sides of the hall, Dr. Albright showed us where there had once been some sort of shop or factory. The furnace and stone boxes failed to yield any signs of bronze casting, which was disappointing, for there must have been hundreds of statues, statuettes, and plaques of bronze in the entrance hall and court.

Dr. Albright next led us outside to see the main wall of the temple, which was somewhat kidney-shaped. It was about thirteen and a half feet thick, constructed of perfectly fit ashlar masonry,

Beginning excavation at Awwam, the Temple of Ilumquh (Mahram Bilqis). At the lower right one of the expedition's Egyptian archaeological foremen directs the Yemeni workers, utilizing teams of oxen to remove the top layers of sand.

This peristyle hall of the Temple of Ilumquh was once covered with a flat roof. Two doors lead from the hall, one into the main oval temple proper on the left, and the other, a large triple door with two massive pillars, to an outer court.

The south arcade of the peristyle hall of Awwam, the Temple of Ilumquh (Mahram Bilqis), showing an interesting series of false windows of imitation lattice in stone

with a sand and rubble fill. In places the wall was preserved to a height of more than twenty-seven feet above the floor of the entrance hall. Unfortunately, there was no way of knowing how high it had originally been or how the top was finished. Portions of the wall displayed variations in workmanship, indicating the different contractors or technicians involved and suggesting that the wall had been built over a long period of time, probably back to the eighth century B.C., although the sections we have uncovered date from about the fifth century B.C.

Dr. Albright believes that this structure may have been used as a kind of walled city after it ceased to function as a temple, presumably after the beginning of the Moslem period. The population would not have been very great at this later time, for after the final destruction of the Marib dam and its associated irrigation system around the sixth century A.D., the land could not support a large number of people.

On the east side of the temple, four small pillars had projected above the sand. Upon excavation, these pillars were found to form the internal supports for a mausoleum contemporary with the temple. There were eleven tombs in all, arranged in tiers three or more deep. The eleventh tomb was smaller than the rest and probably once housed the body of a child. Below the floor level, Dr. Albright showed us where he had completely excavated one chamber and more than half of a second. These rooms had been looted during the ages and supplied us only with broken objects— fragmentary human bones, inscribed tomb covers, a little pottery, incense altars, marble bulls, et cetera, plus part of a sarcophagus, one alabaster face from a tombstone, and one tiny gold globe, which had promptly been seized by Qadi Zeid Inan.

The region surrounding the temple showed evidence of having been densely built up in antiquity. So, in order to save time while the top sand was being removed by oxen from one section of the outer court, most of the workers had been transferred to the area just south of the temple. At first, Frank thought he was uncovering, in this area, a series of houses with each room a complete unit since only a few had one wall in common. But these structures turned out to be tombs built of coarse volcanic cinder block, with the outside walls facing the streets made of well-cut limestone. There were no doors or windows, except some that had been broken through the upper parts of walls at a later period, presumably when the tombs had been used as dwellings. Only a few of the tombs contained human bones, but there were many fragmentary bones of sheep, chickens, and other animals. While they differed somewhat in plan and detail, these tombs were essentially the same as those at Timna, where the bodies were inserted endwise into pigeonhole compartments from a central aisle.

I left the temple site to return to Marib feeling awed and inspired by the things I had seen from the ancient days, the earliest of which go back to only a century to a century and a half after the Biblical Queen of Sheba. If these marvels of antiquity had been revealed after a relatively short period of work, with inadequate forces and under the most difficult circumstances, what could we not do if allowed to excavate around Marib for a full season or two, with co-operation instead of harassment? I made up my mind that, no matter how hopeless it appeared, I was going to do everything in my power to make this possible.

That evening, however, my enthusiasm received a serious damper. Emir Soumsan, Qadi Zeid Inan, and Nagib Muhsin paid a courtesy call upon us. The first hour was passed in pleasantries, but then the real purpose of their visit became apparent. Dr. Jamme could go back to work, I was told, only if he made two additional latex copies of each new inscription discovered, plus latex copies in duplicate of all previous inscriptions. This was an absolute physical impossibility, as they well knew. So I decided to end the latex question once and forever. Dr. Jamme, I announced, would henceforth use only paper and pencil in copying inscriptions. All of our remaining unused latex would be given as baksheesh to Qadi Zeid Inan, who could now go out under the boiling sun and make all the latex squeezes his little heart desired.

Zeid Inan looked horrified, and protested that his sole concern was to facilitate Dr. Jamme's work, while Emir Soumsan laughed heartily at his companion's predicament. I let my announcement stand, for I had not been talking just for effect, and the evening

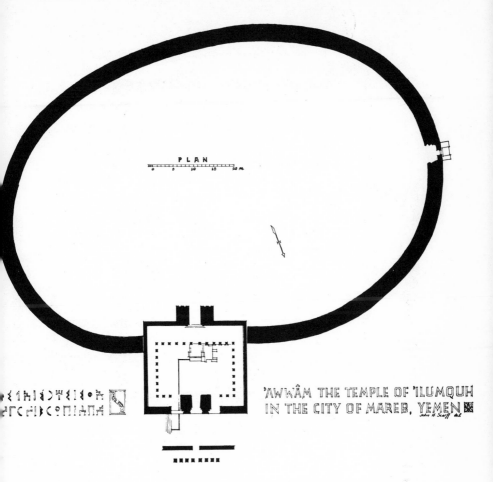

Ground plan of "Mahram Bilqis," the Temple Awwam at Marib. The ovoid
enclosure is probably older in origin than the peristyle structure at its gate,
but the masonry now visible is not earlier than the fifth century B.C.

SECTION

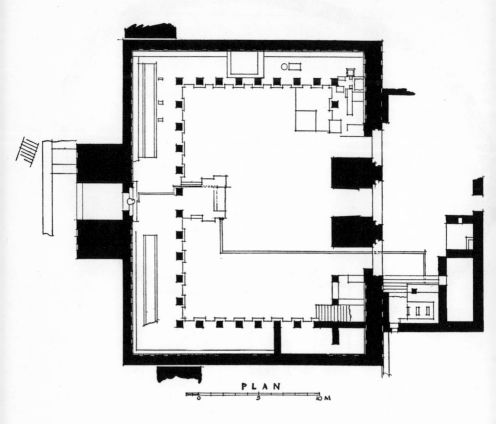

PLAN

Ground plan of the peristyle structure at the entrance to "Mahram Bilqis," the Temple Awwam in Marib

ended, as usual in Yemen, with nothing substantial accomplished and everyone vowing eternal friendship and love through the ages.

The next day being Friday, the Moslem Sabbath, with work shut down at the temple, we concentrated on photographing the bronze and alabaster treasures which had been uncovered and locked up in the storeroom. After a delay of only thirty minutes, Emir Soumsan, Qadi Zeid Inan, and Nagib Muhsin arrived, followed by the governor, who, as usual, was surrounded by a small army of askaris. I began to see that what power the Amel had, rested in his control, such as it was, of the soldiers. He was the man holding the official title of governor, and that meant something to the soldiers, even though they all knew that Zeid Inan was the representative of Prince Hassan.

With appropriate bugle calls and ceremony the door to the archaeological storeroom was unlocked, and we new arrivals were allowed the privilege of inspecting the specimens our expedition had found. The outstanding piece was a three-foot bronze statue of a man walking in rather stiff-kneed fashion. The head was held erect, eyes looking fixedly ahead, while both fists were directed to the front, elbows bent. The right hand probably held at one time a staff or scepter which was now missing, while the left hand still held the official seal, as if ready to stamp an important document. The man wore a short rectangular skirt held up by a broad belt, while draped over his back was a lion skin, fastened by clasped front paws around his neck.

I was particularly struck by a sheathed dagger or jambiya fastened in the man's belt. It was similar to those used today, twenty-five centuries after the time of the statue, except that it was straight at the end where those of this time have points that turn up abruptly. The man's face was broad, and had oversized conventionalized eyes and a large nose and ears. Although no hair was visible beneath a headpiece, a beard of tight curls was indicated by a row of knobs. An inscription ran from the shoulders to the bottom of the skirt, ending at the right knee. It told us this statue of "Ma'adkarib" was dedicated to the moon god, Ilumquh.

Dr. Albright pointed out that while the statue had originally been cast in one piece, probably over a pressed carbon core, he

had found it on New Year's Day at the temple with its left arm
and right foot broken off. The left foot was badly twisted and
almost broken. Dr. Albright had executed an expert repair job
by breaking the left foot off the rest of the way and securing the
two feet and loose arm in their original positions by means of
several half-inch bars and some cement. He had then mounted
the statue on a stone base.

We admired two other remarkable bronze statues in particular
out of the collection of bronzes and alabasters in the storeroom.
One of a young man was preserved down to the knees; he possessed
broad shoulders, very narrow hips, and wore a narrow bracelet
with a flower-like ornament. Around his neck hung a braided
necklace with a pendant disk bearing a crosshatch design.

Statue number three was interesting because its head was probably the work of a different sculptor from the one who made the
rest of the body. It had been welded on in antiquity, turned
slightly to the right and posed gracefully on a very long neck. The
face wore a serious expression, although it was very much alive,
with remarkably good facial muscles and full lips.*

We were interrupted by loud exclamations from outside the
storeroom, where Commander Gilliland was vainly trying to get
at least one movie shot of the statues without Qadi Zeid Inan and
Nagib Muhsin planting themselves directly in the center of the
picture.

I spent the rest of the day going over Dr. Albright's archaeological reports and Dr. Jamme's translations. About nine-thirty
that evening a messenger arrived from the governor informing us
that he would like to see Eileen, Bob, and me immediately. As
soon as Jama joined us—for his advice and counsel were always to
be relied upon—we crossed over to the Amel's residence, which
was elaborately guarded on all sides.

Governor Saiyed Abdul-Rahman was even more polite than
usual. He thanked me for the kind assistance our doctor had given

* Subsequent study by Professor W. F. Albright and Dr. Berta Segall has
brought to light Phoenician affinities. The statues were no slavish imitations
of Phoenician originals, but showed signs of independent South Arabian
development after the original borrowing. The statues themselves belong to
the sixth or fifth century B.C.

Bronze statue of Ma'adkarib (sixth century B.C.) dedicated to the moon god Ilumquh and excavated at the Temple Awwam (Mahram Bilqis). This statue, which was lost to the expedition at Marib, shows signs of independent South Arabian development after the original borrowing from Phoenicia.

Dr. Frank P. Albright holds small bronze head at the expedition headquarters in Marib

him that day, and then wasted little time broaching the subject that was on his mind. He called to my attention the fact that he had at various times advanced Bob money for the expedition. He stated now that he wanted repayment—within a few hours.

Eileen patiently reviewed our understanding with Qadi Al Amri in Taiz and confirmed by the governor on several occasions, that the expedition receive advances from Yemeni officials and pay the American dollar equivalent to the Yemeni legation in Washington. This would facilitate us in the field and help the Yemen government at the same time.

The governor smiled and said that since he was in Marib, not in Washington, he would like to see his money repaid to him in Maria Theresa dollars right away. I pointed out that, in view of the understanding, I had not brought into Yemen a large quantity of M.T. dollars, but added that after arriving in Taiz and learning of the difficulties over money, I had instructed Charlie McCollum to bring funds from Aden when he convoyed the cement, food, medical supplies, and other items to Marib.

The governor could not wait that long, he said. So I suggested that the next morning Bob and I would go to Beihan, where Sherif Hussein would gladly lend us the relatively small sum of two to three thousand Maria Theresa dollars. The governor appeared not to understand, although Eileen's and Jama's Arabic fully covered my simple statement. The Amel went on to say, rather hurriedly, that if we were short of money, he would be pleased to accept a portion of our motor transport in lieu of payment.

Jama whispered in my ear a bit of advice to the effect that if I left for Beihan, some reason would surely be dreamed up to keep me from rejoining the group at Marib, and that would be very bad. Why not send Bob alone, he suggested, as he was the only remaining motor expert at Marib, with both Charlie and George Farrier presumably on their way from Aden.

I made this suggestion, although I was afraid that the Amel would insist on cabling the King for permission and that would lead to more complications. But since his own money was involved, the governor finally agreed that Bob could make the trip.

The next morning we all set out for the temple at eight o'clock, with Emir Soumsan, Qadi Zeid Inan, and Nagib Muhsin. It was apparent that Zeid Inan had been working on the Emir, for that emissary of the King, who was our chief hope for ironing out diffi- culties, began at once to tell me, in no uncertain terms, when, where, and how he wanted the excavations to be carried out.

Dr. Albright and I had decided the night before to begin re- moving sand from inside the main temple walls, for nothing was known of this inner structure. Frank had already been working on this site for an hour when we arrived, with thirty to forty teams of oxen moving sand from this area. The Emir, following Qadi Zeid Inan's instructions, ordered all the oxen shifted to the front part of the temple, where eight tall columns of limestone stood in a partial state of excavation. The Emir explained that he wanted all of the sand cleared away from the base of these columns im- mediately.

Respectfully I pointed out that the only possible result of such action would be the toppling of these columns, which would not only endanger the lives of all Yemenis and expedition members working nearby, but would in all likelihood cause the fall of other pillars. Commander Gilliland demonstrated clearly how these col- umns were already out of alignment and might fall with the slight- est movement of the ground around them.

The power of our combined arguments was finally too much for Emir Soumsan, and he graciously agreed to a compromise solution over the loud protests of Qadi Zeid Inan and his squeaky-voiced assistant, Nagib Muhsin. We were to employ some of the oxen and remove a portion of the sand in front, leaving a protective and supporting margin around the columns. The rest of the oxen were to continue within the main temple walls. It was futile, of course, to use the argument that according to the Imam's agree- ment the expedition and no one else should decide how, when, and where to excavate.

About ten in the morning, the Emir asked us to drive him back to Marib. For the first time I felt that perhaps we were finally on the right track and that the Emir would listen to good sense when it was presented to him. If this were the case we might somehow

Bronze statues discovered at Awwam, the Temple of Ilumquh (Mahram Bilqis) and lost to the expedition at Marib. Around the neck of the young man on the right hangs a braided necklace with a pendent disk bearing a crosshatch design. The head on the statue on the left was probably the work of a sculptor different from the one who made the rest of the body. It dates from about the fifth century B.C.

Sabean inscriptions such as these were discovered in large numbers around the peristyle hall of the Temple Awwam (Mahram Bilqis). In the main these inscriptions mention dedications of bronze statues given in appreciation of favors received from the moon god Ilumquh. They date from the period immediately before and after the Christian era.

make a go of it. Within a week's time Dr. Albright would certainly reach the bottom of the main area within the temple, and
then who could tell what Sabean wonders might be revealed?

Back at headquarters, Emir Soumsan went off to report our
morning's activities to the governor. A few minutes later he returned, looking tired and discouraged. It seems that the Amel had
just left for the temple on horseback, and the Emir was afraid
that Zeid Inan would use his strong influence over the governor
to disrupt everything again. I agreed, and we climbed in the
trucks to drive back to the temple again. By this time it was too
late for Bob to start off on his proposed trip to Beihan, so we
postponed it to the next morning.

As we swung around close to the front of the temple, Dr. Albright ran up to meet us. "The governor, on instructions from
Qadi Zeid Inan," he said, "has just ordered all of the oxen and
workers out of the inside of the temple. He says no more sand
is to be removed there." I looked and saw that every man, boy,
and ox at the site was engaged in removing the protective sand
from the base of the eight tall columns.

Dr. Jamme walked up and explained wearily that the governor
had ordered him to stop copying inscriptions. First no latex, now
no pencil and paper. Dr. Jamme was really through and he knew it.

A moment later the governor greeted me as if I were his long-
lost son, with an audience composed of many soldiers, Zeid Inan,
and "Squeaky." As there was little left to lose, I decided that
I must shoot with everything I had, in front of quite an assemblage
of witnesses. Ignoring Zeid Inan for the moment, I spoke seriously
to the governor.

"If you are sick, very sick, and a hakim, doctor, examines you
and instructs you to take a specific medicine to cure you, and then
if you refuse to follow his instructions and die—whose fault will
it be?"

Without hesitation, the Amel replied, "Mine."

"Excellent conclusion," I said. "Now, Dr. Albright has studied
archaeology for many years and he knows what is right and what is
wrong. He is the doctor, and the temple is his patient. He says

that if you remove all of the sand from around the columns they will collapse and the temple will die. How will you explain going against the doctor's instructions to the King?"

To impress upon the soldiers and workers present the importance of the issue, I got down on my knees in the sand before the governor, demonstrating my recognition of his authority and his total command of the situation. Everyone was shocked speechless, and the governor was horribly embarrassed. He dropped to his knees and helped me to my feet with loud and vehement assurances that I was the leader of the expedition and of course Dr. Albright knew best and things would be done our way from now on.

With this advantage, I decided it was time for Qadi Zeid Inan. So I turned to him and spoke in a loud voice, with Eileen translating word for word.

"Qadi Zeid Inan has accused Dr. Jamme of deciphering an important inscription incorrectly. Thus Qadi Zeid Inan must consider his own scholarship at least equal to that of Dr. Jamme, who is recognized as one of the world's foremost authorities. I therefore propose the following: We shall let Qadi Zeid Inan decipher this inscription in question and immediately thereafter we shall let Dr. Jamme decipher the same inscription and both will be sent to His Majesty the King. Simultaneously we shall publish both decipherings to place them before the world of scholarship for judgment. If Qadi Zeid Inan is proven correct, I will pay him one thousand Maria Theresa dollars and dismiss Dr. Jamme from the expedition."

The assembled soldiers, workers, and even the governor were enormously amused, although I treated the subject with deadly seriousness. They all looked at Qadi Zeid Inan, who could only smile sickly and mumble that I had misunderstood completely his good intentions. There was a difficult silence, ended by Eileen, who thanked the governor for seeing things our way. Without giving him time to change his mind again, I suggested that Dr. Albright shift the oxen back for work inside the temple, as agreed earlier with the Emir.

As everyone went back to work, I walked down into the excavated section of the peristyle entrance with Dr. Jamme, where he had been copying inscriptions. He explained that during the

Stairway and rooms in the northeast corner of the peristyle hall of Awwam, the Temple of Ilumquh (Mahram Bilqis) during excavations. The pillars are pocked with holes in which bronze plaques as votive offerings were fastened in great numbers after the first century B.C.

Wendell Phillips at his expedition headquarters in Marib holding a large bronze sandaled foot. The rest of this statue was never located.

removal of the sand, whole or fragmentary inscriptions had turned up every few feet. By the time they reached the bottom of the fill, the number of inscribed stones was overwhelming. The court was almost completely surrounded by inscribed stones, often piled two or three layers deep. And the floor itself was composed largely of inscribed stones. Fortunately, two large bronze inscriptions had been found complete. The pillars around us were pocked with holes in which bronze plaques had once been fastened. Bronze statues or statuettes had probably surmounted the majority of the inscribed stones, which were usually adorned with ex-voto inscriptions.

Frank Albright explained that the inscribing of dedications on stone or bronze, and setting them up in the temple, must have reached the proportions of a commercial enterprise. In any case, they were a major part of the practice of Sabean religious rites. These dedications were no doubt made by the hundreds, at considerable cost to the dedicator, and they must have been respected and reverenced over the centuries. This custom seems to have reached its height some time after the second century B.C., the date of most of the inscriptions found. After this time, inscribed stones were cut up and used for buildings and other purposes.

Dr. Jamme also pointed out where our excavators had recently uncovered a fine stylized alabaster bull's head. In ancient Sheba, the bull always represented Ilumquh, who was known under other names, one of which was Thor (Bull).

Water, the symbol of life itself in the desert, was apparently closely associated with the Sabean religion. Inside the temple numerous sacrificial altars had been uncovered, all similar in having a drain channel terminating in a spout that was usually decorated with a bull's head. Dr. Albright believes that somewhere within the main unexcavated oval enclosure there remains a well which may have been connected with an earlier structure of religious significance, possibly predating the Biblical Queen of Sheba.

At this point Jama ran up to inform us that the governor was tired and would like to be driven back to Marib. I went to the trucks and found everyone on board and ready to go, including the Emir, Zeid Inan, and Nagib Muhsin, who apparently had their fill of scholarly endeavors for the present.

Thinking that our troubles were over for at least one day, I drove the gentlemen back to Marib happily, but on the way Qadi Zeid Inan and the governor held a long whispered conference that grew increasingly friendly. When we arrived, the governor ushered us all into the room in which, ten months before, my first exploratory party had been held. After a short delay, the Amel walked to the center of the room and announced that from this moment on, Dr. Jamme was to relinquish all further claims to his latex squeezes. It was like asking the great epigrapher to give up his life.

For two hours we argued latex back and forth, before it finally dawned on me that the governor, the Imam, and the Yemen government itself had no interest in these latex copies as such. They had no idea why Dr. Jamme and the expedition valued them so highly. They knew only that we *did* place a high value on them, so they decided to appropriate them to make sure they had everything worthwhile.

Eileen pleaded in vain that they were in no way justified under our agreement with the Imam in demanding Dr. Jamme's latex squeezes. But she might just as profitably have been lecturing to a herd of camels. Eileen had had the deadly task of translating all of the Arabic into English and all of my English into Arabic all morning. Now, after several hours of solid discussion, this young veteran of three major expeditions without the shedding of a tear, finally broke down and left the room crying. The conference was then ended quickly with the usual Yemeni results —nothing accomplished.

Apparently the governor had been concerned when Eileen broke down and left the room, for he took some steps that afternoon to overcome the unpleasantness of the meeting. No, nothing truly helpful, but a gesture of good will in the form of an invitation to Eileen to visit his harem. At the moment Eileen felt that the last thing in the world she wanted to do was see the governor or anything connected with him, and it required a good deal of persuasion to convince her that she should accept this invitation "for the good of thé expedition."

30

ESCAPE!

At dinner that evening it was a welcome relief to hear Eileen's story of her visit to the harem, for it took our minds away from our troubles for a while.

"A tiny slave girl ushered me into a dark hall," she told us, "where all I could hear were muffled sounds with an occasional phrase such as, 'Here is the girl,' and 'What does she look like?' Then someone raised a curtain and I was amazed to find myself in the center of at least twenty women, all elaborately dressed in different kinds of costumes. They stared at me as though I was some new and strange toy to play with.

"The governor's wife finally greeted me, and then the others followed. Everyone was more than surprised to hear me speak Arabic, and it seemed to encourage them to come closer. They were very friendly, but they had never seen a European woman before, and they seemed to think that I must be made of something different. For they touched me, felt my arms, and examined me with the greatest care from head to toe.

"One of the girls noticed my watch, apparently the first she had ever seen. She exclaimed about how beautiful it was, and how small the numbers were. One felt the material of my skirt, another touched my hair, and another put her fingers to my lips to see if they were naturally crimson or colored with some kind of dye. I explained that it was lipstick, and demonstrated with one I had in my handbag. They were delighted, grabbed it gleefully, and smeared it all over their faces—but strangely not on their lips!

"I was wearing two small gold combs in my hair. One girl noticed them, and pointed proudly to her own silver headdress. She said she would like to exchange it for one of my combs. She was overjoyed when I gave them to her as a gift, without taking her beautiful headdress away from her.

"In a little while, tea was served, along with a big plateful of almonds and raisins. The governor's wife sat on the edge of a large bed while the others crowded around me on the floor. She was beautifully dressed, and had a pleasant face with fair skin and very dark hair. Among the others, three were really lovely, each one with a special type of beauty.

"There was a young fourteen-year-old girl dressed in Bedu clothes who was extremely pretty, with rather unusual coloring for an Arabian, with light green eyes, fair hair, and olive complexion. I asked her if she was married and she replied coyly that she had received several proposals but had not accepted any yet. She asked if I didn't think she was too young to be married.

"Next to me sat a slim dark-haired girl with a very attractive, lively face. I noticed her eyes first—large black pools beautifully emphasized with 'kohl,' a kind of black powder the Arabs use a great deal for eye make-up. She was the mother of many children, but she could not have been a day over twenty. I wanted to ask her age, but she probably would not have known it herself and would have been embarrassed.

"The third attractive girl was a local Bedu, the type you read about in the *Arabian Nights*. She was dark, mysterious, and fascinating, with a lovely oval face, long jet-black hair, dark soft eyes, a small nose, and a perfect full mouth. There was not a trace of make-up on her face, and she certainly did not need any. She was tall and graceful, which is rare in Yemen where the women are usually quite small. In her arms lay a baby girl. During my entire visit this beauty never once spoke a word, except to say hello and good-by. She was not trying to be aloof, but contrary to the other women, she was content to listen, with a soft smile on her lips.

"Just before leaving, I explained that I had a lot of work to do, and one of them asked me what I did. They were really surprised when I told them I did office work and translated for the expedition. It was almost impossible for me to explain and demonstrate a typewriter—they had never even heard of one before —but they seemed to appreciate my efforts. What they could not understand above all was that I went unveiled and could remain in the presence of men. They are never allowed to see anyone but their husbands or immediate family and never work outside their homes.

"I presented the governor's wife with a white and gold compact. She thanked me graciously, and in turn offered me a large bag full of almonds and raisins, saying she hoped that I would come again very soon. I thanked her, said good-by to them all, and left.

"Then as I was walking toward our headquarters, Jama met me and told me that one of the Qadi's wives, who had heard about my going to see the Amel's harem, wanted me to come to her house for a short visit. I was so exhausted from the first visit and everything else that has been going on today, that I wasn't ready to face another audience, but I did not want to create any bad feeling by refusing. So up another long flight of steps I climbed, and was delighted to meet this time only four people. The Qadi's wife, a pleasant-looking lady of about forty, greeted me at the entrance, and introduced me to her daughter, a very pretty, shy girl of about eighteen, dressed in green velvet, with a silver belt similar to those in Beihan, and a silver necklace. Then I met the Qadi's niece and another young girl with a baby in her arms. There were no curious stares or questions here, just friendly people who wanted to welcome me in their midst. The mother did most of the talking, in a low sweet voice, saying that this was my home and I was welcome any time I wanted to come.

"Finally she told me that she had severe pains in her arms and legs, and asked me to tell our doctor about it so that he could give me some medicine for her. I explained that it might be necessary for the doctor to examine her, and that I would be happy to come with him. She seemed rather hesitant, as wives are supposed to see no men but their husbands. I am sure she had never been medically examined before. I told her that the doctor was a very fine person, that he was married and had four children of his own. That seemed to make her feel better, though she said she would have to wear a veil in his presence. Again, when I was leaving, I was given a bag of raisins and almonds, for which I thanked her very much. I shook hands all around, and came home."

The friendliness of these people confirmed reports I had received from Dr. Albright, Dr. Jamme, Bob, and others to the effect that the expedition's relations with the local population, the ordinary workers and people, had always been excellent. Only with officials and the soldiers had there been difficulty. And there was more to come, I felt sure, as poor Eileen, Bob, Jama, and I called on the governor again that evening, at his invitation.

I noticed that after he greeted us, the Amel seemed considerably embarrassed, and we soon learned why. There was an important bit of information that he had not mentioned to us before. It seems that when we arrived from Taiz, our chartered plane also brought him a message from the King, to the effect that Charlie McCollum, George Farrier, and Dick Bussey, who were now on their way from Aden, were not to be allowed to enter Marib.

When we just stared at him dumbfounded, the governor apologized and said that he felt very ashamed about this and had cabled to the King, explaining that this convoy carried equipment, gasoline, food, and medical supplies absolutely required by the expedition, as well as the much discussed cement.

"As of this evening," he concluded, "no reply has been received from the Imam."

I understood now why the governor had not been able to wait for his money until the convoy arrived from Aden. He knew it would never get there.

Since there was nothing to say in the face of this news, we walked back to our headquarters. I suddenly realized the full implication of this information when it dawned on me that back in Taiz, just before we had been allowed to leave the airport, Jarmoussi had obtained that permission only when I assured him that Charlie would convoy cement to Marib to repair the broken pillars. Now we knew that the King had ordered this same Jar-moussi, at this same time, to forward instructions to Marib for-bidding the entrance of the convoy carrying the cement. This was more than confusion. It was premeditated and forced isolation of the expedition.

Jama spoke up. "Sahib, if Mr. Charlie and the others are not to be allowed to join us, how can we know that they will let Mr. Bob re-enter Marib with the money from Beihan?"

The answer to this question was obvious. We did not know. And in that event we would be left without a single motor trans-port expert in the party, more cut off from the rest of the world than ever. Bob's departure, scheduled for early the next morn-ing, was canceled on the spot, and we breathed a sigh of relief at the thought that events had delayed his leaving that day.

Meanwhile, there was only one thing to do—keep working and hope for a reversal of the King's order about the convoy from Aden, with perhaps further reversals to come on other matters. The next morning I went to the temple site about an hour and a half after work started there. I found that Emir Soumsan had changed his mind once more during the night. All of the workers and the oxen had been shifted again. The Emir's new order had been, "All of the sand must be removed immediately from around the eight tall columns."

There was nothing to say that had not already been said, noth-ing to do that we had not done. And this was most discouraging, for the man who was supposed to help straighten out matters in Marib had joined the camp of the chief instigator of trouble, Zeid Inan. What worried me most was the knowledge that the Emir, being a personal emissary of the King, would not have taken this step solely because of the influence of Zeid Inan. He must have been acting on the instructions of, or at least with the acquies-cence of, the King.

I returned to headquarters to confer with Bob and Jama. My first thought was to withdraw all expedition personnel from the temple and leave the Yemenis on their own. In this way, we would not be a party to what was certainly going to happen when the Emir's destructive order was carried out.

Jama, however, advised extreme caution. Both he and Bob were more than worried over the actions of the soldiers on the previous night. In reply to Bob's greeting of "Salaam alekum," one of the soldiers stationed at our door had spit at his feet. In the Moslem world, this occurrence was an almost unbelievably defiant insult. On top of that, what would the workers think if all expedition members walked away from the job? Wouldn't they believe their jobs were finished—and at a time when they had money coming to them, money not available to us in Marib?

The only thing to do was keep going at least for a little while, hope for the best at the excavation site, and try to find some way to change the course of events. So after lunch Commander Gilliland, Harry Scarff, and Eileen joined me for a drive out to Marib dam and some photographs. In spite of the presence of several guardian soldiers, it was so beautiful and peaceful at the dam that for a little while we almost forgot our difficulties and relaxed, breathing in the clear desert air. A second and larger section of the dam, which I had seen the year before from the air with Alan and Sarah Scaife, had to be forgotten for the present. I suddenly realized that a second trip would use up fuel, and we did not have much left. There was no way of telling when we could get more.

That evening Jama came to my room, and from the grave expression on his face I knew that something unfavorable had occurred. "Sahib, the governor sends you greetings and his regrets. The King has just cabled from Taiz that unless Dr. Jamme hands over all his latex squeezes tonight, all work must be stopped tomorrow. And the King has again refused the governor's plea to allow Mr. Charlie and the convoy to enter Marib."

Now the intention was clear and unmistakable. There could be no misinterpreting of this latest development. Deliberately and according to plan, the expedition was being deprived of its vitally needed personnel, medical supplies, food, and gasoline. We had food for only about one week. Medicines were running low. Gasoline? I did not know exactly how many gallons were left, but there was little enough. Some trucks, I knew, were standing idle waiting for parts being brought by Charlie. What would happen when the few remaining necessities ran out?

I considered sending cables to the outside world explaining our predicament and asking for help, but I doubted that we could hold out until such help came. Then Jama ended the idea completely by telling me that our messages would probably never be relayed outside of Yemen.

I immediately called a council or war, with Dr. Jamme, Eileen, Bob Carmean, Chester Stevens, and Jama serving as joint chiefs of staff. We all agreed on one thing—the question was no longer one of archaeology at Marib. It was a question of survival, of getting everyone out of Yemen alive.

Dr. Jamme said that although his latex squeezes meant almost more to him than life itself, he would immediately acquiesce in the King's demand if that would allay the final break in relations. If the governor stopped all work at the temple, he pointed out, we would have no further reason for driving around in our trucks and would most certainly be confined to headquarters from that time on. None of us really believed, of course, that surrender of the latex squeezes would end either our difficulties or our danger.

Somehow, we decided, a way must be found to reach the outside world. We all agreed that Bob was the one person who might possibly drive alone across the desert to Beihan and carry my messages of appeal. There was some question about whether or not he would be permitted to leave, but Jama thought that possibly Bob could get away with it, if the excuse were to borrow money from Sherif Hussein so that we could repay the governor and get wages for the workers. So Bob went out to prepare the "reconn" car for an early departure the next morning, while the rest of us composed cables to the President of the United States, the Secretary General of the United Nations, and our Foundation directors. The cable to the President read as follows:

DEAR MR PRESIDENT MY AMERICAN FOUNDATION FOR STUDY OF MAN EXPEDITION TO QUEEN OF SHEBAS CAPITAL MARIB YEMEN IS IN DESPERATE SITUATION STOP MY RELIEF CONVOY WITH NAVY MED-

ICAL SUPPLIES FOOD GASOLINE FORBIDDEN TO REACH US BY KING
AHMED STOP PLEASE PERSONALLY INTERVENE URGENTLY WITH KING
TO HOLD OFF HIS SOLDIERS AND ALLOW ME TO EVACUATE MY AMER-
ICAN SCIENTISTS AND TECHNICIANS STOP UNLESS YOUR IMMEDIATE
ACTION IS TAKEN AMERICAN LIVES WILL BE GRAVELY ENDANGERED
MY GRATEFUL THANKS

                                        WENDELL PHILLIPS

Finally we went to bed and managed to get a little sleep, but the next morning I woke up to learn that Jama had been stopped from entering my room by two soldiers, one of whom handled him quite roughly. There was no doubt that things were reaching a climax.

I decided that if Bob were permitted to leave with the messages, Othman, Jama's brother, would easily be allowed to go along. If Bob were stopped, Othman would somehow be able to make it. I doubted if anything Yemeni on foot could keep up with this Somali, whose speed and endurance were phenomenal.

Bob Carmean carefully stuffed the expedition's archaeological films into two boxes of Post Toasties, hid the messages in his socks and prepared to leave. We did not ask for special permission because the governor had agreed, two days before, that Bob could go to Beihan for money, but we felt sure that he would be searched. And we were right, for a most thorough job was done on him, Othman, and the truck. But they did not look into his socks or the boxes of Post Toasties. After a last-minute delay by the Emir over something whispered in his ear by one of the soldiers, Bob Carmean and Othman were on their way to Beihan —*hamdulillah!*

The understanding was that as soon as Bob had managed to send the cables, he would try to get word to Charlie and the others of his convoy that under no circumstances should they try to reach Marib. This was most important, for Charlie and George would not be easily stopped or turned aside merely by a few Yemeni soldiers if they knew we were in danger. In this instance, however, even Charlie didn't have a chance against the obstacles that confronted all of us. If Bob should succeed in getting all his messages off all right, he would then borrow enough money to handle expenses in Marib, get a supply of gasoline, and return as soon as possible.

We all breathed a good deal easier when Bob was on his way, but we had to face more troubles at once. The Emir insisted that certain inscriptions which had previously been removed from the temple with the governor's approval, must be dragged back again. I patiently agreed to accomplish this senseless, laborious task as soon as Bob returned to operate the Power Wagon winch. As for the King's order that all latex squeezes be turned over to the governor if work were to continue, we decided that the only procedure was to stall the King and his officials for a day or two. We agreed to their original demand—to supply the King with copies of all squeezes made by Dr. Jamme. Thus we were allowed to continue working. By this time we were not so interested in work as in keeping our privilege of getting into trucks and going somewhere.

At the temple, Abdul-Rahman Ghadi, the troublesome labor foreman, poked his hand under an inscription and was greeted by a medium-sized scorpion. His finger swelled rapidly, and Commander Gilliland stopped his photography to rush the moaning patient back to headquarters. Here the Emir produced a charmed stomach stone from a gazelle to apply to the wound, but the victim impolitely knocked it aside in favor of the treatments of the U.S. Navy Bureau of Medicine and Surgery.

After lunch, Jama came to me with startling news. "Sahib! The governor is being recalled to Taiz by the King. This will leave us at the complete mercy of the soldiers."

We all knew that no one but the Amel exercised any real control over them, and that was only tenuous at best. No one else would be the least bit disturbed over any incident the soldiers might provoke.

"What makes this news all the worse," Jama went on, "is something I should have told you about last night. But you were already so worried. Yesterday afternoon I overheard five soldiers discussing the best way to start some kind of argument so they could kill some of us."

"Jama, which one do they want to kill the most?" I asked.

"Number one is probably Dr. Jamme. They have seen that he is the main target of the officials, and they hate him because he works so hard and is not afraid. Or maybe Mr. Bob because he knows too much about Marib and was in charge of things for so long, but of course he is not here. You, Sahib, are next, and then Chester because he has been here too long."

"What about Eileen?"

"They would not hurt her—she would probably disappear into a harem," Jama said. "No one would hear of her again."

"How about the others?"

"They are not important at the moment, as far as the soldiers are concerned, because they would be considered unable to put up a fight without you, and the rest they would kill."

"Jama, tell me, what do you think is likely to happen?"

"Sahib, it will probably start with Dr. Jamme. One of the soldiers will give him some ridiculous order and he will not obey at once. A soldier will pull out his jambiya, and the rest will join in. They will cut Jamme apart, and when you or one of us comes to his rescue, they will have the excuse they are looking for to kill some of us. They will probably do this when you are near because they know you would rush to help Dr. Jamme at once and they would cut you down with rifles from the wall or watchtower. Then they will gather many paid witnesses to swear that we attacked them first and they acted in self-defense. Remember, Sahib, the soldiers who attacked Mr. Bob's convoy swore that the wind smashed in his windows."

Jama was right, of course. Any expedition witnesses who might be left after the incident would not even be listened to. They would be imprisoned if they remained alive at all, with a hundred witnesses to swear the opposite of anything they said. Nothing is so terrifying as to be at the mercy of an Arab mob which once aroused loses all sense of reason. This I knew from experience.

From the point of view of those who wished to get rid of the expedition, it was all very simple. They had been conducting a campaign to discredit the expedition for months. Now an incident blamed on us would rid them of the expedition's most experienced personnel and intimidate the rest. They would trot out all the fantastic charges they had been making against Dr. Jamme and the expedition members, with no one to contradict them. The hated foreigners would no longer be in Yemen, but their excellent airfield, road, and equipment would remain —to the great profit of the officials in control. If by any chance Yemen found itself in international hot water over the incident, this would reflect upon the King, Imam Ahmed, who had given us the concession, and that would strengthen Prince Hassan's position.

Jama was no alarmist, so I had to credit his story about the plot of the soldiers which was one more serious problem confronting us. Jama had been in countless dangerous situations without showing fear. He knew Yemen and the Yemenis well. His mature judgment and advice had always been of great value. Much as I tried to convince myself that we were not actually in danger of our lives, it would not work. We had food for a week and no longer. In a few days there would not be enough gasoline to run one truck. Medical supplies were almost depleted. We had no money. And there was no way of getting any of these necessities. Charlie and his convoy could not reach us. Bob would almost certainly not be allowed to return from Beihan. If we continued working, the pillars would fall at the temple, endangering lives and giving our enemies more excuse for an attack. If we stopped work, we would be virtual prisoners. Somehow we might find a way to get along for three or four days, but no more, if the governor remained in Marib. But with him gone, there was nothing to prevent the soldiers from carrying out their plan at once.

I sent for Chester Stevens and, without telling him what was on my mind, inquired what trucks were left in running condition.

"We have one dump body in first-class condition and one stake bed that needs a battery. Its rear differential is about ready to go, too. The rest need new parts to operate at all."

"How much fuel have we, Chester?"

"By draining all the tanks and shutting off the house generator," he said, "I think we can get by for three or four days."

"About the new route you and Bob developed between Marib and Beihan—I've never been over it. Do you think the dump body can make it alone?"

Chester thought a moment, then shook his head. "No, you have to winch up the dunes in at least two places," he said. "Besides, Bob took our only air hose that connects with the engine for pumping tires. It's next to impossible to hand-pump these sand tires in the sand."

"Could we make it with two trucks with everyone on board, leaving everything else behind?" I asked.

Chester, who never gets overly excited about anything, slowly stood up, and with a smile, held out his hand.

"Wendell, meet your new field director. I think we can make it, and anyway, anything is better than what is going to happen to us right here. What time in the morning do we leave?"

It had not occurred to me that we must leave the next morning, but Chester explained why it was absolutely necessary. If we continued to drive out to the temple for even one more work day, there would probably be insufficient gasoline left to take two trucks to Beihan. It was tomorrow or never. And, the more I thought of it, the more I realized that one more day in Marib would increase the likelihood of the incident we dreaded.

I consulted with Eileen, who at first was completely opposed to our leaving behind all our equipment and possessions. And she felt that we could not possibly get across the sands to Beihan, with heavily loaded trucks, one in doubtful condition, even if we managed somehow to get away from the soldiers who surrounded us and watched every move we made in Marib. I explained the situation as I saw it, then went to inform the others of my decision. Dr. Jamme approved immediately despite the irreparable loss of his precious squeezes, for he had been convinced of the imminent danger for some time.

"The loss of everything is nothing compared to the certain loss of our lives or our freedom if we stay," he said. "The attempt to escape is very risky, but we must take the risk. There is no alternative."

Dr. Albright, who had fortunately escaped many of the personal difficulties encountered by others, agreed heartily. "We could not evacuate our equipment now," he pointed out, "even with the Imam's permission, for we have no gasoline and no way to get any. Some incident could easily panic the soldiers, who are swarming around here as thick as flies."

When I returned to see Eileen I found her stuffing several of her precious French dresses into a pillow case.

"Where do you think you're going?" I asked.

"To Beihan, and the sooner the better," she replied cheerfully. "Won't Sherif Hussein be surprised to see us?"

During the next few hours all arrangements had to be completed without one Yemeni the wiser. With Jama's approval, I decided not even to inform our loyal Somali household staff, for fear one of them would unwittingly give us away.

Later, Chester told me the welcome news that Jama had succeeded in persuading a local official to recharge our truck battery. It would not be ready, however, until six o'clock in the morning, and I had set six-forty as the time of departure from headquarters.

The one big problem that confronted me was to get everyone connected with the expedition out of Yemen alive and safe. Nothing else mattered at this stage. But how could we possibly get the nine staff members, two Egyptian foremen, and eight Somalis away from the swarm of soldiers around us?

Chester and I finally worked out one plan that could succeed if everything went like clockwork. We spread the word, freely and openly, that the next morning Commander Gilliland was going to take movies at the temple. He wanted a picture that would show every person on the expedition in at least one shot, and for that reason everyone's presence would be required.

We felt reasonably sure that this tale would explain taking even our Somalis to the excavation site the next morning. Commander Gilliland had been busy taking movies ever since his arrival, and the Yemenis were fascinated. The officials particularly liked to get into the pictures themselves.

Next I notified every member of the party that he could bring along only his notes, cameras, and the clothes he wore on his back. Absolutely everything else was to be left in Marib. This was essential not only because of lack of space in the trucks but because we could not risk arousing any suspicion by taking to the temple site a single thing that we would not normally take for a day's work.

We had to start our escape from the temple for many reasons. At our headquarters we were surrounded by so many soldiers that making a sudden break for it would bring a hail of bullets on us. Furthermore, even if we got away, the telegraph at Marib would immediately warn the garrison at Harib to intercept us. Starting from the excavation site, we had a slight jump of a few miles and need concern ourselves only with the relatively few soldiers that would accompany the party to the temple and those already stationed there.

I could hardly believe that all preparations could be made by such a large party without arousing suspicion. We had one very important factor in our favor—that the Yemenis could not possibly conceive of our leaving behind priceless equipment and all our possessions which to them far outweighed the value of a few lives.

That evening as Eileen and I walked across the compound, the Emir spoke out from the shadows to inquire where we were going. We told him we were on our way to dinner, but could not help wondering if he suspected what we were planning.

At dinner I carefully assigned to each person a specific place on the trucks for the next morning. Chester had already siphoned out every available drop of gasoline from other trucks and put them in the tanks of the two escape vehicles. This operation had not been noticed, for the soldiers were accustomed to seeing Chester working around the trucks, and they knew about the movie-taking party scheduled for the next morning. Jama arranged for extra water and food to be hidden somewhere on the two trucks. It was almost amusing to watch Ali, one of our hardest-working Somalis, industriously polishing the two Power Wagons for the next day's movies.

I suggested that everyone follow what would seem a normal routine that evening, and get to bed at a reasonable hour in an effort to get as much sleep as possible for the hard trip the next day. Jama collected the Somalis' passports on the pretext that I wanted to inspect them; otherwise they would have been left behind. Eileen went to Bob's and Charlie's rooms and searched their belongings for their field notes and accounts, which could easily be hidden. From then on, throughout the long night, while the others tried to sleep, Chester and Jama labored silently side by side unpacking our remaining Marlins and Winchesters. Each had to be carefully cleaned and loaded in advance for whatever was in store for us when daylight came.

It was still dark at five-thirty when Chester woke me with bad news. Because of the full moon, it had been impossible so far to hide the rifles, ammunition, and water on the trucks. These would have to wait until the soldiers would pay no particular attention to anyone loading things on the trucks—with a prayer that they would not identify what was being loaded.

Jama reported that the battery was ready to go into the stake-bed truck, and Chester disappeared to handle the job himself. I could not help marveling at this former little fat boy, who had joined his first expedition the year before. At that time, he had never even learned to drive a car—and now look at him!

Soon everyone was up and in good spirits, but Eileen chilled me with the remark, "Wouldn't it be horrible if Bob somehow missed us on his way back and, without knowing we had left, entered Marib!" Chester reassured me by stating that he could not possibly miss Bob, for they had both traveled this route together and did not deviate from it. We would meet him even if he had left already, which was very doubtful.

As every member of the expedition went calmly and efficiently about his task, my pride in the group grew and with it my feeling that somehow, despite all the risks and difficulties, we would manage to get away safely. Anyone looking at us would have thought that this day, Tuesday, February 12, 1952—Lincoln's Birthday—was the same as any other day.

I planned to drive from headquarters promptly at six-forty,

with half of the party in the stake-bed truck, to be followed three
or four minutes later by Chester driving the dump body. As this
was ten minutes ahead of our customary working schedule, we
hoped to get away before the Emir, the governor, or Qadi Zeid
Inan appeared.

A glance and a nod from Chester told me that they had managed to get the guns, ammunition, and water into the trucks
without arousing suspicion. I was startled to see Eileen appear
wearing her precious fur coat, which nothing could make her
leave behind. I climbed into my truck and started the engine,
which apparently acted as a signal for Qadi Zeid Inan and Nagib
Muhsin, who immediately appeared. Along with the soldiers,
they climbed aboard and we started off. Fortunately, we left before
the Emir or the governor arrived. The recharged battery had
started the car all right, and I prayed that it would hold out for a
few hours at least.

We rounded the corner and dropped into the dry wadi bed on
our way to the temple. It was a beautiful morning, cool and clear,
and the long shadows stretched across the sand from the sun,
which just showed itself above the horizon. The sand was packed
hard and damp, so we raised little dust. I saw through the rear
window that Chester's truck was bouncing along behind us with
what appeared to be half of the population of Marib hanging on.
I slowed down slightly so that by the time we had driven the two
and a half miles to the temple, both our trucks were side by side.

I pulled up at the far side of the temple, the spot from which
we would have the advantage for a quick departure. With perfect
timing, Dr. Jamme jumped to the ground carrying a half-empty
drum of latex—which he was permitted to use once more. But he
did not move far away. The soldiers followed him to the ground,
and I shouted to the Somalis to keep their places. I gave a helping
hand to Zeid Inan and Nagib Muhsin and, when they were on
the ground, explained, "We are all driving off a short distance
for movies and you, Qadi Zeid Inan, are to act as Mr. Wendell in
my absence."

Dr. Jamme had calmly set down his latex drum and slipped
back into the truck, an act that was not noticed because Chester

at that moment roared off in a cloud of sand, slightly ahead of schedule. Jama had slid behind the wheel of my truck as planned while I spoke casually to Zeid Inan. In the meantime I slowly mounted the right front fender with my last word, and Jama pulled away fast after Chester. I was thus in a position to cover the nearby soldiers if necessary, but they did not make a move. They were too surprised, and merely looked questioningly at Qadi Zeid Inan. I shall never forget the look of blank puzzlement on that gentleman's face. Then the soldiers started to shout something to him, but I could not hear what they said. Their words were lost forever in the wonderful roar of our Power Wagons. I had never doubted for an instant my ability to outgun the handful of Yemeni soldiers near our trucks, should the lives of my party depend on it, for I had on my side the element of surprise plus a Colt for each hand. What I was deathly afraid of was the rifles of the soldiers stationed at the other side of the temple, for my open trucks filled with humanity would afford perfect targets. But we were out of effective range within a minute.

Qadi Zeid Inan may have realized our intentions before we had gone a quarter of a mile. But we figured that he would wait just a little while, to make absolutely certain, before dispatching a runner to the governor. This might take thirty minutes, or it might take less. The governor would then investigate and consult with the Emir. We hoped that this would give us one hour—or, if they were highly bewildered, a maximum of an hour and a half. Then the governor would most certainly cable the Yemeni stronghold of Harib. Our route would of necessity carry us across the mouth of the Wadi Harib, a mere five miles from the governor's fortress there. Could we possibly cross over before the Yemeni camel corps rode down and blocked our way? That was the question, a question to which we could not know the answer until we approached the mouth of the wadi.

Chester and I had debated this question at length the night before. We knew that the wireless operated only until eight-thirty in the morning. Thus it might have been better to leave later, when no message could possibly have reached Harib. But then we would have traveled through soft sand, under a high hot sun. We would certainly have been burdened with the authoritative presence of the Emir and the governor at the temple, making it much more difficult to pull away safely. We had decided that our best gamble was an effort to beat the wireless and cross the Wadi Harib before the camel corps could reach it. We had succeeded already in the first half of our escape—getting away from the temple. But the second half was even more risky.

In about ten minutes I signaled for Jama to stop so that we could change places. For a few seconds no one breathed as I tried to start the engine again. What I wouldn't have given to be armed with Charlie at that moment! On the third try, the battery turned the engine over fast enough to make it roar into life, and we were off again. I promised myself to keep the engine running from then on, no matter how often we had to stop along the way.

Up ahead, Chester located Bob's tracks in the sand, and we drove along for about an hour without running into any trouble. But there ahead lay the first of the high dunes, with Bob's tracks disappearing right over the top. I saw Chester's truck plunge up the slope, hesitate, and then go on over. But my truck could not make it. After two more tries, we unloaded everyone and everything, and I threw into the job every trick of sand driving I had ever learned. My chief concern was that rear differential which was scheduled to go out any second. I didn't want to bring Chester's truck back with the winch for fear of his getting stuck and leaving us completely stranded. Still, try as I might, I simply could not shift in low range from second to first gear and keep up my required speed. Finally, on my seventh attempt, my Power Wagon struggled up the dune and everyone gave a cheer. A quick reloading, and we were off again, but we had lost precious time.

Bob's tracks over the dunes were fairly clear and we made good time for a while. The sun had become hot but there was no wind and consequently little dust. I felt sorry for those riding in the backs of the trucks, for we had to smash ahead at top speed over the crests of the dunes, giving them a rough time of it. You never knew what lay on the other side of these mountains of sand until you were over, and then it was too late to do anything about it.

Often there were rocks, ridges, or holes that almost threw the passengers out.

Next Chester's truck stuck partway up a steep, rocky slope. Fortunately there were large boulders on both sides, since we were approaching the mountains on our right. By tying the winch cable around a huge stone at the top of the rise, we were able to get both trucks over. But thirty precious minutes were lost in the operation, and the Wadi Harib lay only a short distance ahead. Would we find Yemeni soldiers blocking our way?

I took over the lead from Chester at this point, for I wanted to have a clear field of vision as we crossed the Wadi Harib. I knew that Jama, clinging to my right front fender, would not let his sharp eyes miss a thing. We put on all the speed our Power Wagons could take and fairly flew across the wadi. The people in back hung on grimly and looked across the flat earth for a sign of the Harib camel corps.

Over the roar of my Power Wagon I thought I heard Eileen scream. Just at this moment, Eileen, who was riding in the back of the truck, was the first to see a large party of camel corps and horsemen racing down the Wadi Harib attempting to intercept Chester's truck, which had fallen far behind. "Hurry, Chester, hurry!" Eileen kept shouting. She was about to stop me when Chester, now fully aware of his danger, abruptly cut far to the left barely eluding the Yemenis and keeping his truck just out of rifle range.

I had slowed down somewhat, but picked up speed again when I saw that the second truck was safe, and together we roared out of the wadi, leaving the Yemenis to swallow our dust.

We were past the worst danger now, and we all knew it. But there was no time for celebration, for we realized that Yemeni soldiers would not be too reluctant to cross the vague border into Beihan if they thought they might catch us. So we kept going at a steady pace, until Jama pointed to a small Bedu boy up ahead, waving a piece of paper. It was a message from Bob, written in Beihan. He had found Sherif Hussein and Emir Saleh absent when he arrived, so he had flown to Aden on an R.A.F. plane to send out our messages.

We were all relieved to know that Bob was safe. Now, if his messages caught Charlie, George, and Dick in time, every member of the expedition would be out of Yemen, and that meant out of danger.

From this point on it was just a matter of time. Soon we drove into the Wadi Beihan, shimmering in the noonday heat. Never did a parched and dry stretch of desert look so inviting!

31

CHARGES AND
COUNTERCHARGES

Sherif Awad and Sherif Saleh bin Naser were the first to greet us at Beihan al-Qasab. What a difference between this warm reception and the venomous hostility we had just escaped! What a wonderful feeling it was to be free again!

While everyone shook hands and smilingly congratulated one another, Dr. Jamme, more excited than I had ever seen him, got down on his knees to kiss the sand of Beihan, and jubilantly exclaimed to Eileen, *"Béni soit ce sol de liberté!"*

We were all extremely disappointed over the absence in Aden of Sherif Hussein and the Emir, whose comforting presence in Beihan would have meant so much to us at this time. Jama and I went into a closed conference with Sherifs Awad and Saleh bin Naser regarding our security here in Beihan. Only a few months before, I knew, a major tribal war had been in progress between the Yemen and Beihan, and the Yemenis might attack that very night in force, knowing we were all there. Sherif Saleh bin Naser looked grave and admitted that a small war was in progress at that moment.

Both my old warrior friends gave assurances, however, that they had already anticipated my concern and, since we were "back home" now they would defend us with their lives. Jama reported that Sherif Hussein's tribal scouts had been sent out to cover every approach to the capital and that a surprise attack that evening was considered virtually impossible.

Sherif Awad was a wonderful host, and soon made everyone as comfortable as possible in the absent Emir's house. We all sat down to dinner and enjoyed the first really happy meal we had had in a long time. Over coffee, Sherif Awad told Eileen how his spies had reported that two days before, an armed assassin had departed from Sana for Marib with the sole assignment of disposing of me. In view of the previous accuracy of reports of the Sherif's spy system, I had to give some credit to the news, which made me even happier than I had been before to know that I sat in Beihan, among good friends. My greatest satisfaction, however, came as I looked around the room and saw—alive and well, even if tired—every member of the expedition that had been with me in Marib. The safety of an expedition's members is the first responsibility of any expedition leader, and despite the staggering losses in equipment and scientific work, I could take satisfaction in knowing that our people were still alive.

But I was worried about Charlie, George, and Dick. Throughout the night I tried in every way to get a wireless message through to them, for the convoy had to be stopped before it crossed the flat Jol Kudeif, where it would make an ideal target. The Beihani wireless operator first tried Mudia, then Saida, and finally Mufed, points through which the convoy must pass. It was about four in the morning when I finally received a cable from Bob in Aden saying that Charlie had been stopped in time and the convoy was on its way back to Aden. With that welcome news, I could get a bit of sleep.

The next morning we drove to Timna, and beyond a few miles where my tribal father Sheikh Ali and tribal brother Sheikh Abdullah Bahri were overjoyed when we drove up to their encampment. After a real Bedu Bal Harith greeting, we went into Sheikh Ali's tent, where Jama explained what had happened in Marib. Sheikh Ali spoke quietly to his son, and from that minute until I climbed aboard the R.A.F. plane kindly sent by Sir Tom Hickinbotham, the Governor of Aden, to evacuate our party, Sheikh Abdullah never left my side.

On our first evening in Aden, Sherif Hussein visited us, apologizing profusely for being absent from Beihan on our arrival. Then he told us a little story.

"There was once a Sheikh who wanted to get married. He had two proposals. Both girls were very beautiful, of the same age and status. Now each girl's father asked a dowry. The first wanted two thousand M.T. dollars and the second wanted only two hundred M.T. dollars. Without hesitation, the Sheikh chose the first girl and agreed to pay the two thousand M.T. dollars. Both girls were equal in youth and beauty, yet he chose the one that was hardest to get."

Turning to me with a smile, Sherif Hussein continued, "You, Sheikh Hussein, came first to Beihan where you were treated like a king, yet you were not satisfied with this 'two-hundred-dollar girl.' You had to go to Marib for the 'two-thousand-dollar girl.'" Sherif Hussein left the rest of his story untold, while we all applauded.

Sherif Hussein and his son, Emir Saleh, obviously hoped that we would now return to Timna and take up our archaeological work there. I shook my head sadly and explained with grateful thanks that possibly we would return some day, *inshallah*.

After saying farewell to the Sherif and the Emir, I notified the American consul in Aden that, due to circumstances beyond our control, we had left certain unpaid debts behind us in Marib. I asked him to notify the Yemen government that the money would be paid just as soon as definite assurances reached us that it would go to those men on our list and not into the hands of others along the way. The next morning I was besieged with cables from the world's leading news agencies asking for a statement in reply to various charges being leveled at us through Yemen press sources.

The really staggering total of our losses at Marib began to be apparent to all of us. Mild representations through a consul would never succeed in getting that valuable equipment back again. After considerable deliberation, I decided to place an open cable, addressed to the King of Yemen, in the world's leading newspapers, in the hope of impressing upon him the seriousness of the situation. It read as follows:

TO HIS MAJESTY IMAM AHMED KING OF YEMEN ROYAL PALACE
TAIZ YOUR MAJESTY I HAVE JUST SACRIFICED OVER TWO HUNDRED
THOUSAND DOLLARS WORTH OF EQUIPMENT IN YOUR COUNTRY IN
ORDER TO SAVE THE LIVES OF MY AMERICANS EGYPTIANS AND SOMALIS
STOP YOUR RUINS AT MARIB REPRESENT THE GREATEST KNOWN
ARCHAEOLOGICAL TREASURE HOUSE REMAINING ANYWHERE IN THE
WORLD AND THE MONUMENTAL CIRCULAR TEMPLE OF ILUMQUH IS
AN ABSOLUTELY UNIQUE STRUCTURE STOP WE PARTIALLY EXCAVATED
ILUMQUH UNTIL FORCED TO FLEE YEMEN AND UNLESS YOUR MAJESTY
INTERVENES URGENTLY NOTHING WILL SAVE THIS SABEAN MASTER-
PIECE FROM DESTRUCTION FROM YOUR OWN TRIBESMEN AND ITS LOSS
TO THE WORLD OF SCIENCE AND ART WILL BE IRREPLACEABLE STOP
FINALLY I BEG YOUR MAJESTY TO URGENTLY CONSIDER ABOVE THE
VALUE OF OUR TRUCKS SAND CONVEYORS GENERATORS REFRIGER-
ATORS OFFICE EQUIPMENT PHOTO LABORATORY MEDICAL INSTRU-
MENTS RADIOS AND PERSONAL EFFECTS THE UNBELIEVABLE LOSS TO
SCIENCE IF OUR RUBBER LATEX COPIES OF HUNDREDS OF NEW IN-
SCRIPTIONS FALL INTO THE HANDS OF YOUR IRRESPONSIBLE REPRE-
SENTATIVES OR IF THE PRICELESS BRONZE AND ALABASTER STATUES
RECENTLY EXCAVATED AT ILUMQUH ARE DAMAGED OR DESTROYED BY
TRIBESMEN STOP AS MY RECENT PLEAS FOR AN AUDIENCE WITH YOUR
MAJESTY WERE LEFT UNANSWERED I CAN ONLY RESORT TO THIS FINAL
COURT OF APPEAL STOP RESPECTFULLY SUBMITTED WENDELL PHILLIPS
LEADER AMERICAN FOUNDATION FOR THE STUDY OF MAN YEMEN
EXPEDITION

That was the beginning of a year and a half of effort to retrieve
some of our belongings in Yemen. But when Charlie's convoy
returned to Aden with the supplies and equipment destined for
Marib, we realized that we had not been entirely wiped out. We
could still qualify as an expedition, even if a smaller one than
had been intended.

This brought up the question—what next? The most natural
answer seemed to be that we should pack up what we had left and
go back home, licking our wounds, and, after a period of recovery,
start out fresh to gain funds and equipment for a new expedition
elsewhere. This obvious answer did not appeal to me, however. I

wondered if there might be some way to salvage something worthwhile from this catastrophe, to snatch victory from this temporary defeat.

That is when my thoughts turned to my friend Sultan Said bin Taimur, Sultan of Muscat and Oman. Back in 1949, during our audience in Muscat, the Sultan had expressed his willingness to have me bring an expedition to explore and excavate in the little-known Dhofar province of Oman. At the time, Timna had beckoned first and then Marib, where we knew for sure that we could find really ancient pre-Himyaritic cities to excavate. I thought that there must be such in Oman, too, even though no one had ever found them. But would we still be welcome in Oman? After this lapse of time would the Sultan still permit us to come and work? Would our bad experience in Yemen influence other Arab countries against us?

There was only one way to find an answer to these questions, so I sent a cable to the Sultan of Muscat and Oman. While waiting for a reply the Yemeni legations in Cairo, London, and Washington erupted simultaneously with an amazing series of conflicting stories about our expedition. My open cable had received front-page headlines and the King issued orders to dream up something that would get bigger headlines and discredit the expedition.

The Cairo legation came up with a beauty. It accused me of smuggling out of Yemen a solid gold statue of the Queen of Sheba! The Washington legation couldn't quite go that far, however, and when pressed by newsmen refused to sanction this ridiculous charge. As the entire population of Marib, its officials and its soldiers all knew, we had discovered no statue or even concrete reference to the Biblical Queen of Sheba. And the largest piece of gold found in all our Sabean excavations had been the tiny globe appropriated on the spot by Qadi Zeid Inan. The portion of the Temple of Ilumquh (Awwam) that we excavated, dates from about the fifth century B.C., while the Biblical Queen lived around 950 B.C., a minor point, possibly, in higher Yemen diplomatic circles, but a major consideration in archaeology.

The money question, as handled by the different Yemeni authorities, was even more confused. Simultaneously the Cairo legation stated that we owed 3,620 M.T. dollars, the Washington legation said 2,800 M.T. dollars, the Arab press in Aden quoted official Yemen sources at 1,670 M.T. dollars. At the same time the American consul in Aden was officially notified that the sum was 5,442½ M.T. dollars.

In this last total we were charged rent on the storeroom in which our archaeological discoveries were locked away from us, and for the services of the soldiers who threatened Dr. Jamme, killed Charlie's pet dog, smashed Bob's convoy windows, and made the nights miserable for everyone. Actually Bob's field records, as signed in red ink by the governor of Marib, totaled 2,995.79 M.T. dollars.

After looking at some of the Yemeni statements, I thought it might be a good idea to submit to the Yemen government a bill for supervising construction of their airfield and roads, for the use of our trucks and labor in building several storehouses, plus the entire cost of bringing the major party in January, under the false promises that we would be allowed to work in Marib.

The Yemen government also expressed its concern over the archaeological methods employed by Dr. Albright. It appeared that he was not using the latest Yemeni-approved techniques in archaeology. These can best be demonstrated not only by our own experience with such "experts" as Qadi Zeid Inan, but by the visit to Marib in 1947 of the eminent Egyptian archaeologist Dr. Ahmed Fakhry. He published that to his horror the Yemeni government had recently ordered more than a dozen irreplaceable ancient Sabean structures torn down to obtain cut building stones for their ugly present-day fortress.

Saiyid Abdurrahman Abu Taleb, Yemen chargé d'affaires, in a Washington press conference insisted that at no time was the expedition in any danger. Yet this same official would never think of stepping outside his own well-guarded home in Yemen without soldiers to protect him. Saiyid Abu Taleb also forgot to mention to the assembled reporters that his own king, for security reasons, had yet to visit his own capital of Sana since the assassination of his father several years before.

Apparently the charges of the Yemen government were not

taken very seriously in most quarters, as was shown by two illu-
minating articles in the Arabic paper, *Al Fadhl*. The first story,
sent direct from an Arab observer in Taiz, said:

Taiz circles were well aware of the decision taken to harass the American Mission and expel it. Consultations on this matter were carried
on for two months between Taiz and Sana. Prince Abdullah's sole purpose in going to Marib was to give verbal instructions to his agents
there. Eminent persons of the court in Taiz whisper that the entrance
of the Americans to Marib was regretted from the beginning. What
happened was necessary to correct that mistake. Governor Yadomi,
Chief Justice and friend of the Imam, says, "These antiquities were
the window through which the eyes of the world would have looked
at us. Now we have closed it." It is well established here that His
Majesty the King had changed his mind, even though he had given
the Mission signed permission to excavate in Marib.

The editor of *Al Fadhl* commented:

Our London representative, Hassan Ibrahim's only defense is that
"the Yemeni guards acted only to prevent the smuggling of antiquities to the outside world." We might have believed the Yemen authorities if we had seen in their long history in treating people one example of logic or one precedent of right or truth. Can this representative
or those whom he represents explain to the people what these supposed
antiquities are that made them spoil the name of Yemen by their disgraceful actions to the Mission? It is good that the Americans excavated the site of Sheba and with it uncovered the dilemma suffered by
the Yemeni people for the last forty years.

In a second article, *Al Fadhl* stated:

Yemen is the only country in which savagery still prevails. The worst
enemy of Yemen could not have succeeded in spoiling its name to the
same degree accomplished by our own incompetent and ill-behaved
Yemeni authorities. People had high hopes when the Mission was given
permission to excavate for antiquities in Yemen. They thought it was
a good step forward, that would lead Yemen out of the state of isolation, darkness and doubt.

Today every decent Yemeni is disgraced to be related to Yemen for
fear of being described as a barbaric savage. God is witness that the

Yemenis are innocent of this shame and that they are dissatisfied with their authorities' conduct toward the American scientists. The rulers of Yemen could have found it easy to delegate the question of supervision to honest experts from the Arab countries; but good counsel is difficult to find its way towards such rulers. They entrusted a band of commoners and ignorants with the duty of supervising the Mission and its excavations. These men might have imagined when they saw some of the antiquities uncovered by the Mission that the Americans had discovered mountains of gold and communicated their illusions to their higher authorities. Those higher authorities, illiterate and senseless as they are, being persecuted by the desire to secure for themselves mountains of gold and treasures of diamonds, committed the shameful follies against the members of the Mission and its scientists.

This, in our view, is the reason behind the catastrophe which befell the American Mission, and the shames that were inflicted on the name of Yemen. But what disappointment will fall on the heads of those dreamers when they find the fallacy of what they imagined! No mountains of gold, no treasures of diamonds. Nothing but ruins and antiquities—worthless when stripped of their archaeological value. Yes, what disappointment and how unlucky are these antiquities and the rubber squeezes of Sheba, when they become in Marib patches in the boots of the hungry armed bands.

32

UNKNOWN OMAN

"The heat was so intense that it burned the marrow in the bones, the sword in its scabbard melted like wax, and the gems that adorned the handle of the dagger were reduced to coal. In the plains the chase became a matter of perfect ease, for the desert was filled with roasted gazelles!"

So wrote Abd-er-Razak, a Persian, describing Muscat in the year 1442. In August of 1949, during my first visit, this old weather report was credible, but when Commander Gilliland and I went to Muscat in February, 1952, the evenings, at least, were cool and comfortable.

In answer to my cable, I had received word from the Sultan of Muscat and Oman that permission had been granted for an audience. Unable to find faster transportation, Commander Gilliland and I took passage on a Dutch-owned Liberty ship, the SS *Enganno,* and arrived in Muscat five days later. The rest of our party remained in Aden, anxiously awaiting the results of my negotiations and hoping they were still an archaeological expedition. I was worried about Bob Carmean, who had succumbed to malaria and was in the R.A.F. hospital, along with Chester Stevens, who had come down with a liver ailment. One small patch of silver lining in these clouds made us all thankful—if they had to be sick, how fortunate it was that they were not stricken in Yemen.

In Muscat, we were welcomed to the delightful home of Dr.

and Mrs. W. Wells Thoms, medical missionaries of the Dutch Reformed Church of America. In the spirit of the miracle of Calvary, the doctor and his charming wife, Beth, aided by their locally trained staff, treat more than twelve thousand patients a year on an annual budget of around $20,000. Certainly few endeavors anywhere in the world can approach this record of worthwhile dollar expenditure.

From our mission window in Matrah, sister city to Muscat, we could see on all sides the influence of the Portuguese, who had for years commanded this entrance to the Persian Gulf, until they were expelled in 1650, to be followed by a hundred years of Persian occupation. During the first half of the nineteenth century, Oman was the most powerful state in Arabia. Today it is an independent nation, ruled by Sultan Said bin Taimur, who succeeded his father in 1932 as the thirteenth of his dynasty.

At ten o'clock on the morning after our arrival, Commander Gilliland and I were warmly greeted by the Sultan and made to feel at home in his beautiful palace. What a pleasure it was to talk to this ruler who was intelligent, cultured, honest, and friendly! With the Sultan's perfect knowledge of English, there was no language barrier. Even more important, there was no barrier of court advisers and sycophants motivated by personal ambition, fear, and prejudice. We could deal directly with the Sultan, who understood what we were talking about and was sympathetic with our aims.

We explained the unfortunate events of Yemen, and all agreed that things might have turned out quite differently if only I had accepted his generous invitation to excavate in Oman two and a half years before.

The next two days of discussion resulted in what is probably the fairest archaeological concession granted in the Middle East for many years. The Sultan graciously allowed us to set up operations immediately at Dhofar, and to explore and excavate for three years. At the end of each season, all archaeological objects were to be divided on a fifty-fifty basis, the division to be made with a view to the quantity and uniqueness of each object as well as the total number of objects.

Sultan Said bin Taimur, Sultan of Muscat and Oman

Sheikh Hamoud bin Hamid, governor (*wali*) of the province of Dhofar, Sultanate of Muscat and Oman

I cabled the wonderful news to George Farrier in Aden, who immediately arranged for a special Air Djibouti charter to fly the entire party from Aden to Salalah, capital of Dhofar. Trucks and other heavy equipment that had not been abandoned in Yemen would have to come by boat.

Traveling from Muscat to Salalah was almost more difficult than moving the rest of the expedition from Aden. I finally had to get a chartered plane from the island of Bahrein, near the head of the Gulf, to fly Commander Gilliland and me to Salalah via Masira Island.

The province of Dhofar is 640 sea miles west of Muscat—with a coastline extending approximately two hundred miles between the points of land called Ras Darbat Ali and Ras Shuwamiyah.* We faced the task of exploring this isolated area of approximately 38,000 square miles, almost as large as the state of Ohio, larger than all of Portugal. Nineteen hundred years ago, the author of the *Periplus of the Erythrean Sea* described the area as follows:

The land recedes greatly and there follows a very deep bay stretching a great way across, which is called Sachalites; and the Frankincense Country mountainous and hard to cross, wrapped in thick clouds and fog, yielding frankincense from trees. These incense-bearing trees are not of great size or height; they bear frankincense sticking in drops on the bark, just as the trees in Egypt weep their gums. The frankincense is gathered by the King's slaves and those who are sent out by way of punishment.

The hills and mountains behind Salalah, then, had in ancient times been the major source of the fabulous aromatic riches which traveled the long road across southern Arabia and up beside the Red Sea to the Mediterranean, giving rise to great kingdoms on

* The eastern boundary of Dhofar Province runs inland from Ras Shuwamiyah 160 miles to Ramlat Mughshin. On the north it runs along the great sands (Al Rimal) for about 200 miles as far west as the Ramlat Shuait. Here the boundary turns south across wadis Shuait, Khawat, and Mitan, from there to Jabal Sadakh at Wadi Habrut down to Ras Darbat Ali on the coast. This boundary line divides the tribes of Dhofar from those of the Eastern Aden Protectorate. Reference to the above is clearly shown on W. Thesiger's excellent map of his journeys through South Arabia including the Mahra country during March and April, 1947, as published by the Royal Geographical Society.

the way and the cities of Shabwa, Timna, and Marib. If these cities had been made large and prosperous by the incense traffic, what could we expect in the country that had produced most of the incense? It was reasonable to hope for wealthy cities here, too, and the ruins of an ancient civilization of power and importance. But no one had ever undertaken archaeological work in Oman before. No one had found ancient inscriptions or stones protruding through the sand as the gravestones of buried cities of antiquity. The narrow coastal plain was dotted with limestone ruins, but all surface indications had shown them to date from medieval Arab times, after the coming of Islam.

Ancient writers such as Claudius Ptolemy and Arrian, among others, had written of the Dhofar region as a center of Arabian civilization in the great days of Timna and Marib. Though this evidence was second- or third-hand, it must have had some basis in fact, and served to confirm what common sense told us. Nevertheless, we were shooting in the dark for the first time. On previous expeditions our targets had been known, if not clearly revealed. Timna and Marib actually existed, and their locations were known. We could go there and dig. Now, in Oman, the situation was different. We looked upon the broad land of plains, hills, mountains, and desert, and said, "Somewhere in this region there must exist ancient ruins, cities with temples, tombs, houses, carved inscriptions, pottery, and statues—all lying buried beneath the sands of many centuries. Where are they? Can we find them and discover their secrets?"

After Yemen, we were a materially poor expedition, and now we were plunging into the unknown. Still, that was better than giving in to disaster, better than admitting defeat.

That was plainly the spirit of all members of the expedition, who welcomed the generous opportunity given us by the Sultan and were eager to buckle down to work again. The knowledge that Oman was a complete archaeological *terra incognita* served as a spur and a challenge, and we were a happy group that gathered in Salalah.

The city itself gave us encouragement and hope. We had all become a little bitter about the human race in Yemen, but here

The first pre-Islamic inscription discovered in Dhofar Province, Oman, this bronze plaque, deciphered by Dr. Albert Jamme, dates from about the second century A.D. and gives the name of the Hadhramaut moon god Sin and the name Sumhuram, a long-lost city. The lines read from right to left. Line six can partly be made out on the plaque's lower edge: 1) SHAFSAY AND HIS MOTHER, 2) NADRAT DEDICATED TO, 3) THEIR LORD SIN, HE OF (THE TEMPLE OF), 4) 'ILUM, IN (THE CITY OF) SUMHURAM, 5) FOR THE PROTECTION OF THEIR PERSONS, 6) AND OF THEIR KING

Bronze female dancer excavated at Khor Rory, Dhofar Province, Oman. It was probably imported from India about the second century A.D.

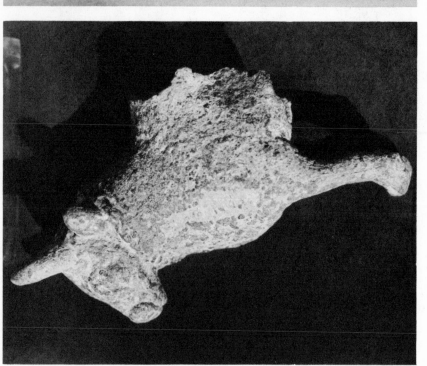

Bronze bull representing the moon god excavated in Dhofar Province, Oman, the frankincense capital of the ancient world

in Dhofar we met friendly people, ruled by the Sultan's wali (governor), Sheikh Hamoud bin Hamid. They were relaxed and unafraid, and went about their work and pleasures in peace.

The city itself was relatively clean, and its streets wider than those of many Arab towns. Palm trees swayed gracefully in the pleasant breeze from the ocean, and the town lay in a bed of green foliage. We all felt clean, invigorated, and secure.

A few minutes from the center of town lay the large and beautiful house which the Sultan had offered us as headquarters, shaded by palm trees and looking over the sea.

We began our reconnaissance of the region, searching for a site for our work. A quick trip to the foothills of the mysterious Qara Mountains encircling the Dhofar plain made us want to survey the entire region up to the vast sands of the Empty Quarter on the north. This limestone paradise, with its forested slopes, lakes, and waterfalls—Murbat Falls being over five hundred feet high— must certainly contain the solutions to innumerable archaeological mysteries. As our first site, however, Dr. Frank Albright chose a spot much closer at hand, a high mound of the extensive ruin called al-Balid, situated along the shore. In Moslem times this city had existed under the name of Mansura. Previous to its destruction in A.D. 618, it had probably been the location of the ancient city of Zufar, whose prince had an exclusive monopoly of the frankincense trade and who put to death anyone who dared to infringe on his domain. In subsequent months Dr. Albright started work at three other sites, but by the time the first conclusive results were found, I was back in New York, where Foundation business required my attention. Bob Carmean, who had recovered from his attack of malaria, returned to the States with us, after eighteen months in Arabia.

Then by cable came good news from George Farrier, who was serving as Oman field director—the news that despite our great troubles and great losses we were indeed an archaeological expedition once more, an expedition making significant discoveries about the history of the ancient world. Dr. Jamme had deciphered a newly uncovered bronze inscription mentioning the name of the Hadhramaut moon god Sin and giving for the first time the name SMHRM (Sumhuram), a long-lost city. Next came a strange inscription on a stone trough, running from left to right, and with peculiar forms of letters found previously only in inscriptions belonging to the Biblical Chaldeans.

About twenty-nine miles east of Salalah, overlooking beautiful Lake Khor Rory, Dr. Albright had discovered our first pre-Islamic city in Oman. Some twenty centuries or more ago, this impregnable fortress city guarded the best harbor on the coast of Dhofar, from which the principal export was frankincense.

Against the city wall and near its northern gate, lay the ruins of an important temple with huge massive walls. Dr. Albright excavated this temple in its entirety, the first time in Arabia that a pre-Islamic temple has been completely unveiled. In addition to an elaborate ablution system, two sacrificial altars, and a cache of bronze coins, seven important inscriptions were discovered, carved on the walls of the inner city gate.

Several of these inscriptions mentioned King Ilazz of the Hadhramaut, well known in the *Periplus* and other classical writings as Eleazus, king of the incense country. They mentioned also the city of Shabwa and the local Hadhrami province and governor. Here, more than seven hundred miles away from the cities made great by the incense trade, was the first concrete evidence linking the Dhofar region in ancient times with those capitals of kingdoms far to the west. Here was strong indication that shortly before the time of Christ, the Kingdom of Hadhramaut extended all the way from Beihan to Dhofar. No wonder that kingdom had been called the frankincense country! It was no longer necessary to conjecture about forests of incense-bearing trees in the Wadi Hadhramaut where little evidence of such forests exists today. Hadhramaut was the incense country because it was a kingdom of great extent, reaching halfway across Arabia to include the greatest producer of incense—Dhofar.

Oman was no longer an archaeological question mark. The question had been answered by our expedition. As our own Professor Albright said recently, "The historical importance of these Oman discoveries is very great indeed, since no one thought that South Arabian civilization extended so far east. Even I was skeptical!"

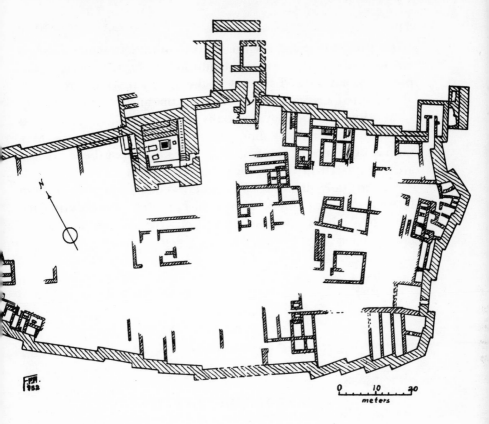

Ground plan of the ancient spice port Sumhuram near Khor Rory, Dhofar
Province, Oman, as far as excavated. Inscriptions date it to the last centuries
B.C. and the first three centuries A.D. and prove that it was then a Hadhrami
colony.

That important and exciting work continues to move ahead, as our expedition goes farther inland into the heart of the incense-producing forests and beyond to the great Empty Quarter.

Our quest has carried us far along the ancient Biblical spice routes. Buried cities have partially unveiled their hidden secrets and have suggested new lines of exploration for the future. Mysterious kingdoms of the past and their kings, long believed lost, are now placed in their proper historical setting.

We can only dream of what our reception would have been like had our visit to Sheba's capital city taken place during the reign of Arabia's most famous Queen. For she too was an explorer at heart.

THE END

EL-HAMDU LILLAH!

AFTERWORD
BIRTH PAINS OF AN EXPEDITION

Two of the most common queries to me after a showing of my lecture film, "Exploring Shebaland," or in private conversations are: "How do you become the organizer and leader of scientific expeditions?" and "How do you raise money and equipment for expeditions?"

The answer to both questions is much the same—desire, hard work, unlimited faith, enthusiasm, and a certain amount of luck with the added essential of knowing or meeting the right people. These generalizations, however, are no more enlightening than most generalizations. The queries can best be answered, I think, by a brief summary of my own experiences in getting started as a leader of expeditions and in raising funds and obtaining equipment for major projects in Africa, Sinai, and South Arabia.

As far back as I can remember, I always wanted to be an explorer. This childhood ambition of mine was given every conceivable encouragement by my mother, who as a girl, had prospected the gold dust trail by pack mule with her father and mother throughout California's High Sierras.

During the Depression years one developed early an ability to speak with speed and precision while selling newspapers and magazines on the street corners of Oakland, California, at the advanced age of ten. Later this ability was put to the acid test while painting house numbers on street curbings in Antioch,

California, at fifty cents a house. How was I to know that this house in question belonged to the chief of police, who felt quite capable of finding his own dwelling without my beautiful numbers?

As H. G. Wells once told me in wartime London, "Wendell, the only way to learn to write is to write," and I can testify the only way to learn to speak well is to stand up and do it as often as possible. During the San Francisco World's Fair on Treasure Island, I was given an unparalleled opportunity as chief lecturer at the "Lost World," to relate to thousands daily the wonders of the geologic past.

At graduation time from the University of California with a degree in paleontology, I already had tasted field life as the youngest member on three University fossil-hunting expeditions to Arizona, Utah, and Oregon.

My wartime career as a merchant mariner carried me to every major theater of operations and was concluded after the Okinawa invasion with infantile paralysis. During the "back-on-my-feet" months that followed, I conceived the idea of an extensive continent-wide African expedition, which appealed immediately to my alma mater's farsighted president, Robert Gordon Sproul, and to University of California regent, John Francis Neylan. My extensive wartime travels which had found me inside Paris on liberation day, behind the Japanese lines on Okinawa, and reported missing in the South Pacific, had also enabled me to meet many of the world's foremost scientists and scholars. This afforded me a firm basis for the future selection of an unsurpassed international staff.

I have always credited famed Gobi Desert explorer Roy Chapman Andrews with giving me the early stimulus and basic techniques of fund raising, of which he is past master. For Dr. Andrews' expeditions to Central Asia on behalf of the American Museum of Natural History were models which I hoped I might copy in Africa. However, it was soon evident that setting up an expedition is in many ways like having a child—easy to conceive but hard to deliver.

The busy months that followed were filled with anxiety and frequently with failure. I had to make constant apologies. Why had I never written any books? Was it true that I had never even been in Africa? Didn't I know that a Ph.D. was considered an essential academic union card in the world today? And why wasn't I home with mother, studying until ready to take my rightful place among the other laboratory assistants at the University?

At this time, late in 1946, Field Marshal Jan Christian Smuts, Prime Minister of the Union of South Africa, was representing his country at the United Nations meeting at Lake Success. Armed with a letter of introduction from President Sproul, I hitched a ride to New York and presented myself before one of the truly great men of all time, fighting general of the nineteenth-century Boer War, master statesman, scholar, and philosopher. The world owes the late Jan Smuts a great debt, not only for his own brilliant career, but for his once having spared the life of a rash young war correspondent who lived on to become the greatest Englishman of our age—Sir Winston Churchill.

General Smuts listened attentively as I unfolded my plans, then with a broad sweep of his hand—a sign that I learned later to be characteristic of him—said that he would be proud to accept honorary chairmanship of our advisory board and gave me an all-important letter of introduction which said in part:

The beginnings of man in his early surroundings could today probably best be studied in South Africa, which is a veritable museum of prehistoric material and perhaps the prehistoric cradle of the human race, and these beginnings are one of the most fascinating chapters of the latest science now being written. We judge the tree not only by its fruits but also by its roots, and the knowledge of our far-off beginnings, and our progress through the geological ages before the dawn of history, may be expected to throw light on many of the scientific and other problems which trouble us today.

Support from such an outstanding source was unexpected manna from heaven, and within ten days it was possible to add such contributions as ten new trucks, fifty thousand gallons of gasoline, steamship transportation, electrical supplies, recording equipment, and hundreds of thousands of dollars' worth of other basic essentials for an expedition in the field.

But much travel, worry, hard work, and talk came between this major support from General Smuts and the launching of the expedition. There was a trip to Africa, covering 40,000 miles, through the courtesy of Samuel F. Pryor, vice-president of Pan American World Airways, and a veteran African big-game hunter who had long had a very special interest in exploration. During this journey I attended, as the only American delegate, the first Pan-African Congress on Prehistory, which met at Nairobi in January, 1947.

Back in the United States, I started the hectic fun of fund raising. My father had pounded into me long before that the key to success in any undertaking requiring the presentation of an idea by one person to another was the proper combination of personal enthusiasm, split-second timing, and perfect organization, together with a certain amount of colorful imagination, self-confidence, luck, and, above all, faith. I needed them all to accomplish the large and extensive expedition I envisioned. I had been cautioned many times by various well-meaning scientists not to make the expedition too large. ("Keep it small, Wendell, keep it small!") And yet my one fear at this time was that I could not make the project impressive enough to appeal to the really big men whose support was needed to make my dream come true.

Many were the not-too-hushed whispers circulated through the University that the expedition was getting out of hand and would collapse from overexpansion, and that the idea of attacking Africa from various different geographical points simultaneously in several phases of study could not possibly work out. This type of criticism actually gave me my greatest stimulus. It is significant to note that the men who had faith in the expedition were also those of the greatest stature, men who in their own lifetimes had overcome many of the same kind of petty obstacles.

I'll never forget the time I walked in on General James H. Doolittle, who had become vice-president of the Shell Oil Company. He looked up from his crowded desk and said, somewhat abruptly, "You have just sixty seconds to state your business, young man." For once in my life I was *almost* speechless, but at the end of the allotted time I rushed out soon to be richer by 50,000 gallons of gasoline. I had encountered a trait common to all of the world's great men whom I have been privileged to meet—the ability to make immediate decisions.

Allan Sproul, President of the Federal Reserve Bank in New York, had already introduced me to several important General Motors officials, with the result that that firm contributed ten new trucks. Since we now had the gas to make them run, the expedition could be considered mobile.

With most people still shuddering with horror at the thought of sending an expedition of record size to Africa under the leadership of a 26-year-old "child," John Francis Neylan, as usual, was enthusiastically far ahead of me, and suggested that I approach the Navy. Fleet Admiral Chester W. Nimitz, then Chief of Naval Operations, had an impressive Washington suite, but for a time it looked as if I would have to remain impressed with its outer and not its inner office. I am not inferring that his aides and assistants were not co-operative when I stated that I wished to see the Admiral. I merely seemed unable to convince them that I really meant Admiral Nimitz. I passed from a commander to a captain to a rear admiral, which should have been enough to satisfy anyone on his first visit to the Navy Department. But I was insistent, and finally was admitted to the presence of the C.N.O., whose sympathy, understanding, and co-operation helped so much in the difficult years to follow. This first visit resulted in an introduction to General Carl Spaatz, after which I was richer by one airplane. Then Admiral Nimitz sent me to see the Commandant of the Marine Corps, General A. A. Vandergrift, who with words of encouragement passed me along to Major General W. P. T. Hill, who had been with Roy Chapman Andrews in the Gobi Desert.

With the expedition augmented by Marine Corps officers, enlisted men, and equipment, Admiral Nimitz sent me next to see the Navy's Surgeon General, C. A. Swanson, and his deputy, Rear Admiral Lamont Pugh. While my request was only for a medical officer, Admiral Pugh's keen vision saw that there were unique opportunities for naval research in a more active association with the expedition. This brought a $58,000 naval research contract for the expedition to conduct medical studies throughout Africa on behalf of the Navy's Bureau of Medicine and Surgery, plus a team of nine medical officers, enlisted technicians, and civilian specialists for our expedition.

Meetings with General Dwight D. Eisenhower, Dr. Dana Co-man, and Dr. Paul Siple of the Army's Research and Development Board resulted in our obtaining the loan of a fleet of army trucks, trailers, a motorboat, and thousands of dollars worth of essential field equipment.

It was a most important day for me when I called on the noted E. Roland Harriman, partner in the banking firm of Brown Brothers, Harriman and Company, to see if he might possibly be interested. He was, and his enthusiastic and generous support not only for our African expedition but for our later projects has enabled many a scholar and scientist to leave his study and make major contributions to the world's knowledge from regions which otherwise would have remained as inaccessible to them as the moon.

Another supporter, with a generous contribution at this time as well as in later expeditions, was International Business Machines' famed Thomas J. Watson, who has always been warmly interested in everything I have undertaken.

Two of my most enthusiastic backers were Dr. Gilbert Darlington, whose American Bible Society has in the past 134 years produced some 400,000,000 Bibles or portions of Scriptures, and Rear Admiral Richard E. Byrd, whose Antarctic expeditions remain unsurpassed in conception, organization, and execution.

Finally the time came when Rear Admiral M. L. Royar loaded our equipment on Navy ships for transport to Alexandria, Egypt, and the regents of the University of California made up the final sum needed to finance the expedition by appropriating $20,000, proving that great institutions are not without a heart.

A year later the California papers stated, "It is with local pride that we note that the National Geographic Society has listed our expedition first in its annual review of scientific expeditions for 1948." And twenty-six solid months later the University of California African Expedition was ended—and in the words of Admiral Pugh, "the most extensive medical survey of Africa ever accomplished by a single expedition has come to a successful conclusion."

Then came the expeditions to Mount Sinai and South Arabia, under the auspices of my newly formed American Foundation for

the Study of Man, whose board of directors was made up primarily of men who had aided so greatly in getting the African
work started. But I was faced once more with the task of obtaining funds and equipment for several large-scale projects.

Armed with an introduction from Pan American's Sam Pryor,
who always knows the right people at the right time, I invaded
the Detroit office of K. T. Keller, President of the Chrysler Corporation. In my mind at the time was our need for ten Dodge
Power Wagons, with twelve as the ideal at which to aim. This
was, however, before I met the renowned K. T. Keller, who, after
briefly listening to my plans with all of its research possibilities,
phoned L. L. ("Tex") Colbert, then president of the Dodge Division of Chrysler (now president of Chrysler Corporation). I'll
never forget K.T.'s words, "Say, Tex, thought you'd be interested
to know you've just given away fifteen Dodge Power Wagons." I
could well imagine Mr. Colbert's reply to this startling announcement. In any case, Mr. Keller beamed on me and shortly afterward in rushed Tex Colbert with a strange expression on his face.
I had the feeling that I was being examined as a possible new
species of gangster, but Mr. Colbert and one of his top truck experts, Joe Berr, soon put together a magnificent fleet of Power
Wagons for us, and I can safely say that no similar expedition has
ever been supplied with field transport which could equal ours.

A few days later my old friend Ben Conner, President of Colt's
Manufacturing Company, who had kept the African expedition
supplied with six-shooters, introduced me to Walter E. Ditmars,
President of the Gray Manufacturing Company. Only occasionally have I met anyone whose enthusiasm for the project ever
surpassed my own, but such was Walter Ditmars', who not only
supplied us with his wonderful Audograph Electronic Soundwrit-
ers, which made the first draft of this book possible from Mt.
Sinai, but approached his many friends for needed contributions.
One of these was Al N. Seares, Vice President of Remington Rand,
who supplied us with all of our office equipment for the field.

It might be thought by some that great corporations are generous only to the extent that their contributed products are used
exclusively. I did not find this to be the case however, as illus-

trated by Presidents John Olin and Roger Kenna, whose respective Winchesters and Marlins, supplied us in quantity, spelled expedition security, fresh meat, recreation, and American goodwill gifts par excellence for the Arabs.

Clarence Francis, Board Chairman of General Foods, not only made available large quantities of his own corporation's products, but introduced me to Stokely-Van Camp, Hormel, and Borden's with the result that we not only ate the best in the field, but we also found their empty containers the best for target practice.

The photographic aspects of an expedition are all-important, not only for the portrayal of scientific results but for the human interest value unique pictures create. Thus, a visit in Rochester with Eastman Kodak's President T. J. Hargraves and General E. P. Curtis resulted in a Ciné Special movie camera. That same day I called on G. E. Whitacker, President of Graflex, Inc., who kindly made available an assortment of Speed Graphic, Graphic View, and Graflex cameras.

The Library of Congress backed the Sinai project, which made its success a certainty, and then W. Alton Jones, President of Cities Service Oil Company, kindly offered us fuel supplies. When I explained that the Shell Company was again keeping us afloat in petrol, Mr. Jones, through Burl Watson (now president of Cities Service) kindly donated funds, a two-engine Cessna airplane and some motor oil.

One of the last equipment items needed was a radio transmitter, which was kindly supplied by the Chief of Naval Operations, Admiral Forrest Sherman. Together with our Zenith, Link, and Hallicrafter sending and receiving sets, this meant that our only remaining requirement was someone who knew how to make the stuff work in the field.

The day before the final shipload of supplies and personnel was to sail for Aden, our specially built Fairbanks Morse generators were still in Chicago. President Robert Morse came to the rescue with a chartered plane, and this essential equipment arrived on board just minutes before sailing time.

In many ways the hardest part of an expedition is over the day it sails fully equipped, staffed, and financed for the field of science and adventure. The strain begins to tell on an expedition leader, however, when his expedition sails equipped and staffed, but not financed. This was my exact problem at the start of the first Arabian expedition, where our chief controlling factor was climate. We had to work during the so-called "cool" season, and it took over six weeks to transport the expedition and personnel from New York to Aden and then on to Mukalla. I had to send off the equipment and most of the staff even before I had all the money, if we were going to get any work done at all.

With the expedition safely on the high seas, thanks to A. E. King, Vice-President of the Isthmian Steamship Company, Walter Ditmars telephoned Robert G. Tait, President of the Stromberg Carlson Company, who in turn telephoned Jack Heinz, President of the H. J. Heinz Company in Pittsburgh. So I flew to meet the fabulous H.J.

Now there is nothing worse in approaching a wealthy man for money than to seem to need it too badly, for this might signify that there was some small doubt of the success of your project. Furthermore, you should normally never come out crudely and ask for what you are really after. By a process of good indirect presentation, your prospect should soon anticipate your desires, and if he has been infected with your enthusiasm, he may or may not succumb and make a substantial contribution. Obtaining contributions of supplies is one thing. Obtaining green folding money is something else again, for although I have never stressed the publicity to be exchanged for any contribution of equipment, it goes without saying that it is our duty to supply what pictures and public relations material we can make available from the field about the various items which have contributed to our success.

I was patiently waiting outside the office of the president of the Heinz Company trying to get the number "57" out of my mind, when a good-looking young man walked up and apologized for having kept me waiting, ushering me into a handsome office. I thought to myself, "Mr. Heinz certainly has a superior assistant here." To my amazement the young man in question sat down behind a beautiful desk in a comfortable position as though he owned the place, and suddenly it dawned on me that he did, that this was the president of the H. J. Heinz Company—Mr. H.J. himself. His first words were, "You have a lot of important friends. Why haven't you been to see me before?"

Now this was the first time in my hectic career that I had ever had anyone who was being approached for a contribution begin the conversation with, "Why haven't you been to see me before?" I was so shaken by this unique opening that my presentation was not as smooth, I am afraid, as it should have been. However, it was soon my turn to give Mr. Heinz a jolt, for when he politely inquired what quantities of food products the expedition would require, I replied that I was really not after his products at this time, since the expedition was already on the high seas, but that I would be keenly interested in getting hold of some of his money.

The next day, through an introduction from Jack Heinz, Wallace Richards, Director of the great Carnegie Museum of Pittsburgh, established a grant-in-aid for the expedition. Thus, with generous support from Adolph W. Schmidt, representing the A. W. Mellon Educational and Charitable Trust, from the Sarah Mellon Scaife Foundation, from the Gulf Oil Corporation, and from Jack Heinz, the Arabian expedition finally became solvent, and I flew immediately to Cairo and on to Aden.

This brief narrative will perhaps give some idea of the trials, tribulations, and surprises to be encountered in organizing and financing an expedition. But for every instance of generosity told here there are countless others in my experience, for which there could not possibly be space in a volume of this size. The complete list of substantial contributors, those business firms, trusts, organizations, institutions, and individuals, which have made our Sinai and Arabian expeditions possible follows, but no words or acknowledgments in cold type can ever express the full appreciation of myself, my staff, and the many scientists who have been able to do significant work because of their help. The general public cannot realize how much good is accomplished in this world through the farsightedness and altruism of such people.

SUBSTANTIAL CONTRIBUTORS
American Foundation for the Study of Man

Governmental & Academic Organizations	American Geographical Society Carnegie Museum Leon Falk Trust Howard Heinz Endowment Humanities Fund, Inc. Library of Congress A. W. Mellon Educational and Charitable Trust Sarah Mellon Scaife Foundation United States Navy Trinity Church (N. Y.) University of Alexandria University of California The Johns Hopkins University University of Louvain University of Redlands St. Andrews University
Corporations & Companies	American Anode Company American Trust Company Barber-Greene Company Borden Company Brush Development Company Chrysler Corporation California Texas Oil Co. Ltd. Cities Service Oil Company Coca-Cola Corporation Colgate-Palmolive-Peet Company Colt's Manufacturing Company Eastman Kodak Company Fairbanks Morse & Company General Foods Corporation Goodyear Tire and Rubber Company

Corporations &   Graflex, Inc.
Companies   Gray Manufacturing Company
(contd)   Griffin & Howe, Inc.
                       Gulf Oil Corporation
                       Hallicrafters Company
                       H. J. Heinz Company
                       Geo. A. Hormel & Company
                       International Business Machines Corp.
                       International General Electric Co.
                       Isthmian Steamship Company
                       R. G. LeTourneau, Inc.
                       Link Radio Corporation
                       Lyman Gun Sight Corporation
                       Marine Transport Line, Inc.
                       Marlin Firearms Company
                       Olin Industries, Inc.
                       Pan American World Airways
                       Plymouth Oil Company
                       Remington Rand, Inc.
                       Richfield Oil Corporation
                       Royal Typewriter Company, Inc.
                       Associated Oil Companies in the Royal Dutch Shell Group
                       Socony-Vacuum Oil Company
                       Square D Company
                       E. R. Squibb & Sons
                       Stokely-Van Camp, Inc.
                       The Texas Company
                       United States Steel Corporation
                       V-M Corporation
                       Willys Overland Motors, Inc.
                       Zenith Radio Corporation

Individuals   Paul G. Benedum
                       Helen W. Buckner
                       Walker G. Buckner
                       S. Bayard Colgate
                       W. W. Crocker
                       Dr. Gilbert Darlington
                       Walter E. Ditmars
                       Sidney Erhman
                       Clarence Francis
                       E. Roland Harriman
                       H. J. Heinz, II
                       Samuel S. Himmell
                       Lester W. Hink
                       Col. Charles F. H. Johnson
                       Dr. Harry Katz
                       H.H. The Aga Khan

Individuals
(*contd*)

James Lochead
George D. Lockhart
J. K. Moffitt
Lenord Mudge
John I. Moore
H. H. Phillips
Samuel F. Pryor
James C. Rea
Alan and Sarah Scaife
John B. Trevor

INDEX

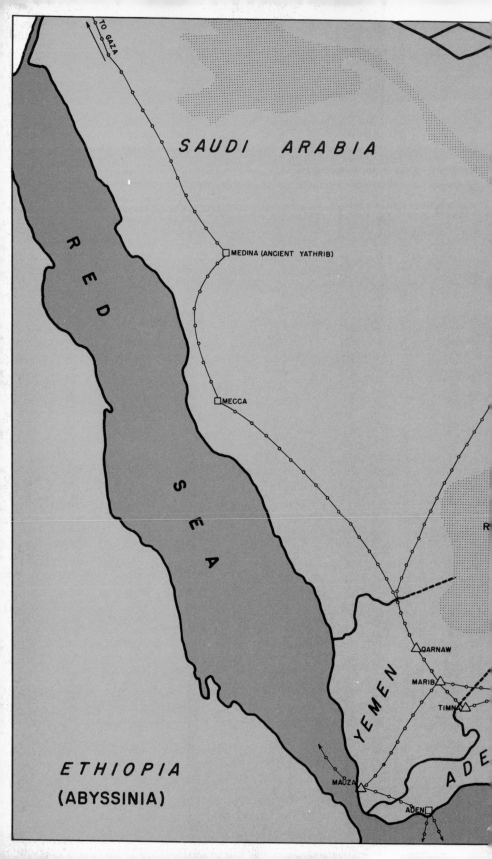